W9-DFE-310

The Nature of God

The Nature of God

ARTHUR W. PINK

MOODY PRESS
CHICAGO

© 1975, 1999 by
MOODY BIBLE INSTITUTE
OF CHICAGO

Original Title: *Gleanings in the Godhead*

All rights reserved. No part of this book may be reproduced in any form without permission in writing from the publisher, except in the case of brief quotations embodied in critical articles or reviews.

All Scripture quotations, unless indicated, are taken from the King James Version.

Scripture quotations marked (RV) are taken from *The Holy Bible, The Revised Version,* The Universities of Oxford and Cambridge, 1904.

Scripture quotations marked (RSV) are taken from the *Revised Standard Version* © 1946, 1952, 1971 by the Division of Christian Education of the National Council of Churches of Christ in the United States of America.

ISBN: 0-8024-6571-4

1 3 5 7 9 10 8 6 4 2

Printed in the United States of America

CONTENTS

Part 2
Excellencies Which Pertain to God the Son as Christ

EDITOR'S PREFACE

These studies relating to the Persons of the Godhead are selections from the works of Arthur W. Pink, beloved pastor and Bible expositor, whose ministry extended from Great Britain to the United States and to Australia. The articles were compiled by I. C. Herendeen from various sources, mainly from the monthly periodical *Studies in the Scriptures,* of which Mr. Pink was editor and publisher. Mr. Pink died July 15, 1952, but his writings continue to have a wide ministry.

For some time this book was part of the Gleanings series published by Moody Press. It is now being reissued with the new title *The Nature of God,* but retaining the King James Version as the basic Scripture text and including some very minor typographical changes.

THE PUBLISHERS

Part 1

EXCELLENCIES WHICH PERTAIN TO THE GODHEAD AS GOD

Chapter 1

THE SOLITARINESS OF GOD

*P*erhaps the title of the chapter is not sufficiently explicit to indicate its theme. This is partly because so few are accustomed to meditate upon the personal perfections of God. Comparatively few who occasionally read the Bible are aware of the awe-inspiring and worship-provoking grandeur of the divine character. That God is great in wisdom, wondrous in power, yet full of mercy is assumed by many as common knowledge. But to entertain anything approaching an adequate conception of His being, nature, and attributes, as revealed in the Scripture, is something which very few people in these degenerate times have done. God is solitary in His excellency. "Who is like unto thee, O LORD, among the gods? who is like thee, glorious in holiness, fearful in praises, doing wonders?" (Exodus 15:11).

"In the beginning God" (Genesis 1:1). There was a time, if "time" it could be called, when God, in the unity of His nature (though subsisting equally in three Persons), dwelt all alone. "In the beginning God." There was no heaven where His glory is now particularly manifested. There was no earth to engage His attention. There were no angels to sing His praises. There was no universe to be upheld by the word of His power. There was nothing, no one, but God; and that not for a day, a year, or an age, but "from everlasting." During a past eternity God was alone—self-contained, self-sufficient, in need of nothing. Had a universe, or angels, or humans been necessary to Him in any way, they also would have been called into existence from all eternity. Creating them when He did added nothing to God essentially. He changes not (Malachi 3:6); therefore His essential glory can be neither augmented nor diminished.

God was under no constraint, no obligation, no necessity to create. That He chose to do so was purely a sovereign act on His part, caused by nothing outside Himself, determined by nothing but His own good pleasure; for He "worketh all things after the counsel of his own will" (Ephesians 1:11). That He did create was simply for His manifestative glory. Do some of our readers imagine that we have gone beyond what Scripture warrants? Then we appeal to the Law and the testimony: "Stand up and bless the LORD your God for ever and ever: and blessed be thy glorious name, which is exalted above all blessing and praise" (Nehemiah 9:5). God is no gainer even from our worship. He was in no need of that external glory of His grace which arises from His redeemed, for He is glorious enough in Himself without that. What was it that moved Him to predestinate His elect to the praise of the glory of His grace? It was "according to the good pleasure of his will" (Ephesians 1:5). *Eph 1:5-14*

We are well aware that the high ground we tread here is new and strange to almost all of our readers, so it is well to move slowly. Let us appeal again to the Scriptures. As the apostle brings to a close a long argument on salvation by sovereign grace, he asks, "For who hath known the mind of the Lord? or who hath been his counsellor? or who hath first given to him, and it shall be recompensed unto him again?" (Romans 11:34–35). The force of this is that it is impossible to bring the Almighty under obligation to the creature. God gains nothing from us. "If thou be righteous, what givest thou him? or what receiveth he of thine hand? Thy wickedness may hurt a man as thou art; and thy righteousness may profit the son of man" (Job 35:7–8). But it certainly cannot affect God, who is all-blessed in Himself. "When ye shall have done all those things which are commanded you, say, We are unprofitable servants" (Luke 17:10)—our obedience has profited nothing.

We go farther: Our Lord Jesus Christ added nothing to God in His essential being and glory, either by what He did or suffered. True, gloriously true, He manifested that glory of God to us, but He added nothing to God. He Himself expressly declares so, and there is no appeal from His words: "My goodness extendeth not to thee" (Psalm 16:2). The whole of that psalm is a psalm of Christ. Christ's goodness or righteousness reached unto His saints in the earth (v. 3), but God was high above and beyond it all.

It is true that God is both honored and dishonored by men, not in His essential being, but in His official character. It is equally true that God has been glorified by creation, by providence, and by redemption. We do not dare dispute this for a moment. But all of this has to do with His manifestative glory and the recognition of it by us. Yet, had God so pleased, He might have continued alone for all eternity, without making known His glory unto creatures. Whether He should do so or not He determined solely by His own will. He was perfectly blessed in Himself before the first creature was called into being. And what are all the creatures of His hands unto Him even now? The Scripture again answers:

> Behold, the nations are as a drop of a bucket, and are counted as the small dust of the balance: behold, he taketh up the isles as a very little thing. And Lebanon is not sufficient to burn, nor the beasts thereof sufficient for a burnt offering. All nations before him are as nothing; and they are counted to him less than nothing, and vanity. To whom then will ye liken God? or what likeness will ye compare unto him? (Isaiah 40:15–18)

That is the God of Scripture; but He is still "the unknown God" (Acts 17:23) to heedless multitudes.

> It is he that sitteth upon the circle of the earth, and the inhabitants thereof are like grasshoppers; that stretcheth out the heavens as a curtain, and spreadeth them out as a tent to dwell in: that bringeth the princes to nothing; he maketh the judges of the earth as vanity. (Isaiah 40:22–23)

Read all of Isa. 40

How vastly different is the God of Scripture from the god of the average pulpit!

Nor is the testimony of the New Testament any different from that of the Old. How could it be since both have one and the same Author? There too we read:

Which in his times he shall shew, who is the blessed and only Potentate, the King of kings, and Lord of lords; who only hath immortality, dwelling in the light which no man can approach unto; whom no man hath seen, nor can see; to whom be honour and power everlasting. Amen. (1 Timothy 6:15–16)

Such a One is to be revered, worshiped, and adored. He is solitary in His majesty, unique in His excellency, and peerless in His perfections. He sustains all, but is Himself independent of all. He gives to all and is enriched by none.

Such a God cannot be found out by searching. He can be known only as He is revealed to the heart by the Holy Spirit through the Word. It is true that creation demonstrates a Creator, and so plainly that men are "without excuse." Yet we still have to say with Job, "Lo, these are parts of his ways: but how little a portion is heard of him? but the thunder of his power who can understand?" (Job 26:14). The so-called argument from design by well-meaning apologists has, we believe, done much more harm than good. It has attempted to bring the great God down to the level of finite comprehension, and thereby has lost sight of His solitary excellence.

Analogy has been drawn between a savage who finds a watch upon the sands, and from a close examination of it infers a watchmaker. So far so good. But attempt to go farther. Suppose the savage sits on the sand and endeavors to form a conception of this watchmaker, his personal affections and manners, his disposition, acquirements, and moral character, all that goes to make up a personality. Could he ever think or reason out a real man, the man who made the watch, so he could say, "I am acquainted with him"? It seems trifling to ask, but is the eternal and infinite God so much more within the grasp of human reason? No, indeed. The God of Scripture can be known only by those to whom He makes Himself known.

Nor is God known by the intellect. "God is a Spirit" (John 4:24), and therefore can only be known spiritually. But fallen man is not spiritual; he is carnal. He is dead to all that is spiritual. Unless he is born again, supernaturally brought from death unto life, miraculously translated out of darkness into light, he cannot even see the things of God (John 3:3), still less apprehend them (1 Corinthians 2:14). The Holy Spirit has to shine in our hearts (not intellects) to give us "the knowledge of the glory of God in the face of Jesus Christ" (2 Corinthians 4:6). But even that spiritual knowledge is fragmentary. The regenerated soul has to "grow in grace, and in the knowledge of our Lord and Saviour Jesus Christ" (2 Peter 3:18).

The principal prayer and aim of Christians should be to "walk worthy of the Lord unto all pleasing, being fruitful in every good work, and increasing in the knowledge of God" (Colossians 1:10).

John 4:24

"God is Spirit, and Those who worship Him must worship in spirit and Truth"

[This is who God seeks.
                John 4:23]

Chapter 2

THE DECREES OF GOD

The Scriptures mention the decrees of God in many passages, and in a variety of terms. The word "decree" is found in Psalm 2:7. In Ephesians 3:11 we see His "eternal purpose"; in Acts 2:23, His "determinate counsel and foreknowledge"; in Ephesians 1:9, the mystery of His "will"; in Romans 8:29, that He also did "predestinate"; in Ephesians 1:9, His "good pleasure." God's decrees are called His "counsel" to signify that they are consummately wise. They are called God's "will" to show that He was under no control, but acted according to His own pleasure. When a man's will is the rule of his conduct, it is usually capricious and unreasonable; but wisdom is always associated with will in the divine proceedings, and accordingly, God's decrees are said to be "the counsel of his own will" (Ephesians 1:11).

The decrees of God relate to all future things without exception; whatever is done in time was foreordained before time began. God's purpose was concerned with everything, whether great or small, whether good or evil. But with reference to the latter we must be careful to state that while God is the Orderer and Controller of sin, He is not the Author of it in the same way that He is the Author of good. Sin could not proceed from a Holy God by positive and direct creation, but only by decretive permission and negative action. God's decree, as comprehensive as His government, extends to all creatures and events. It was concerned about our life and death; about our state in time; and about our state in eternity. As God works all things after the counsel of His own will, we learn from His works what His counsel is (was), as we judge an architect's plan by inspecting the building erected under his direction.

God did not merely decree to make man, place him upon the earth, then leave him to his own uncontrolled guidance. Instead, He fixed all the circumstances in the lot of individuals, and all the particulars which comprise the history of the human race from commencement to close. He did not merely decree that general laws should be established for the government of the world, but He settled the application of those laws to all particular cases. Our days are numbered, and so are the hairs of our heads. We may learn what is the extent of the divine decrees from the dispensations of Providence in which they are executed. The care of Providence reaches to the most insignificant creatures, and the most minute events—the death of a sparrow, the fall of a hair.

Let us now consider some of the properties of the divine decrees. First, they are *eternal*. To suppose any of them to be made in time is to suppose that some new occasion has occurred, some unforeseen event or combination of circumstances has arisen, which has induced the Most High to form a new resolution. This would argue that the knowledge of the Deity is limited, and that He grows wiser in the progress of time—which would be horrible blasphemy. No man who believes that the divine understanding is infinite, comprehending the past, the present, and the future, will ever assent to the erroneous doctrine of temporal decrees. God is not ignorant of future events which will be executed by human volitions; He has foretold them in innumerable instances, and prophecy is but the manifestation of His eternal prescience. Scripture affirms that believers were chosen in Christ before the world began (Ephesians 1:4); yes, that grace was "given" to them then (2 Timothy 1:9).

Second, the decrees of God are *wise*. Wisdom is shown in the selection of the best possible ends and the fittest means to accomplish them. That this character belongs to the decrees of God is evident from what we know of them. They are disclosed to us by their execution, and every proof of wisdom in the works of God is a proof of the wisdom of the plan, in conformity to which they are performed. As the psalmist declared, "O LORD, how manifold are thy works! in wisdom hast thou made them all" (Psalm 104:24). It is indeed but a very small part of them which falls under our observation; yet, we ought to proceed here as we do in other cases and judge of the whole by the specimen, of what is unknown by what is known. He who sees the workings of admirable skill in the parts of a machine which he has an opportunity to examine is naturally led to believe that the other parts are equally admirable. In like manner should we satisfy our minds as to God's works when doubts obtrude themselves upon us and repel the objections which may be suggested by something we cannot reconcile to our notions of what is good and wise. When we reach the bounds of the finite and gaze toward the mysterious realm of the infinite, let us exclaim, "O the depth of the riches both of the wisdom and knowledge of God!" (Romans 11:33).

Third, they are *free*. "Who hath directed the Spirit of the LORD, or being his counsellor hath taught him? With whom took he counsel, and who instructed him, and taught him in the path of judgment, and taught him knowledge, and shewed to him the way of understanding?" (Isaiah 40:13–14). God was alone when He made His decrees, and His determinations were influenced by no external cause. He was free to decree or not to decree, and to decree one thing and not another. This liberty we must ascribe to Him who is supreme, independent, and sovereign in all His doings.

Fourth, they are *absolute* and *unconditional*. The execution of them is not suspended upon any condition which may, or may not be, performed. In every instance where God has decreed an end, He has also decreed every means to that end. The One who decreed the salvation of His elect also decreed to work faith in them (2 Thessalonians 2:13). "My counsel shall stand, and I will do all my pleasure" (Isaiah 46:10); but that could not be, if His counsel depended upon a condition which might not be performed. But God "worketh all things after the counsel of his own will" (Ephesians 1:11).

Side by side with the immutability and invincibility of God's decrees, Scripture plainly teaches that man is a responsible creature and answerable for his actions. If our thoughts are formed from God's Word, the maintenance of the one will not lead to the denial of the other. That there is a real difficulty in defining where the one ends and the other begins is freely granted. This is always the case where there is a conjunction of the divine and the human. Real prayer is composed by the Spirit, yet it is also the cry of a human heart. The Scriptures are the inspired Word of God, yet they were written by men who were something more than machines in the hand of the Spirit. Christ is both God and man. He is omniscient, yet "increased in wisdom" (Luke 2:52). He is almighty, yet was "crucified through weakness" (2 Corinthians 13:4). He is the Prince of life, yet He died. High mysteries all—yet faith receives them unquestioningly.

It has been pointed out often in the past that every objection against the eternal decrees of God applies with equal force against His eternal foreknowledge. Jonathan Edwards said:

> Whether God has decreed all things that ever come to pass or not, all that own the being of a God, own that He knows all things beforehand. Now, it is self-evident that if He knows all things beforehand, He either doth approve of them or doth not approve of them; that is, He either is willing they should be, or He is not willing they should be. But to will that they should be is to decree them.

Finally, attempt to assume and then contemplate the opposite. To deny the divine decrees would be to predicate a world and all its concerns regulated by undesigned chance or blind fate. Then what peace, what assurance, what comfort would there be for our poor hearts and minds? What refuge would there be to fly to in the hour of trial? None at all. There would be nothing better than the black darkness and abject horror of atheism. How thankful we should be that everything is determined by infinite wisdom and goodness! What praise and gratitude are due unto God for His divine decrees. Because of them, "We know that all things work together for good to them that love God, to them who are the called according to his purpose" (Romans 8:28). Well may we exclaim, "For of him, and through him, and to him, are all things: to whom be glory for ever. Amen" (11:36).

Romans 8: 28-30

Chapter 3

THE
KNOWLEDGE
OF GOD

God is omniscient. He knows everything; everything possible, everything actual; all events, all creatures; of the past, of the present, and of the future. He is perfectly acquainted with every detail in the life of every being in heaven, in earth, and in hell. "He knoweth what is in the darkness" (Daniel 2:22). Nothing escapes His notice; nothing can be hidden from Him, nothing is forgotten by Him. Well may we say with the psalmist, "Such knowledge is too wonderful for me; it is high, I cannot attain unto it" (Psalm 139:6). His knowledge is perfect. He never errs, never changes, never overlooks anything. "Neither is there any creature that is not manifest in his sight: but all things are naked and opened unto the eyes of him with whom we have to do" (Hebrews 4:13). Such is the God with whom we "have to do"!

"Thou knowest my downsitting and mine uprising, thou understandest my thought afar off. Thou compasseth my path and my lying down, and art acquainted with all my ways. For there is not a word in my tongue, but, lo, O LORD, thou knowest it altogether" (Psalm 139:2–4). What a wondrous Being is the God of Scripture! Each of His glorious attributes should render Him honorable in our esteem. In apprehension of His omniscience we ought to bow in adoration before Him. Yet how little do we meditate upon this divine perfection! Is it because the very thought of it fills us with uneasiness?

How solemn is this fact: Nothing can be concealed from God! "For I know the things that come into your mind, every one of them" (Ezekiel 11:5). Though He be invisible to us, we are not so to Him. Neither the darkness of night, the closest curtains, nor the deepest dungeon can hide the sinner from the eyes of Omniscience. The trees of the garden were not able to conceal our first parents. No human eye beheld Cain murder his brother, but his Maker witnessed his crime. Sarah might laugh derisively in the seclusion of her tent, yet Jehovah heard it. Achan stole a wedge of gold and carefully hid it in the earth, but God brought it to light. David took great pains to cover up his wickedness, but the all-seeing God sent one of His servants to say to him, "Thou art the man" (2 Samuel 12:7). To writer and reader also is said, "Be sure your sin will find you out" (Numbers 32:23).

Men would strip Deity of His omniscience if they could—what a proof that "the carnal mind is enmity against God" (Romans 8:7). The wicked do as naturally hate this divine perfection as much as they are naturally compelled to acknowledge it. They wish there might be no Witness of their sins, no Searcher of their hearts, no Judge of their deeds. They seek to banish such a God from their thoughts: "They consider not in their hearts that I remember all their wickedness" (Hosea 7:2). How solemn is Psalm 90:8. Good reason has every Christ-rejecter for trembling before it. "Thou hast set our iniquities before thee, our secret sins in the light of thy countenance."

But to the believer, the fact of God's omniscience is a truth fraught with much comfort. In times of perplexity he says with Job, "But he knoweth the way that I take" (23:10). It may be profoundly mysterious to me, quite incomprehensible to my friends, but "he knoweth"! In times of weariness and weakness believers assure themselves, "He knoweth our frame; he remembereth that we are dust" (Psalm 103:14). In times of doubt and suspicion they appeal to this very attribute, saying, "Search me, O God, and know my heart: try me, and know my thoughts: and see if there be any wicked way in me, and lead me in the way everlasting" (Psalm 139:23–24). In times of sad failure, when our actions have belied our hearts, when our deeds have repudiated our devotion, and the searching question comes to us, "Lovest thou Me?" we say, as Peter did, "Lord, thou knowest all things; thou knowest that I love thee" (John 21:17).

Here is encouragement to prayer. There is no cause to fear that the petitions of the righteous will not be heard, or that their tears will escape the notice of God, since He knows the thoughts and intents of the heart. There is no danger of the individual saint being overlooked amidst the multitude of supplicants who hourly present their petitions, for an infinite Mind is as capable of paying the same attention to millions as if only one were seeking its attention. So, too, the lack of appropriate language, the inability to give expression to the deepest longing of the soul, will not jeopardize our prayers, for "it shall come to pass, that before they call, I will answer; and while they are yet speaking, I will hear" (Isaiah 65:24).

"Great is our Lord, and of great power: his understanding is infinite" (Psalm 147:5). God knows whatsoever has happened in the past in every part of His vast domains, and He is thoroughly acquainted with everything that now transpires throughout the entire universe. But He also is perfectly cognizant with every event, from the least to the greatest, that will happen in ages to come. God's knowledge of the future is as complete as His knowledge of the past and the present, for the future depends entirely upon Himself. Were it in anywise possible for something to occur apart from either the direct agency or permission of God, then that something would be independent of Him, and He would at once cease to be supreme.

Now the divine knowledge of the future is not a mere abstraction, but something inseparably connected with and accompanied by His purpose. God designed whatsoever shall yet be, and what He has designed must be effected. As His most sure Word affirms, "He doeth according to his will in the army of heaven, and among the inhabitants of the earth: and none can stay his hand" (Daniel 4:35). Again, "There are many devices in a man's heart; nevertheless the counsel of the LORD, that shall stand" (Proverbs 19:21). The wisdom and power of God being alike infinite, the accomplishment of whatever He hath purposed is absolutely guaranteed. It is no more possible for the divine counsels to fail in their execution than it would be for the thrice-holy God to lie.

Nothing relating to the future is uncertain so far as the actualization of God's counsels are concerned. None of His decrees are left contingent either upon creatures or secondary causes. There is no future event which is only a mere possibility, that is, something which may or may not come to pass, "Known unto God are all his works from the beginning" (Acts 15:18). Whatever God has decreed is inexorably certain, for He is without variableness, or shadow of turning (James 1:17). Therefore, we are told at the very beginning of that book which unveils to us so much of the future that it will deal with "things which must shortly come to pass" (Revelation 1:1).

The perfect knowledge of God is exemplified and illustrated in every prophecy recorded in His Word. In the Old Testament, scores of predictions concerning the history of Israel were fulfilled to their minutest detail, centuries after they were made. Scores more foretold the earthly career of Christ, and they, too, were accomplished literally and perfectly. Such prophecies could only have been given by One who knew the end from the beginning, whose knowledge rested upon the unconditional certainty of the accomplishment of everything foretold. In like manner, both Old and New Testaments contain many other announcements yet future. They, too, "must be fulfilled" (Luke 24:44) because they were foretold by Him who decreed them.

It should, however, be pointed out that neither God's knowledge nor His cognition of the future, considered simply in themselves, are causative. Nothing has ever come to pass, or ever will, merely because God knew it. The cause of all things is the will of God. The man who really believes the Scriptures knows beforehand that the seasons will continue to follow each other with unfailing regularity to the end of earth's history (Genesis 8:22), yet his knowledge is not the cause of their succession. So God's knowledge does not arise from things because they are or will be, but because He has ordained them to be. God knew and foretold the crucifixion of His Son many hundreds of years before He became incarnate, and this because in the Divine purpose He was a Lamb slain from the foundation of the world; hence we read of His being "delivered by the determinate counsel and foreknowledge of God" (Acts 2:23).

A word or two of application. The infinite knowledge of God should fill us with amazement. How far exalted above the wisest man is the Lord! None of us knows what a day may bring forth, but all futurity is open to His omniscient gaze. The infinite knowledge of God ought to fill us with holy awe. Nothing we do, say, or even think, escapes the knowledge of Him with whom we have to do: "The eyes of the LORD are in every place, beholding the evil and the good" (Proverbs 15:3). What a curb this would be to us, if we meditated upon it more frequently! Instead of acting recklessly, we should say with Hagar, "Thou God seest me" (Genesis 16:13). The apprehension of God's infinite knowledge should fill the Christian with adoration. The whole of my life stood open to His view from the beginning. He foresaw my every fall, my every sin, my every backsliding; yet He fixed His heart upon me. Oh, how the realization of this should bow me in wonder and worship before Him!

Chapter 4

THE FOREKNOWLEDGE OF GOD

*W*hat controversies have been engendered by this subject in the past! But what truth of Holy Scripture is there which has not been the occasion of theological and ecclesiastical battles? The deity of Christ, His virgin birth, His atoning death, His second advent; the believer's justification, sanctification, security; the church, its organization, officers, discipline; baptism, the Lord's Supper, and a score of other precious truths might be mentioned. Yet, the controversies which have been waged over them did not close the mouths of God's faithful servants. Why, then, should we avoid the vexing question of God's foreknowledge because some will charge us with fomenting strife? Let others contend if they will; our duty is to bear witness according to the light given us.

There are two things concerning the foreknowledge of God about which many are in ignorance: the meaning of the term and its scriptural scope. Because this ignorance is so widespread, it is easy for preachers and teachers to palm off perversions of this subject, even upon the people of God. There is only one safeguard against error: that is to be established in the faith. For that there has to be prayerful, diligent study and a receiving with meekness the engrafted Word of God. Only then are we fortified against the attacks of those who assail us. There are those who misuse this very truth to discredit and deny the absolute sovereignty of God in the salvation of sinners. Just as higher critics repudiate the divine inspiration of the Scriptures; and evolutionists, the work of God in creation; so some pseudo Bible teachers pervert His foreknowledge to set aside His unconditional election unto eternal life.

When the blessed subject of divine fore*ordination* is expounded, when God's eternal choice of certain ones to be conformed to the image of His Son is set forth, the Enemy sends along someone to argue that election is based upon the fore*knowledge* of God. This foreknowledge is interpreted to mean that God foresaw certain ones who would be more pliable than others and would respond more readily to the strivings of the Spirit. So, because God knew they would believe, He predestinated them unto salvation. But such logic is radically wrong. It repudiates the truth of total depravity, for it argues that there is something good in some men. It takes away the independency of God, for it makes His decrees rest upon what He discovers in the creature.

It completely turns things upside down, for saying God foresaw certain sinners who would believe in Christ, and because of this He predestinated them unto salvation, is the very reverse of the truth. Scripture affirms that God, in His sovereignty, singled out certain ones to be recipients of His distinguishing favors (Acts 13:48); therefore, He determined to bestow upon them the gift of faith. False theology makes God's foreknowledge of our believing the cause of His election to salvation. However, God's election is the *cause,* and our believing in Christ the *effect.*

Before we proceed further with this much misunderstood theme, let us define our terms. What is meant by *foreknowledge?* "To know beforehand" is the ready reply of many. But we must not jump to conclusions, nor must we turn to Webster's dictionary as the final court of appeal, for it is not a matter of the etymology of the term employed. What we need is to find out how the word is used in Scripture. The Holy Spirit's usage of an expression always defines its meaning and scope. Failure to apply this simple rule is responsible for much confusion and error. So many people assume they already know the significance of a certain word used in Scripture, and then they are too dilatory to test their assumptions with a concordance. Let us amplify:

Take the word *flesh*. Its meaning appears so obvious that many would regard it as a waste of time to look up its various connections in Scripture. It is hastily assumed that the word is synonymous with the physical body, so no inquiry is made. But, in fact, *flesh* in Scripture frequently includes far more than what is corporeal; all that is embraced by the term can only be ascertained by a diligent comparison of every occurrence of it in the Bible and by a study of each separate context.

Take the word *world*. The average Bible reader imagines this word is the equivalent for the human race; and, consequently, many passages where the term is found are wrongly interpreted.

Take the word *immortality*. Surely it requires no study! Obviously it has reference to the indestructibility of the soul. Ah, but it is wrong to assume anything where the Word of God is concerned. If the reader will take the trouble to carefully examine each passage where *mortal* and *immortal* are found, it will be seen these words are never applied to the soul but always to the body.

Now what has just been said on *flesh*, the *world*, and *immortality* applies with equal force to the terms *know* and *foreknow*. Instead of imagining that these words signify no more than a simple cognition, carefully weigh the different passages in which they occur. The word *foreknowledge* is not found in the Old Testament. But *know* occurs there frequently. When that term is used in connection with God, it often signifies to regard with favor, denoting not mere cognition but an affection for the object in view. "I know thee by name" (Exodus 33:17). "Ye have been rebellious against the LORD from the day that I knew you" (Deuteronomy 9:24). "Before I formed thee in the belly I knew thee" (Jeremiah 1:5). "They have made princes, and I knew it not" (Hosea 8:4). "You only have I known of all the families of the earth" (Amos 3:2). In these passages *knew* signifies either "loved" or "appointed."

In like manner, the word *know* is frequently used in the New Testament in the same sense as in the Old. "Then will I profess unto them, I never knew you" (Matthew 7:23). "I am the good shepherd, and know my sheep, and am known of mine" (John 10:14). "If any man love God, the same is known of him" (1 Corinthians 8:3). "The Lord knoweth them that are his" (2 Timothy 2:19).

Now the word *foreknowledge* as it is used in the New Testament is less ambiguous than in its simple form, *to know*. If you carefully study every passage in which it occurs, you will discover that it is a moot point whether it ever has reference to the mere perception of events yet to take place. The fact is that *foreknowledge* is never used in Scripture in connection with events or actions; instead, it always refers to persons. It is to persons God is said to "foreknow," not to the actions of those persons. To prove this we will quote each passage where this expression is found.

The first occurs in Acts 2:23:"Him, being delivered by the determinate counsel and foreknowledge of God, ye have taken, and by wicked hands have crucified and slain." Careful attention to the wording of this verse shows that the apostle was not speaking of God's foreknowledge of the act of the crucifixion, but of the Person crucified:"Him [Christ], being delivered by."

The second is Romans 8:29–30:"For whom he did foreknow, he also did predestinate to be conformed to the image of his Son, that he might be the firstborn among many brethren. Moreover whom he did predestinate, them he also called." Weigh well the pronoun used here. It is not *what* He did foreknow, but *whom* He did. It is not the surrendering of their wills, nor the believing of their hearts, but the persons themselves, which is in view.

"God hath not cast away his people which he foreknew" (Romans 11:2). Once more, the plain reference is to persons, and to persons only.

The last mention is in 1 Peter 1:2:"Elect according to the foreknowledge of God the Father."Who are "elect according to the foreknowledge of God the Father"? The previous verse tells us the reference is to the "strangers scattered," i.e., the diaspora, the dispersion, the believing Jews. Thus, the reference is to persons and not to their foreseen acts.

Now, in view of these passages (and there are no more), what scriptural ground is there for anyone to say God "foreknew" the acts of certain ones, i.e., their "repenting and believing," and that because of those acts He elected them unto salvation? The answer is, None whatever. Scripture never speaks of repentance and faith as being foreseen or foreknown by God. Truly, He did know from all eternity that certain ones would repent and believe, yet this is not what Scripture refers to as the object of God's foreknowledge. The word uniformly refers to God's foreknowing *persons;* then let us "hold fast the form of sound words" (2 Timothy 1:13).

Another thing we want to call particular attention to is that the first two passages quoted above show plainly and teach implicitly that God's foreknowledge is not causative; that instead, something else lies behind, *precedes* it—something that is His own sovereign decree. Christ was "delivered by the [1] determinate counsel and [2] foreknowledge of God" (Acts 2:23). His counsel or decree was the ground of His foreknowledge. So again in Romans 8:29. That verse opens with the word *for,* which tells us to look back to what immediately precedes. What, then, does the previous verse say? This: "All things work together for good to them . . . who are the called according to his purpose." Thus God's *foreknowledge* is based upon His *purpose,* or decree (see Psalm 2:7).

God foreknows what will be because He has decreed it. It is therefore a reverse order of Scripture, putting the cart before the horse, to affirm that God elects because He foreknows people. The truth is, He foreknows because He has elected. This removes the cause of election from outside the creature and places it in God's own sovereign will. God purposed in Himself to elect a certain people, not because of anything good in them or from them, either actual or foreseen, but solely out of His own pleasure.

Why He chose the ones He did, we do not know. We can only say, "Even so, Father: for so it seemed good in thy sight" (Matthew 11:26). The plain truth of Romans 8:29 is that God, before the foundation of the world, singled out certain sinners and appointed them unto salvation (2 Thessalonians 2:13). This is clear from Romans 8:29: "For whom he did foreknow, he also did predestinate to be conformed to the image of his Son." God did not predestinate those whom He foreknew were conformed. On the contrary, those whom He foreknew (i.e., loved and elected) He predestinated "to be conformed." Their conformity to Christ is not the *cause,* but the effect of God's foreknowledge and predestination.

God did not elect any sinner because He foresaw that he would believe, for the simple but sufficient reason that no sinner ever believes until God gives him faith, just as no man sees until God gives him sight. *Sight* is God's gift; *seeing* is the consequence of my using His gift. So faith is God's gift (Ephesians 2:8–9) and believing is the consequence of my using His gift. If it were true that God had elected certain ones to be saved because in due time they would believe, that would make believing a meritorious act. In that event, the saved sinner would have ground for "boasting," which Scripture emphatically denies (v. 9).

Surely God's Word is plain enough in teaching that believing is not a meritorious act. It affirms that Christians are a people "which had believed through grace" (Acts 18:27). If, then, they have believed "through grace," there is absolutely nothing meritorious about believing; if nothing meritorious, it could not be the ground or cause which moved God to choose them. No! God's choice proceeds not from anything in or from *us*, but solely from His own sovereign pleasure. Once more, we read of "a remnant according to the election of grace" (Romans 11:5). There it is, plain enough; election itself is of grace, and grace is unmerited favor, something for which we had no claim upon God whatsoever.

It is highly important for us to have clear and scriptural views of the foreknowledge of God. Erroneous conceptions about it lead inevitably to thoughts most dishonoring to Him. The popular idea of divine foreknowledge is altogether inadequate. God not only knew the end from the beginning, but also He planned, fixed, and predestinated everything from the beginning. And, as cause stands to effect, so God's purpose is the ground of His prescience. If, then, the reader is a true Christian, he is so because God chose him in Christ before the foundation of the world (Ephesians 1:4); and chose you not because He *foresaw* you would believe, but simply because it *pleased Him to choose;* chose you notwithstanding your natural unbelief. This being so, all glory and praise belongs alone to Him. You have no ground for taking any credit to yourself. You have "believed through grace" (Acts 18:27), and that, because your very election was "of grace" (Romans 11:5).

Chapter 5

THE SUPREMACY OF GOD

*I*n one of his letters to Erasmus, Luther said, "Your thoughts of God are too human." Probably that renowned scholar resented such a rebuke, the more so, since it proceeded from a miner's son. Nevertheless, it was thoroughly deserved. We, too, prefer the same charge against the vast majority of the preachers of our day and against those who, instead of searching the Scriptures for themselves, lazily accept their teachings. The most dishonoring conceptions of the rule and reign of the Almighty are now held almost everywhere. To countless thousands, even professing Christians, the God of Scriptures is quite unknown.

Of old, God complained to an apostate Israel, "Thou thoughtest that I was altogether such an one as thyself" (Psalm 50:21). Such must now be His indictment against apostate Christendom. Men imagine the Most High is moved by sentiment, rather than by principle. They suppose His omnipotency is such an idle fiction that Satan can thwart His designs on every side. They think that if He has formed any plan or purpose at all, then it must be like theirs, constantly subject to change. They openly declare that whatever power He possesses must be restricted, lest He invade the citadel of man's free will and reduce him to a machine. They lower the all-efficacious atonement, which redeems everyone for whom it was made, to a mere remedy, which sin-sick souls may use if they feel so disposed. They lessen the strength of the invincible work of the Holy Spirit to an offer of the Gospel which sinners may accept or reject as they please.

The god of this century no more resembles the Sovereign of Holy Writ than does the dim flickering of a candle the glory of the midday sun. The god who is talked about in the average pulpit, spoken of in the ordinary Sunday school, mentioned in much of the religious literature of the day, and preached in most of the so-called Bible conferences, is a figment of human imagination, an invention of maudlin sentimentality. The heathen outside the pale of Christendom form gods of wood and stone, while millions of heathen inside Christendom manufacture a god out of their carnal minds. In reality, they are but atheists, for there is no other possible alternative between an absolutely supreme God and no God at all. A god whose will is resisted, whose designs are frustrated, whose purpose is checkmated, possesses no title to deity and, far from being a fit object of worship, merits nothing but contempt.

The supremacy of the true and living God might well be argued from the infinite distance which separates the mightiest creatures from the Creator. He is the Potter; they are but the clay in His hands, to be molded into vessels of honor or to be dashed into pieces (Psalm 2:9) as He pleases. Were all the denizens of heaven and all the inhabitants of earth to combine in open revolt against Him, it would cause Him no uneasiness. It would have less effect upon His eternal, unassailable throne than the spray of the Mediterranean's waves has upon the towering rocks of Gibraltar. So puerile and powerless is the creature to affect the Most High, Scripture tells us that when the Gentile heads unite with apostate Israel to defy Jehovah and His Christ, "He that sitteth in the heavens shall laugh" (Psalm 2:4).

The absolute and universal supremacy of God is plainly affirmed in many Scriptures. "Thine, O LORD, is the greatness, and the power, and the glory, and the victory, and the majesty: for all that is in the heaven and in the earth is thine; thine is the kingdom, O LORD, and thou art exalted as head above all. . . . And thou reignest over all" (1 Chronicles 29:11–12). Note "reignest" *now*, not "will do so in the Millennium." "O

LORD God of our fathers, art not thou God in heaven? and rulest not thou over all the kingdoms of the heathen? and in thine hand is there not power and might, so that none [not even the devil himself] is able to withstand thee?" (2 Chronicles 20:6). Before Him presidents and popes, kings and emperors, are less than grasshoppers.

"But he is in one mind, and who can turn him? and what his soul desireth, even that he doeth" (Job 23:13). My reader, the God of Scripture is no make-believe monarch, no imaginary sovereign, but King of kings, and Lord of lords. "I know that thou canst do every thing, and that no thought can be withholden from thee" (Job 42:2); or, another translator, "no purpose of thine can be thwarted" (RSV). All that He has designed, He does. All that He has decreed, He perfects. All that He has promised, He performs. "But our God is in the heavens: he hath done whatsoever he hath pleased" (Psalm 115:3). Why has He? Because "there is no wisdom nor understanding nor counsel against the Lord" (Proverbs 21:30).

God's supremacy over the works of His hands is vividly depicted in Scripture. Inanimate matter, irrational creatures, all perform their Maker's bidding. At His pleasure, the Red Sea divided and its waters stood up as walls (Exodus 14); the earth opened her mouth, and guilty rebels went down alive into the pit (Numbers 16). When He so ordered, the sun stood still (Joshua 10:1–13); and on another occasion it went backward ten degrees on the dial of Ahaz (2 Kings 20:1–11). To exemplify His supremacy, God made ravens carry food to Elijah (1 Kings 17); iron to float on the waters (2 Kings 6:1–7); lions to be tame when Daniel was cast into their den (Daniel 6); fire to burn not when three Hebrews were flung into its flames (Daniel 3). Thus, "Whatsoever the LORD pleased, that did he in heaven, and in earth, in the seas, and all deep places" (Psalm 135:6).

God's supremacy is also demonstrated in His perfect rule over the wills of men. Ponder carefully Exodus 34. Three times in the year all the males of Israel were required to leave their homes and go up to Jerusalem. They lived in the midst of hostile people, who hated them for having appropriated their lands. What, then, was to hinder the Canaanites from seizing the opportunity, during the absence of the men, to enslave the women and children and take possession of their farms? If the hand of the Almighty was not upon the wills even of wicked men, how could He make this promise beforehand, that none should so much as "desire" their lands (v. 24)? "The king's heart is in the hand of the LORD, as the rivers of water: he turneth it whithersoever he will" (Proverbs 21:1).

But, some may object, do we not read again and again in Scripture how men defied God, resisted His will, broke His commandments, disregarded His warnings, and turned a deaf ear to all His exhortations? Certainly we do. Does this nullify all we have said? If so, then plainly the Bible contradicts itself. But that cannot be. What the objector refers to is simply the wickedness of men against the external word of God. We have mentioned what God has purposed in Himself. The rule of conduct He has given us to walk by is perfectly fulfilled by none of us. His own eternal counsels are accomplished to their minutest details.

The absolute and universal supremacy of God is affirmed with equal positiveness in the New Testament. We are told that God "worketh all things after the counsel of his own will" (Ephesians 1:11)—the Greek for "worketh" means "to work effectually." For this reason we read, "For of him, and through him, and to him, are all things: to whom be glory forever. Amen" (Romans 11:36). Men may boast they are free agents, with a will of their own, and are at liberty to do as they please. But Scripture says to those who boast, "We will go into such a city, and continue there a year, and buy and sell," that they ought to say, "If the Lord will" (James 4:13, 15).

Here then is a sure resting place for the heart. Our lives are neither the product of blind fate nor the result of capricious chance. Every detail of them was ordained from all eternity and is now ordered by the living, reigning God. Not a hair of our heads can be touched without His permission. "A man's heart deviseth his way: but the LORD directeth his steps" (Proverbs 16:9). What assurance, what strength, what comfort this should give the real Christian! "My times are in thy hand" (Psalm 31:15). Then let me "rest in the LORD, and wait patiently for him" (37:7).

Chapter 6

THE SOVEREIGNTY OF GOD

*T*he sovereignty of God may be defined as the exercise of His supremacy (see preceding chapter). Infinitely elevated above the highest creature, He is the Most High, Lord of heaven and earth; subject to none, influenced by none, absolutely independent. God does as He pleases, only as He pleases, always as He pleases. None can thwart Him; none can hinder Him. So His own Word expressly declares: "My counsel shall stand, and I will do all my pleasure" (Isaiah 46:10); "he doeth according to his will in the army of heaven, and among the inhabitants of the earth: and none can stay his hand" (Daniel 4:35). Divine sovereignty means that God is God in fact as well as in name; that He is on the throne of the universe, directing all things, working all things "after the counsel of his own will" (Ephesians 1:11).

Rightly did the late Charles Haddon Spurgeon say in his sermon on Matthew 20:15:

> There is no attribute more comforting to His children than that of God's Sovereignty. Under the most adverse circumstances, in the most se-

vere trials, they believe that Sovereignty has ordained their afflictions, that Sovereignty overrules them, and that Sovereignty will sanctify them all. There is nothing for which the children ought more earnestly to contend than the doctrine of their Master over all creation—the Kingship of God over all the works of His own hands—the Throne of God and His right to sit upon that Throne.

On the other hand, there is no doctrine more hated by worldings, no truth of which they have made such a football, as the great, stupendous, but yet most certain doctrine of the Sovereignty of the infinite Jehovah. Men will allow God to be everywhere except on His throne. They will allow Him to be in His workshop to fashion worlds and make stars. They will allow Him to be in His almonry to dispense His alms and bestow His bounties.

They will allow Him to sustain the earth and bear up the pillars thereof, or light the lamps of heaven, or rule the waves of the evermoving ocean; but when God ascends His throne, His creatures then gnash their teeth, and we proclaim an enthroned God, and His right to do as He wills with His own, to dispose of His creatures as He thinks well, without consulting them in the matter; then it is that we are hissed and execrated, and then it is that men turn a deaf ear to us, for God on His throne is not the God they love. But it is God upon the throne that we love to preach. It is God upon His throne whom we trust.

"Whatsoever the LORD pleased, that did he in heaven, and in earth, in the seas, and all deep places" (Psalm 135:6). Such is the mighty Potentate revealed in Holy Writ: unrivalled in majesty, unlimited in power, unaffected by anything outside Himself. But we are living in a day when even the most orthodox seem afraid to admit the proper Godhood of God. They say that to press the sovereignty of God excludes human responsibility, whereas human responsibility is based upon divine sovereignty and is the product of it.

"But our God is in the heavens: he hath done whatsoever he hath pleased" (Psalm 115:3). He sovereignly chose to place each of His creatures on that particular footing which seemed good in His sight. He created angels. Some He placed on a conditional footing; others He gave an immutable standing before Him (1 Timothy 5:21), making Christ their head (Colossians 2:10). Let it not be overlooked that the angels which sinned (2 Peter 2:4) were as much His creatures as the angels that sinned not. Yet God foresaw they would fall. Nevertheless He placed them on a mutable, creature, conditional footing, and suffered them to fall, though He was not the Author of their sin.

Too, God sovereignly placed Adam in the Garden of Eden upon a conditional footing. Had He so pleased, He could have placed him upon an unconditional footing; He could have placed him on a footing as firm as that occupied by the unfallen angels; He could have placed him upon a footing as sure and as immutable as that which His saints have in Christ. Instead, He chose to set him in Eden on the basis of creature responsibility, so that he stood or fell according to how he measured up or failed to measure up to his responsibility—obedience to his Maker. Adam stood accountable to God by the Law which his Creator had given him. Here was responsibility, unimpaired responsibility, tested under the most favorable conditions.

God did not place Adam upon a footing of conditional, creature responsibility because it was right He should so place him. No, it was right because God did it. God did not even give creatures being because it was right for Him to do so, i.e., because He was under any obligations to create; but it was right because He did so. God is sovereign. His will is supreme. So far from God being under any law of right, He is a law unto Himself, so that whatever He does is right. Woe be to the rebel who calls His sovereignty into question: "Woe unto him that striveth with his Maker! Let the potsherd strive with the potsherds of the earth. Shall the clay say to him that fashioneth it, What makest thou?" (Isaiah 45:9).

Again, the Lord sovereignly placed Israel upon a conditional footing. Exodus 19, 20, and 24 afford a full proof of this. They were placed under a covenant of works. God gave them certain laws. National blessing for them depended upon their observance of His statutes. But Israel was stiff-necked and uncircumcised in heart. They rebelled against Jehovah, forsook His Law, turned unto false gods, apostatized. In consequence, divine judgment fell upon them; they were delivered into the hands of their enemies, dispersed abroad throughout the earth, and remain under the heavy frown of God's displeasure to this day.

It was God in the exercise of His sovereignty who placed Satan and his angels, Adam, and Israel in their respective responsible positions. But so far from His sovereignty taking away responsibility from the creature, it was by the exercise of it that He placed them on this conditional footing, under such responsibilities as He thought proper. By virtue of this sovereignty, He is seen to be God over all. Thus, there is perfect harmony between the sovereignty of God and the responsibility of the creature. Many have more foolishly said that it is quite impossible to show where divine sovereignty ends and creature accountability begins. Here is where creature responsibility begins: in the sovereign ordination of the Creator. As to His sovereignty, there is not, and never will be, any end to it!

Let us see further proofs that the responsibility of the creature is based upon God's sovereignty. How many things are recorded in Scripture which were right because God commanded them—which would not have been right had He not so commanded! What right had Adam to eat of the trees of the garden? The permission of his Maker (Genesis 2:16); without such, he would have been a thief! What right had Israel to borrow of the Egyptians' jewels and raiment (Exodus 12:35)? None, unless Jehovah had authorized it (3:22). What right had Israel to slay so many lambs for sacrifice? None, except that God commanded it. What right had Israel to kill off all the Canaanites? None, only as Jehovah had bidden them (Deuteronomy 20:17). What right has the husband to require submission from his wife? None, unless God had appointed it (Ephesians 5:22; Colossians 3:18). So we might go on. Human responsibility is based on divine sovereignty.

One more example of the exercise of God's absolute sovereignty: God placed His elect upon a different footing than Adam or Israel. He placed them upon an *unconditional* footing. In the Everlasting Covenant Jesus Christ was appointed their Head, took their responsibilities upon Himself, and wrought out a righteousness for them which is perfect, indefeasible, eternal. Christ was placed upon a conditional footing, for He was "made under the law, to redeem them that were under the law" (Galatians 4:4–5), but with this infinite difference: The others failed, but He did not and could not. Who placed Christ upon that conditional footing? The Triune God. It was sovereign will that appointed Him, sovereign love that sent Him, sovereign authority that assigned His work.

Certain conditions were set before the Mediator. He was to be made in the likeness of sin's flesh; He was to magnify the Law and make it honorable; He was to bear all the sins of all God's people in His own body on the tree; He was to make full atonement for them; He was to endure the outpoured wrath of God; He was to die and be buried. On the fulfillment of those conditions He was promised a reward (Isaiah 53:10–12). He was to be the firstborn among many brethren; He was to have a people who should share His glory. Blessed be His name forever, He fulfilled those conditions.

Because He did so, the Father stands pledged, on solemn oath, to preserve through time and bless throughout eternity every one of those for whom His incarnate Son mediated. Because He took their place, they now share His. His righteousness is theirs. His standing before God is theirs. His life is theirs. There is not a single condition for them to meet, not a single responsibility for them to discharge in order to attain their eternal bliss. "By one offering he hath perfected for ever them that are sanctified" (Hebrews 10:14).

Here then is the sovereignty of God openly displayed before all, displayed in the different ways in which He has dealt with His creatures. Part of the angels, Adam, and Israel were placed upon a conditional footing. Continued blessing was dependent upon their obedience and fidelity to God. But in sharp contrast, the "little flock" (Luke 12:32) have been given an unconditional, an immutable standing in God's covenant, God's counsels, God's Son; their blessing is dependent upon what Christ did for them. "The foundation of God standeth sure, having this seal, The Lord knoweth them that are his" (2 Timothy 2:19). The foundation on which God's elect stand is a perfect one; nothing can be added to it, nor anything taken from it (Ecclesiastes 3:14). Here, then, is the highest and grandest display of the absolute sovereignty of God. He has "mercy on whom he will have mercy, and whom he will he hardeneth" (Romans 9:18).

Chapter 7

THE IMMUTABILITY OF GOD

*T*his is one of the divine perfections which is not sufficiently pondered. It is one of the excellencies of the Creator which distinguishes Him from all His creatures. God is perpetually the same: subject to no change in His being, attributes, or determinations. Therefore God is compared to a rock (Deuteronomy 32:4) which remains immovable when the entire ocean surrounding it is continually in a fluctuating state. Even so, though all creatures are subject to change, God is immutable. Because God has no beginning and no ending, He can know no change. He is everlastingly "the Father of lights, with whom is no variableness, neither shadow of turning" (James 1:17).

First, God is immutable in His essence. His nature and being are infinite, and so, subject to no mutations. There never was a time when He was not; there never will come a time when He shall cease to be. God has neither evolved, grown, nor improved. All that He is today, He has ever been, and ever will be. "I am the LORD, I change not" (Malachi 3:6) is His own unqualified affirmation. He cannot change for the better, for He is already perfect; being perfect, He cannot change for the worse. Altogether unaffected by anything outside Himself, improvement or deterioration is impossible. He is perpetually the same. He only can say, "I AM THAT I AM" (Exodus 3:14). He is altogether uninfluenced by the flight of time. There is no wrinkle upon the brow of eternity. Therefore His power can never diminish, nor His glory ever fade.

Second, God is immutable in His attributes. Whatever the attributes of God were before the universe was called into existence, they are precisely the same now, and will remain so forever. Necessarily so; for they are the very perfections, the essential qualities of His being. *Semper idem* (always the same) is written across every one of them. His power is unabated, His wisdom undiminished, His holiness unsullied. The attributes of God can no more change than deity can cease to be. His veracity is immutable, for His Word is "for ever . . . settled in heaven" (Psalm 119:89). His love is eternal: "I have loved thee with an everlasting love" (Jeremiah 31:3), and, "Having loved his own which were in the world, he loved them unto the end" (John 13:1). His mercy ceases not, for it is "everlasting" (Psalm 100:5).

Third, God is immutable in His counsel. His will never varies. Perhaps some are ready to object when we read "It repented the LORD that he had made man" (Genesis 6:6). Our first reply is, Do the Scriptures contradict themselves? No, that cannot be. Numbers 23:19 is plain enough: "God is not a man, that he should lie; neither the son of man, that he should repent." The explanation is simple. When speaking of Himself, God frequently accommodates His language to our limited capacities. He describes Himself as clothed with bodily members, as eyes, ears, hands.

He speaks of Himself as "waking" (see Psalm 78:65), as "rising up early" (Jeremiah 7:13); yet He neither slumbers nor sleeps. When He institutes a change in His dealings with men, He describes His course of conduct as "repenting" (see Genesis 6:6).

Yes, God is immutable in His counsel. "The gifts and calling of God are without repentance" (Romans 11:29). It must be so, for "he is in one mind, and who can turn him? and what his soul desireth, even that he doeth" (Job 23:13).

> Change and decay in all around we see,
> May He who changeth not abide with thee.

God's purpose never alters. One of two things causes a man to change his mind and reverse his plans: want of foresight to anticipate everything, or lack of power to execute them. But as God is both omniscient and omnipotent, there is never any need for Him to revise His decrees. No: "The counsel of the LORD standeth for ever, the thoughts of his heart to all generations" (Psalm 33:11). Therefore we read of "the immutability of his counsel" (Hebrews 6:17).

Here we may perceive the infinite distance which separates the highest creature from the Creator. Creaturehood and mutability are correlative terms. If the creature was not mutable by nature, it would not be a creature; it would be God. By nature we tend to nothing, as we came from nothing. Nothing stays our annihilation but the will and sustaining power of God. None can sustain himself a single moment. We are entirely dependent on the Creator for every breath we draw. We gladly own with the psalmist, "God . . . holdeth our soul in life" (Psalm 66:8–9). The realization of this ought to make us lie down under a sense of our own nothingness in the presence of Him "in [whom] we live, and move, and have our being" (Acts 17:28).

As fallen creatures we are not only mutable, but also everything in us is opposed to God. As such we are "wandering stars" (Jude 13), out of our proper orbit. The wicked are "like the troubled sea, when it cannot rest" (Isaiah 57:20). Fallen man is inconstant. The words of Jacob concerning Reuben apply with full force to all of Adam's descendants: "unstable as water" (Genesis 49:4). Thus it is not only a mark of piety, but also the part of wisdom to heed that injunction, "Cease ye from man" (Isaiah 2:22). No human being is to be depended on. "Put not your trust in princes, nor in the son of man, in whom there is no help" (Psalm 146:3). If I disobey God, then I deserve to be deceived and disappointed by my fellows. People who like you today, may hate you tomorrow. The multitude who cried, "Hosanna to the Son of David," speedily changed to "Away with him, crucify him" (Matthew 21:9; John 19:15).

Here is solid comfort. Human nature cannot be relied upon; but God can! However unstable I may be, however fickle my friends may prove, God changes not. If He varied as we do, if He willed one thing today and another tomorrow, if He were controlled by caprice, who could confide in Him? But He is ever the same. His purpose is fixed, His will stable, His word is sure. Here then is a rock on which we may fix our feet, while the mighty torrent sweeps away everything around us. The permanence of

God's character guarantees the fulfillment of His promises: "For the mountains shall depart, and the hills be removed; but my kindness shall not depart from thee, neither shall the covenant of my peace be removed, saith the LORD that hath mercy on thee" (Isaiah 54:10).

Here is encouragement to prayer. "What comfort would it be to pray to a god that, like the chameleon, changed colour every moment? Who would put up a petition to an earthly prince that was so mutable as to grant a petition one day, and deny it another?" (S. Charnock, 1670). Should someone ask what is the use of praying to One whose will is already fixed, we answer, because He requires it. What blessings has God promised without our seeking them? "If we ask any thing according to his will, he heareth us" (1 John 5:14). He has willed everything that is for His child's good. To ask for anything contrary to His will is not prayer, but rank rebellion.

Here is terror for the wicked. Those who defy Him, break His laws, have no concern for His glory, but live their lives as though He did not exist, must not suppose that, when at the last they shall cry to Him for mercy, He will alter His will, revoke His word, and rescind His awful threatenings. No, He has declared, "Therefore will I also deal in fury: mine eye shall not spare, neither will I have pity: and though they cry in mine ears with a loud voice, yet will I not hear them" (Ezekiel 8:18). God will not deny Himself to gratify their lusts. God is holy, unchangingly so. Therefore God hates sin, eternally hates it. Hence the eternality of the punishment of all who die in their sins.

> The divine immutability, like the cloud which interposed between the Israelites and the Egyptian army, has a dark as well as a light side. It insures the execution of His threatenings, as well as the performance of His promises; and destroys the hope which the guilty fondly cherish, that He will be all lenity to His frail and erring creatures, and that they will be much more lightly dealt with than the declarations of His own Word would lead us to expect. We oppose to these deceitful and presumptuous speculations the solemn truth, that God is unchanging in veracity and purpose, in faithfulness and justice. (J. Dick, 1850)

Chapter 8
THE
HOLINESS
OF GOD

"Who shall not fear thee, O Lord, and glorify thy name? for thou only art holy" (Revelation 15:4). He only is independently, infinitely, immutably holy. In Scripture, He is frequently styled "the Holy One." He is so because the sum of all moral excellency is found in Him. He is absolute purity, unsullied even by the shadow of sin. "God is light, and in him is no darkness at all" (1 John 1:5). Holiness is the very excellency of the divine nature; the great God is "glorious in holiness" (Exodus 15:11). Therefore we read, "Thou art of purer eyes than to behold evil, and canst not look on iniquity" (Habakkuk 1:13).

As God's power is the opposite of the native weakness of the creature, as His wisdom is in complete contrast from the least defect of understanding or folly, so His holiness is the very antithesis of all moral blemish or defilement. Of old God appointed singers in Israel "that should praise the beauty of holiness" (2 Chronicles 20:21). "Power is God's hand or arm, omniscience His eye, mercy His bowels, eternity His duration, but holiness is His beauty" (S. Charnock). It is this, supremely, which renders Him lovely to those who are delivered from sin's dominion.

A chief emphasis is placed upon this perfection of God.

> God is oftener styled Holy than Almighty, and set forth by this part of His dignity more than by any other. This is more fixed on as an epithet to His name than any other. You never find it expressed "His mighty name" or "His wise name," but His great name, and most of all, His holy name. This is the greatest title of honour; in this latter cloth the majesty and venerableness of His name appear. (S. Charnock)

This perfection, as none other, is solemnly celebrated before the throne of heaven, the seraphim crying, "Holy, holy, holy, is the LORD of hosts" (Isaiah 6:3). God Himself singles out this perfection, "Once have I sworn by my holiness" (Psalm 89:35). God swears by His holiness because that is a fuller expression of Himself than anything else.

Therefore we are exhorted, "Sing unto the LORD, O ye saints of his, and give thanks at the remembrance of his holiness" (Psalm 30:4). "This may be said to be a transcendental attribute, that, as it were, runs through the rest, and casts lustre upon them. It is an attribute of attributes" (A. Howe, 1670). Thus we read of "the beauty of the LORD" (Psalm 27:4), which is none other than "the beauty of holiness" (Psalm 29:2; 96:9; 110:3).

> As it seems to challenge an excellency above all His other perfections, so it is the glory of all the rest: as it is the glory of the Godhead, so it is the glory of every perfection in the Godhead; as His power is the strength of them, so His holiness is the beauty of them; as all would be weak without almightiness to back them, so all would be uncomely without holiness to adorn them. Should this be sullied, all the rest would lose their honour; as at the same instant the sun should lose its light, it would lose its heat, its strength, its generative and quickening virtue. As sincerity is the lustre of every grace in a Christian, so is purity the splendour of every attribute in the Godhead. His justice is a holy justice, His wisdom a holy wisdom, His power a "holy arm" (Psalm 98:1). His truth or promise a "holy promise" (Psalm 105:42). His name, which signifies all His attributes in conjunction, is "holy" (Psalm 103:1). (S. Charnock)

God's holiness is manifested in His works. "The LORD is righteous in all his ways, and holy in all his works" (Psalm 145:17). Nothing but what is excellent can proceed from Him. Holiness is the rule of all His actions. At the beginning He pronounced all that He made "very good" (Genesis 1:31), which He could not have done had there been anything imperfect or unholy in them. Man was made "upright" (Ecclesiastes 7:29), in the image and likeness of his Creator. The angels that fell were created holy, for we are told that they "kept not their first estate, but left their own habitation" (Jude 6). Of Satan it is written, "Thou wast perfect in thy ways from the day that thou wast created, till iniquity was found in thee" (Ezekiel 28:15).

God's holiness is manifested in His Law. That Law forbids sin in all of its modifications—in its most refined, as well as its grossest forms, the intent of the mind as well as the pollution of the body, the secret desire as well as the overt act. Therefore we read, "The law is holy, and the commandment holy, and just, and good" (Romans 7:12). Yes, "the commandment of the LORD is pure, enlightening the eyes. The fear of the LORD is clean, enduring for ever: the judgments of the LORD are true and righteous altogether" (Psalm 19:8–9).

God's holiness is manifested at the Cross. Wondrously, and yet most solemnly does the atonement display God's infinite holiness and abhorrence of sin. How hateful must sin be to God for Him to punish it to its utmost deserts when it was imputed to His Son!

> Not all the vials of judgment that have or shall be poured out upon the wicked world, nor the naming furnace of a sinner's conscience, nor the irreversible sentence pronounced against the rebellious demons, nor the groans of the damned creatures, give such a demonstration of God's hatred of sin, as the wrath of God let loose upon His Son. Never did Divine holiness appear more beautiful and lovely than at the time our Saviour's countenance was most marred in the midst of His dying groans. This Himself acknowledges in Psalm 22. When God had turned His smiling face from Him, and thrust His sharp knife into His heart, which forced that terrible cry from Him, "My God, My God, why hast thou forsaken me?" He adores this perfection—"Thou art holy" (v. 3). (S. Charnock)

Because God is holy He hates all sin. He loves everything which is in conformity to His laws, and loathes everything contrary to them. His Word plainly declares, "The froward is abomination to the LORD" (Proverbs 3:32). And again, "The thoughts of the wicked are an abomination to the LORD" (Proverbs 15:26). It follows, therefore, that He must necessarily punish sin. Sin can no more exist without demanding His punishment than it can without requiring His hatred of it. God has often forgiven sinners, but He never forgives sin; the sinner is only forgiven on the ground of Another having borne his punishment; for "without shedding of blood is no remission" (Hebrews 9:22). Therefore we are told "The LORD will take vengeance on his adversaries, and he reserveth wrath for his enemies" (Nahum 1:2). For one sin God banished our first parents from Eden; for one sin all the posterity of Canaan fell under a curse which remains over them to this day; for one sin Moses was excluded from the promised land; Elisha's servant smitten with leprosy; Ananias and Sapphira were cut off from the land of the living.

Here we find proof for the divine inspiration of the Scriptures. The unregenerate do not really believe in the holiness of God. Their concept of His character is altogether one-sided. They fondly hope that His mercy will override everything else. "Thou thoughtest that I was altogether such an one as thyself" (Psalm 50:21) is God's charge against them. They think only of a god patterned after their own evil hearts, hence their continuance in a course of mad folly. Such is the holiness ascribed to the divine nature and character in Scripture that it clearly demonstrates their superhuman origin.

The character attributed to the gods of the ancients and of modern heathendom are the very reverse of that immaculate purity which pertains to the true God. An ineffably holy God, who has the utmost abhorrence of all sin, was never invented by any of Adam's fallen descendants! The fact is that nothing reveals more of the terrible depravity of man's heart and his enmity against the living God than to have set before him One who is infinitely and immutably holy. His own idea of sin is practically limited to what the world calls crime. Anything short of that, man palliates as "defects," "mistakes," "infirmities." And even where sin is owned at all, man makes excuses and extenuations for it.

The god which the vast majority of professing Christians love is looked upon very much like an indulgent old man, who himself has no relish for folly, but leniently winks at the indiscretions of youth. But the Word says, "Thou hatest all workers of iniquity" (Psalm 5:5). And again, "God is angry with the wicked every day" (Psalm 7:11). But men refuse to believe in this God, and gnash their teeth when His hatred of sin is faithfully pressed upon their attention. No, sinful man was no more likely to devise a holy God than to create the lake of fire in which he will be tormented forever and ever.

Because God is holy, acceptance with Him on the ground of creature doings is utterly impossible. A fallen creature could sooner create a world than produce that which would meet the approval of infinite Purity. Can darkness dwell with light? Can the Immaculate One take pleasure in "filthy rags" (Isaiah 64:6)? The best that sinful man brings forth is defiled. A corrupt tree cannot bear good fruit. God would deny Himself, vilify His perfections, were He to account as righteous and holy that which is not so in itself; and nothing is so which has the least stain upon it contrary to the nature of God. But that which His holiness demanded His grace has provided in Christ Jesus our Lord. Every poor sinner who has fled to Him for refuge stands "accepted in the beloved" (Ephesians 1:6).

Because God is holy, the utmost reverence becomes our approaches to Him. "God is greatly to be feared in the assembly of the saints, and to be had in reverence of all them that are about him" (Psalm 89:7). Then, "Exalt ye the LORD our God, and worship at his footstool; for he is holy" (Psalm 99:5). Yes, "at His footstool," in the lowest posture of humility, prostrate before Him. When Moses would approach unto the burning bush, God said, "Put off thy shoes from off thy feet" (Exodus 3:5). He is to be served "with fear" (Psalm 2:11). Of Israel His demand was, "I will be sanctified in them that come nigh me, and before all the people I will be glorified" (Leviticus 10:3). The more our hearts are awed by His ineffable holiness, the more acceptable will be our approaches to Him.

Because God is holy, we should desire to be conformed to Him. His command is "Be ye holy; for I am holy" (1 Peter 1:16). We are not bidden to be omnipotent or omniscient as God is, but we are to be holy, and that "in all manner of [deportment]" (v. 15). "This is the prime way of honouring God. We do not so glorify God by elevated admirations, or eloquent expressions, or pompous services of Him, as when we aspire to a conversing with Him with unstained spirits, and live to Him in living like Him" (S. Charnock). Then, as God alone is the source and fount of holiness, let us earnestly seek holiness from Him; let our daily prayer be that He may "sanctify [us] wholly: and I pray God [our] whole spirit and soul and body be preserved blameless unto the coming of our Lord Jesus Christ" (1 Thessalonians 5:23).

Chapter 9

THE
POWER
OF GOD

e cannot have a right conception of God unless we think of Him as all-powerful, as well as all-wise. He who cannot do what he will and perform all his pleasure cannot be God. As God has a will to resolve what He deems good, so He has power to execute His will.

The power of God is that ability and strength whereby He can bring to pass whatsoever He pleases, whatsoever His infinite wisdom may direct, and whatsoever the infinite purity of His will may resolve. . . . As holiness is the beauty of all God's attributes, so power is that which gives life and action to all the perfections of the Divine nature. How vain would be the eternal counsels, if power did not step in to execute them. Without power His mercy would be but feeble pity, His promises an empty sound, His threatenings a mere scare-crow. God's power is like Himself: infinite, eternal, incomprehensible; it can neither be checked, restrained, nor frustrated by the creature. (S. Charnock)

"God hath spoken once; twice have I heard this; that power belongeth unto God" (Psalm 62:11). "God hath spoken once"; nothing more is necessary! Heaven and earth shall pass away, but His word abides forever. "God hath spoken once"; how befitting His divine majesty! We poor mortals may speak often and yet fail to be heard. He speaks but once and the thunder of His power is heard on a thousand hills.

> The LORD also thundered in the heavens, and the Highest gave his voice; hail stones and coals of fire. Yea, he sent out his arrows, and scattered them; and he shot out lightnings, and discomfited them. Then the channels of waters were seen and the foundations of the world were discovered at thy rebuke, O LORD, at the blast of the breath of thy nostrils. (Psalm 18:13–15)

"God hath spoken once." Behold His unchanging authority. "For who in the heaven can be compared unto the Lord? who among the sons of the mighty can be likened unto the LORD?" (Psalm 89:6). "And all the inhabitants of the earth are reputed as nothing: and he doeth according to his will in the army of heaven, and among the inhabitants of the earth: and none can stay his hand, or say unto him, What doest thou?" (Daniel 4:35). This was openly displayed when God became incarnate and tabernacled among men. To the leper He said, "I will; be thou clean. And immediately his leprosy was cleansed" (Matthew 8:3). To one who had lain in the grave four days He cried, "Lazarus, come forth," and the dead came forth (John 11:43). The stormy wind and the angry waves hushed at a single word from Him (Mark 4:35–39). A legion of demons could not resist His authoritative command (Mark 5:1–17; Luke 8:26–36).

"Power belongeth unto God," and to Him alone. Not a creature in the entire universe has an atom of power save what God delegates. But God's power is not acquired, nor does it depend upon any recognition by any other authority. It belongs to Him inherently.

> God's power is like Himself, self-existent, self-sustained. The mightiest of men cannot add so much as a shadow of increased power to the omnipotent One. He sits on no buttressed throne and leans on no assisting arm. His court is not maintained by His courtiers, nor does it borrow its splendor from His creatures. He is Himself the great central source and Originator of all power. (C. H. Spurgeon)

Not only does all creation bear witness to the great power of God, but also to His entire independency of all created things. Listen to His own challenge: "Where wast thou when I laid the foundations of the earth? declare, if thou hast understanding. Who hath laid the measures thereof, if thou knowest? or who hath stretched the line upon it? Whereupon are the foundations thereof fastened? or who laid the corner stone thereof?" (Job 38:4–6). How completely is the pride of man laid in the dust!

> Power is also used as a name of God: "the Son of man sitting on the right hand of power" (Mark 14:62), that is, at the right hand of God. God and power are so inseparable that they are reciprocated. As His essence is immense, not to be confined in place; as it is eternal, not to be measured in time; so it is almighty, not to be limited in regard of action. (S. Charnock)

"Lo, these are parts of his ways: but how little a portion is heard of him? but the thunder of his power who can understand?" (Job 26:14). Who is able to count all the monuments of His power? Even that which is displayed of His might in the visible creation is utterly beyond our powers of comprehension, still less are we able to conceive of omnipotence itself. There is infinitely more power lodged in the nature of God than is expressed in all His works.

"Parts of his ways" we behold in creation, providence, redemption; but only a "little" part of His might is seen in them. Remarkably this is brought out in Habakkuk 3:4: "and there was the hiding of his power." It is scarcely possible to imagine anything more grandiloquent than the imagery of this whole chapter; yet nothing in it surpasses the nobility of this statement. The prophet (in a vision) beheld the mighty God scattering the hills and overturning the mountains, which one would think afforded an amazing demonstration of His power. Nay, says our verse, that is rather the "hiding" than the displaying of His power. What does it mean? So inconceivable, so immense, so uncontrollable is the power of Deity, that the fearful convulsions which He works in nature conceal more than they reveal of His infinite might!

It is very beautiful to link together the following passages: "[He] treadeth upon the waves of the sea" (Job 9:8), which expresses God's uncontrollable power. "[He] walketh in the circuit of heaven" (Job 22:14), which tells of the immensity of His presence. "[He] walketh upon the wings of the wind" (Psalm 104:3), which signifies the amazing swiftness of His operations. This last expression is very remarkable. It is not that He "flieth," or "runneth," but that He "walketh," and that, on the very "wings of the wind"—on the most impetuous of the elements, tossed into utmost rage, and sweeping along with almost inconceivable rapidity; yet they are under His feet, beneath His perfect control!

Let us now consider God's power in creation. "The heavens are thine, the earth also is thine: as for the world and the fulness thereof, thou hast founded them. The north and the south thou hast created them" (Psalm 89:11–12). Before man can work he must have both tools and materials. But God began with nothing, and by His word alone out of nothing He made all things. The intellect cannot grasp it. God "spake, and it was done; he commanded, and it stood fast" (Psalm 33:9). Primeval matter heard His voice. "God said, Let there be: . . . and it was so" (Genesis 1). Well may we exclaim, "Thou hast a mighty arm: strong is thy hand, and high is thy right hand" (Psalm 89:13).

> Who, that looks upward to the midnight sky; and, with an eye of reason, beholds its rolling wonders; who can forbear enquiring, Of what were their mighty orbs formed? Amazing to relate, they were produced without materials. They sprung from emptiness itself. The stately fabric of universal nature emerged out of nothing. What instruments were used by the Supreme Architect to fashion the parts with such exquisite niceness, and give so beautiful a polish to the whole? How was it all connected into one finely-proportioned and nobly finished structure? A bare fiat accomplished all. Let them be, said God. He added no more; and at once the marvelous edifice arose, adorned with every beauty, displaying innumerable perfections, and declaring amidst enraptured seraphs its great Creator's praise. "By the word of the LORD were the heavens made; and all the host of them by the breath of his mouth" (Psalm 33:6). (James Hervey, 1789)

Consider God's power in preservation. No creature has power to preserve itself. "Can the rush grow up without mire? can the flag grow without water?" (Job 8:11). Both man and beast would perish if there were not herbs for food, and herbs would wither and die if the earth were not refreshed with fruitful showers. Therefore is God called the Preserver of "man and beast" (Psalm 36:6). He upholds "all things by the word of his power" (Hebrews 1:3).

The preservation of the earth from the violence of the sea is another plain instance of God's might. How is that raging element kept confined within those limits where He first lodged it, continuing its channel, without overflowing the earth and dashing in pieces the lower part of the creation? The natural situation of the water is to be above the earth, because it is lighter, and to be immediately under the air, because it is heavier. Who restrains the natural quality of it? Certainly man does not, and cannot. It is the fiat of its Creator which alone bridles it: "And said, Hitherto shalt thou come, but no further: and here shall thy proud waves be stayed" (Job 38:11). What a standing monument of the power of God the preservation of the world is!

Consider God's power in government. Take His restraint of the malice of Satan. "The devil, as a roaring lion, walketh about, seeking whom he may devour" (1 Peter 5:8). He is filled with hatred against God, and with fiendish enmity against men, particularly the saints. He who envied Adam in paradise, envies us the pleasure of enjoying any of God's blessings. Could he have his will, he would treat us all the same way he treated Job; he would send fire from heaven on the fruits of the earth, destroy the cattle, cause a wind to overthrow our houses, and cover our bodies with boils. But, little as men may realize it, God bridles him to a large extent, prevents him from carrying out his evil designs, and confines him within His ordinations.

Too, God restrains the natural corruption of men. He suffers sufficient outbreaks of sin to show what fearful havoc has been wrought by man's apostasy from his Maker. But who can conceive the frightful lengths to which men would go were God to remove His curbing hand? "[Their] mouth is full of cursing and bitterness: their feet are swift to shed blood" (Romans 3:14–15) is the nature of every descendant of Adam. Then what unbridled licentiousness and headstrong folly would triumph in the world, if the power of God did not interpose to lock down the floodgates of it (see Psalm 93:3–4).

Consider God's power in judgment. When He smites, none can resist Him (see Ezekiel 22:14). How terribly this was exemplified at the Flood! God opened the windows of heaven and broke up the great fountains of the deep, and (excepting those in the ark) the entire human race, helpless before the storm of His wrath, was swept away. A shower of fire and brimstone from heaven, and the cities of the plain were exterminated. Pharaoh and all his hosts were powerless when God blew upon them at the Red Sea. What a terrific word is in Romans 9:22: "What if God, willing to shew his wrath, and to make his power known, endured with much longsuffering the vessels of wrath fitted to destruction." God is going to display His mighty power upon the reprobate, not merely by incarcerating them in Gehenna, but by supernaturally preserving their bodies as well as souls amid the eternal burnings of the lake of fire.

Well may all tremble before such a God. To treat with disrespect One who can crush us more easily than we can a moth is a suicidal policy. To openly defy Him who is clothed with omnipotence, who can rend in pieces or cast into hell any moment He pleases, is the very height of insanity. To put it on its lowest ground, it is but the part of wisdom to heed His command, "Kiss the Son, lest he be angry, and ye perish from the way, when his wrath is kindled but a little" (Psalm 2:12).

Well may the enlightened soul adore such a God! The wondrous, infinite perfections of such a Being call for fervent worship. If men of might and renown claim the admiration of the world, how much more should the power of the Almighty fill us with wonderment and homage. "Who is like unto thee, O LORD, among the gods? who is like thee, glorious in holiness, fearful in praises, doing wonders?" (Exodus 15:11).

Well may the saint trust such a God! He is worthy of implicit confidence. Nothing is too hard for Him. If God were stinted in might and had a limit to His strength we might well despair. But seeing that He is clothed with omnipotence, no prayer is too hard for Him to answer, no need too great for Him to supply, no passion too strong for Him to subdue, no temptation too powerful for Him to deliver from, no misery too deep for Him to relieve. "The Lord is the strength of my life; of whom shall I be afraid?" (Psalm 27:1). "Now unto him that is able to do exceeding abundantly above all that we ask or think, according to the power that worketh in us, unto him be glory in the church by Christ Jesus throughout all ages, world without end. Amen" (Ephesians 3:20–21).

Chapter 10

THE FAITHFULNESS OF GOD

Unfaithfulness is one of the most outstanding sins of these evil days. In the business world, a man's word is, with rare exceptions, no longer his bond. In the social world, marital infidelity abounds on every hand, the sacred bonds of wedlock are broken with as little regard as discarding an old garment. In the ecclesiastical realm, thousands who have solemnly covenanted to preach the truth have no scruples about attacking and denying it. Nor can reader or writer claim complete immunity from this fearful sin. How many ways have we been unfaithful to Christ, and to the light and privileges which God has entrusted to us! How refreshing, then, and how blessed, to lift our eyes above this scene of ruin, and behold One who is faithful, faithful in all things, at all times.

"Know therefore that the LORD thy God, he is God, the faithful God" (Deuteronomy 7:9). This quality is essential to His being, without it He would not be God. For God to be unfaithful would be to act contrary to His nature, which is impossible. "If we believe not, yet he abideth faithful: he cannot deny himself" (2 Timothy 2:13). Faithfulness is one of the glorious perfections of His being. He is clothed with it: "O

LORD God of hosts, who is a strong LORD like unto thee? or to thy faithfulness round about thee?" (Psalm 89:8). So too when God became incarnate it was said, "Righteousness shall be the girdle of his loins, and faithfulness the girdle of his reins" (Isaiah 11:5).

What a word in Psalm 36:5: "Thy mercy, O LORD, is in the heavens; and thy faithfulness reacheth unto the clouds." Far above all finite comprehension is the unchanging faithfulness of God. Everything about God is great, vast, incomparable. He never forgets, never fails, never falters, never forfeits His word. To every declaration of promise or prophecy the Lord has exactly adhered; every engagement of covenant or threatening He will make good, for "God is not a man, that he should lie; neither the son of man, that he should repent: hath he said, and shall he not do it? or hath he spoken, and shall he not make it good?" (Numbers 23:19). Therefore does the believer exclaim, "His compassions fail not. They are new every morning: great is thy faithfulness" (Lamentations 3:22–33).

Scripture abounds in illustrations of God's faithfulness. More than four thousand years ago He said, "While the earth remaineth, seedtime and harvest, and cold and heat, and summer and winter, and day and night shall not cease" (Genesis 8:22). Every year furnishes a fresh witness to God's fulfillment of this promise. In Genesis 15, Jehovah declared unto Abraham, "Thy seed shall be a stranger in a land that is not theirs, and shall serve them. . . . But in the fourth generation they shall come hither again" (vv. 13, 16). Centuries ran their weary course. Abraham's descendants groaned amid the brick kilns of Egypt. Had God forgotten His promise? No, indeed. Exodus 12:41, "And it came to pass at the end of the four hundred and thirty years, even the selfsame day it came to pass, that all the hosts of the LORD went out from the land of Egypt." Through Isaiah the Lord declared, "Behold, a virgin shall conceive, and bear a son, and shall call his name Immanuel" (Isaiah 7:14). Again centuries passed, but "when the fulness of the time was come, God sent forth his Son, made of a woman" (Galatians 4:4).

God is true. His Word of promise is sure. In all His relations with His people God is faithful. He may be safely relied upon. No one ever yet really trusted Him in vain. We find this precious truth expressed almost everywhere in the Scriptures, for His people need to know that faithfulness is an essential part of the divine character. This is the basis of our confidence in Him. But it is one thing to accept the faithfulness of God as a divine truth, yet quite another to act upon it. God has given us many "exceeding great and precious promises" (2 Peter 1:4), but are we really counting on His fulfillment of them? Do we actually expect Him to do for us all that He has said? Are we resting with implicit assurance on these words: "He is faithful that promised" (Hebrews 10:23).

There are seasons in the lives of all when it is not easy, not even for Christians, to believe that God is faithful. Our faith is sorely tried, our eyes dimmed with tears, and we can no longer trace the outworking of His love. Our ears are distracted with the noises of the world, harassed by the atheistic whisperings of Satan, and we can no longer hear the sweet accents of His still small voice. Cherished plans have been thwarted, friends on whom we relied have failed us, a professed brother or sister in Christ has betrayed us. We are staggered. We sought to be faithful to God, and now a dark cloud hides Him from us.

We find it difficult, yes, impossible, for carnal reasons to harmonize His frowning providence with His gracious promises. Ah, faltering soul, seek grace to heed Isaiah 50:10: "Who is among you that feareth the LORD, that obeyeth the voice of his servant, that walketh in darkness, and hath no light? let him trust in the name of the LORD, and stay upon his God."

When you are tempted to doubt the faithfulness of God, cry out, "Get thee hence, Satan." Though you cannot now harmonize God's mysterious dealings with the avowals of His love, wait on Him for more light. In His own good time He will make it plain to you. "What I do thou knowest not now; but thou shalt know hereafter" (John 13:7). The sequel will demonstrate that God has neither forsaken nor deceived His child. "And therefore will the LORD wait, that he may be gracious unto you, and therefore will he be exalted, that he may have mercy upon you: for the LORD is a God of judgment: blessed are all they that wait for him" (Isaiah 30:18).

> Judge not the Lord by feeble sense,
> But trust Him for His grace,
> Behind a frowning providence He hides a smiling face.
> Ye fearful saints, fresh courage take,
> The clouds ye so much dread,
> Are rich with mercy, and shall break
> In blessing o'er your head.

"Thy testimonies that thou hast commanded are righteous and very faithful" (Psalm 119:138). God has not only told us the best, but also He has not withheld the worst. He has faithfully described the ruin which the Fall effected; He has faithfully diagnosed the terrible state which sin produced; He has faithfully made known His inveterate hatred of evil, and that He must punish the same; He has faithfully warned us that He is "a consuming fire" (Hebrews 12:29). Not only does His Word abound in illustrations of His fidelity in fulfilling His promises, but also it records numerous examples of His faithfulness in making good His threatenings. Every stage of Israel's history exemplifies that solemn fact. So it was with individuals: Pharaoh, Korah, Achan, and a host of others are many proofs. Thus it will be with you. Unless you have fled, or flee, to Christ for refuge, the everlasting burning of the lake of fire will be your certain portion. God is faithful.

God is faithful in preserving His people. "God is faithful, by whom ye are called unto the fellowship of his Son" (1 Corinthians 1:9). In the previous verse a promise was made that God would confirm unto the end His own people. The apostle's confidence in the absolute security of believers was founded not on the strength of their resolutions or ability to persevere, but on the veracity of the One who cannot lie. Since God has promised to His Son a certain people for His inheritance, to deliver them from sin and condemnation, and to become the participants of eternal life in glory, it is certain that He will not allow any of them to perish.

God is faithful in disciplining His people. He is faithful in what He withholds, no less than in what He gives. He is faithful in sending sorrow as well as in giving joy. The faithfulness of God is a truth to be confessed by us not only when we are at ease, but also when we are smarting under the sharpest rebuke. Nor must this confession be merely of our mouths, but of our hearts also. When God smites us with the rod of chastisement, it is faithfulness which wields it. To acknowledge this means that we humble ourselves before Him, own that we fully deserve His correction; and instead of murmuring, thank Him for it. God never afflicts without a reason: "For this cause many are weak and sickly among you" (1 Corinthians 11:30) illustrates this principle. When His rod falls on us, let us say with Daniel, "O LORD, righteousness belongeth unto thee, but unto us confusion of faces" (Daniel 9:7).

"I know, O LORD, that thy judgments are right, and that thou in faithfulness hast afflicted me" (Psalm 119:75). Trouble and affliction are not only consistent with God's love pledged in the everlasting covenant, but also they are parts of the administration of the same. God is not only faithful, notwithstanding afflictions, but faithful in sending them. "Then will I visit their transgression with the rod, and their iniquity with stripes. Nevertheless my lovingkindness will I not utterly take from him, nor suffer my faithfulness to fail" (Psalm 89:32–33). Chastening is not only reconcilable with God's loving-kindness, but also it is the effect and expression of it. It would quiet the minds of God's people if they would remember that His covenant love binds Him to lay on them seasonable correction. Afflictions are necessary for us: "In their affliction they will seek me early" (Hosea 5:15).

God is faithful in glorifying His people. "Faithful is he that calleth you, who also will do it" (1 Thessalonians 5:24). The immediate reference here is to saints being "preserved blameless unto the coming of our Lord Jesus Christ" (v. 23). God treats us not on the ground of our merits (for we have none), but for His own great name's sake. God is constant to Himself and to His own purpose of grace: "Whom he also called, . . . them he also glorified" (Romans 8:30). God gives a full demonstration of the constancy of His everlasting goodness toward His elect by effectually calling them out of darkness into His marvelous light. This should fully assure them of the certain continuance of it. "The foundation of God standeth sure" (2 Timothy 2:19). Paul rested on the faithfulness of God when he said, "I know whom I have believed, and am persuaded that he is able to keep that which I have committed unto him against that day" (1:12).

Apprehension of this blessed truth will preserve us from worry. To be full of care, to view our situation with dark forebodings, to anticipate the morrow with sad anxiety is to reflect upon the faithfulness of God. He who has cared for His child through all the years will not forsake him in old age. He who has heard your prayers in the past will not refuse to supply your need in the present emergency. Rest on Job 5:19: "He shall deliver thee in six troubles: yea, in seven there shall no evil touch thee."

Apprehension of this truth will check our murmurings. The Lord knows what is best for each of us. One effect of resting on this truth will be to silence our petulant complainings. God is greatly honored when, under trial and chastening, we have good thoughts of Him, vindicate His wisdom and justice, and recognize His love in His rebukes.

Apprehension of this truth will breed increasing confidence in God. "Wherefore let them that suffer according to the will of God commit the keeping of their souls to him in well doing, as unto a faithful Creator" (1 Peter 4:19). The sooner we trustfully resign ourselves and all our affairs into God's hands, fully persuaded of His love and faithfulness, the sooner we will be satisfied with His providences and realize, with Fanny Crosby, that He "doeth all things well."

Chapter 11

THE LOVING-KINDNESS OF GOD

*W*e propose to engage the reader with another of His excellencies —of which every Christian receives innumerable proofs. We turn to a consideration of God's loving-kindness because our aim is to maintain a due proportion in treating of the divine perfections, for all of us are apt to entertain one-sided views of them. A balance must be preserved here (as everywhere), as it appears in those two statements of the divine attributes: "God is light" (1 John 1:5); "God is love" (4:8). The sterner, more awe-inspiring aspects of the divine character are offset by the gentler, more winsome ones. It is to our irreparable loss if we dwell exclusively on God's sovereignty and majesty, or His holiness and justice; we need to meditate frequently, though not exclusively, on His goodness and mercy. Nothing short of a full-orbed view of the divine perfections —as revealed in Holy Writ—should satisfy us.

Scripture speaks of "the multitude of his lovingkindnesses," and who is capable of numbering them? (Isaiah 63:7). Said the psalmist, "How excellent is thy lovingkindness, O God!" (Psalm 36:7). No pen of man, no tongue of angel, can adequately express it. Familiar as this blessed attribute of God's may be to people, it is something entirely peculiar to divine revelation. None of the ancients ever dreamed of investing his gods with such endearing perfection as this. None of the objects worshiped by present-day heathen possess gentleness and tenderness; very much the reverse is true, as the hideous features of their idols exhibit. Philosophers regard it as a serious reflection upon the honor of the Absolute to ascribe such qualities to it. But the Scriptures have much to say about God's loving-kindness, or His paternal favor to His people, His tender affection toward them.

The first time this divine perfection is mentioned in the Word is in that wondrous manifestation of deity to Moses, when Jehovah proclaimed His "Name," i.e., Himself as made known. "The LORD, the LORD God, merciful and gracious, longsuffering, and abundant in goodness and truth" (Exodus 34:6), though much more frequently the Hebrew word *chesed* is rendered "kindness" and "lovingkindness." In our English Bibles the initial reference, as connected with God, is Psalm 17:7, where David prayed, "Shew thy marvellous lovingkindness, O thou that savest by thy right hand them which put their trust in thee." Marvelous it is that One so infinitely above us, so inconceivably glorious, so ineffably holy, should not only notice such worms of the earth, but also set His heart upon them, give His Son for them, send His Spirit to indwell them, and so bear with all their imperfections and waywardness as never to remove His loving-kindness from them.

Consider some of the evidences and exercises of this Divine attribute unto the saints. "In love: having predestinated us unto the adoption of children by Jesus Christ to himself" (Ephesians 1:4–5). As the previous verse shows, that love was engaged on their behalf before this world came into existence: "He hath chosen us . . . before the foundation of the world" (v. 4). "In this was manifested the love of God toward us, because that God sent His only begotten Son into the world, that we might live through him" (1 John 4:9), which was His amazing provision for us fallen creatures. "I have loved thee with an everlasting love: therefore with lovingkindness have I drawn thee" (Jeremiah 31:3), by the quickening operations of My Spirit, by the invincible power of My grace, by creating in you a deep sense of need, by attracting you by My winsomeness. "I will betroth thee unto me for ever; yea, I will betroth thee unto me in righteousness, and in judgment, and in lovingkindness, and in mercies" (Hosea 2:19). Having made us willing in the day of His power to give ourselves to Him, the Lord enters into an everlasting marriage contract with us.

This loving-kindness of the Lord is never removed from His children. To our reason it may *appear* to be so, yet it never is. Since the believer be in Christ, nothing can separate him from the love of God (Romans 8:39). God has solemnly engaged Himself by covenant, and our sins cannot make it void. God has sworn that if His children "keep not [His] commandments," He will "visit their transgression with the rod, and their iniquity with stripes" (Psalm 89:31–32). Yet He adds, "Nevertheless my lovingkindness will I not utterly take from him, nor suffer my faithfulness to fail. My covenant will I not break" (vv. 33–34). Observe the change of number from "their" and "them" to "him." The loving-kindness of God toward His people is centered in Christ. Because His exercise of loving-kindness is a covenant engagement, it is repeatedly linked to His "truth" (40:11; 138:2), showing that it proceeds to us by promise. Therefore we should never despair.

"For the mountains shall depart, and the hills be removed; but my kindness shall not depart from thee, neither shall the covenant of my peace be removed, saith the LORD that hath mercy on thee" (Isaiah 54:10). No, that covenant has been ratified by the blood of its Mediator, by which blood the enmity (occasioned by sin) has been removed and perfect reconciliation effected. God knows the thoughts which He entertains for those embraced in His covenant and who have been reconciled to Him; namely, "thoughts of peace, and not of evil" (Jeremiah 29:11). Therefore we are assured, "The LORD will command his lovingkindness in the daytime, and in the night his song shall be with me" (Psalm 42:8). What a word that is! Not merely that the Lord will give or bestow, but *command* His loving-kindness. It is given by decree, bestowed by royal engagement, as He also commands "deliverances" (44:4), "the blessing, even life for evermore" (133:3), which announces that nothing can possibly hinder these bestowments.

What ought our response to be? First, "Be ye therefore followers [imitators] of God, as dear children; and walk in love" (Ephesians 5:1–2). "Put on therefore, as the elect of God, holy and beloved, bowels of mercies, kindness" (Colossians 3:12). Thus it was with David: "Thy lovingkindness is before mine eyes: and I have walked in thy truth" (Psalm 26:3). He delighted to ponder it. It refreshed his soul to do so, and it molded his conduct. The more we are occupied with God's goodness, the more careful we will be about our obedience. The constraints of God's love and grace are more powerful to the regenerate than the terrors of His Law. "How excellent is thy lovingkindness, O God! therefore the children of men put their trust under the shadow of thy wings" (Psalm 36:7). Second, a sense of this divine perfection strengthens our faith and promotes confidence in God.

Third, it should stimulate the spirit of worship. "Because thy lovingkindness is better than life, my lips shall praise thee" (Psalm 63:3; cf. 138:2). Fourth, it should be our cordial when depressed. "Let . . . thy merciful kindness [same Hebrew word] be for my comfort" (119:76). It was so with Christ in His anguish (69:17). Fifth, it should be our plea in prayer, "Quicken me, O LORD, according to thy lovingkindness" (119:159). David applied to that divine attribute for new strength and increased vigor. Sixth, we should appeal to it when we have fallen by the wayside. "Have mercy upon me, O God, according to thy lovingkindness" (51:1). Deal with me according to the gentlest of Thy attributes; make my case an exemplification of Thy tenderness. Seventh, it should be a petition in our evening devotions. "Cause me to hear thy lovingkindness in the morning" (Psalm 143:8). Arouse me with my soul in tune therewith; let my waking thoughts be of Thy goodness.

Chapter 12

THE GOODNESS OF GOD

$\mathcal{T}$he goodness of God endureth continually" (Psalm 52:1). The goodness of God respects the perfection of His nature: "God is light, and in him is no darkness at all" (1 John 1:5). There is such an absolute perfection in God's nature and being that nothing is wanting to it or defective in it; nothing can be added to it to make it better.

> He is originally good, good of Himself, which nothing else is; for all creatures are good only by participation and communication from God. He is essentially good; not only good, but goodness itself: the creature's good is a superadded quality, in God it is His essence. He is infinitely good; the creature's good is but a drop, but in God there is an infinite ocean or gathering together of good. He is eternally and immutably good, for He cannot be less good than He is; as there can be no addition made to Him, so no subtraction from Him. (Thomas Manton)

God is *summum bonum,* the chiefest good.

The original Saxon meaning of our English word *God* is "The Good." God is not only the greatest of all beings, but the best. All the goodness there is in any creature has been imparted from the Creator, but God's goodness is un-derived, for it is the essence of His eternal nature. As God is infinite in power from all eternity, before there was any display thereof, or any act of omnipotence put forth; so He was eternally good before there was any communication of His bounty, or any creature to whom it might be imparted or exercised. Thus, the first manifestation of this divine perfection was in giving being to all things. "Thou art good, and doest good" (Psalm 119:68). God has in Himself an infinite and inexhaustible treasure of all blessedness, enough to fill all things.

All that emanates from God—His decrees, His creation, His laws, His providences—cannot be otherwise than good: as it is written,. "And God saw every thing that he had made, and, behold, it was very good" (Genesis 1:31). Thus, the goodness of God is seen, first, in creation. The more closely the creature is studied, the more the beneficence of his Creator becomes apparent. Take the highest of God's earthly creatures, man. Abundant reason he has to say with the psalmist, "I will praise thee; for I am fearfully and wonderfully made: marvellous are thy works; and that my soul knoweth right well" (Psalm 139:14). Everything about the structure of our bodies attests to the goodness of their Maker. How suited the hands to perform their allotted work! How good of the Lord to appoint sleep to refresh a wearied body! How benevolent His provision to give the eyes lids and brows for their protection! So we might continue indefinitely.

Nor is the goodness of the Creator confined to man; it is exercised toward all His creatures. "The eyes of all wait upon thee; and thou givest them their meat in due season. Thou openest thine hand, and satisfiest the desire of every living thing" (Psalm 145:15–16). Whole volumes might be written, and have been, to amplify this fact. Whether it is the birds of the air, the beasts of the forest, or the fish in the sea, abundant provision has been made to supply their every need. God "giveth food to all flesh: for his mercy endureth for ever" (136:25). Truly, "The earth is full of the goodness of the LORD" (33:5).

The goodness of God is seen in the variety of natural pleasures which He has provided for His creatures. God might have been pleased to satisfy our hunger without the food being pleasing to our palates—how His benevolence appears in the varied flavors He has given to meats, vegetables, and fruits! God has not only given us senses, but also that which gratifies them; this too reveals His goodness. The earth might have been as fertile as it is without being so delightfully variegated. Our physical lives could have been sustained without beautiful flowers to regale our eyes and exhale sweet perfumes. We might have walked the fields without our ears being saluted by the music of the birds. Whence then, this loveliness, this charm, so freely diffused over the face of nature? Verily, "His tender mercies are over all his works" (Psalm 145:9).

The goodness of God is seen in that when man transgressed the law of his Creator a dispensation of unmixed wrath did not at once commence. God might well have deprived His fallen creatures of every blessing, every comfort, every pleasure. Instead, He ushered in a regime of a mixed nature, of mercy and judgment. This is very wonderful if it be duly considered; and the more thoroughly that regime is examined the more it will appear that "mercy rejoiceth against judgment" (James 2:13). Notwithstanding all the evils which attend our fallen state, the balance of good greatly preponderates. With comparatively rare exceptions, men and women experience a far greater number of days of health than they do of sickness and pain. There is much more creature-happiness than creature-misery in the world. Even our sorrows admit of considerable alleviation, and God has given to the human mind a pliability which adapts itself to circumstances and makes the most of them.

Nor can the benevolence of God be justly called into question because there is suffering and sorrow in the world. If man sins against the goodness of God, if he despises "the riches of his goodness and forbearance and longsuffering," and after the hardness and impenitency of his heart treasures up unto himself "wrath against the day of wrath" (Romans 2:4–5), who is to blame but himself? Would God be "good" if He did not punish those who ill-use His blessings, abuse His benevolence, and trample His mercies beneath their feet? It will be no reflection upon God's goodness, but rather the brightest exemplification of it, when He will rid the earth of those who have broken His laws, defied His authority, mocked His messengers, scorned His Son, and persecuted those for whom He died.

The goodness of God appeared most illustriously when He "sent forth his Son, made of a woman, made under the law, to redeem them that were under the law, that we might receive the adoption of sons" (Galatians 4:4–5). It was then that a multitude of the heavenly host praised their Maker and said, "Glory to God in the highest and on earth peace, good will toward men" (Luke 2:14). Yes, in the Gospel the "grace

(Greek, *benevolence* or *goodness*) of God that bringeth salvation hath appeared to all men" (Titus 2:11). Nor can God's benignity be called into question because He has not made every sinful creature a subject of His redemptive grace. He did not do so with the fallen angels. Had God left all to perish it had been no reflection on His goodness. To any who challenge this statement we remind him of our Lord's sovereign prerogative: "Is it not lawful for me to do what I will with mine own? Is thine eye evil, because I am good?" (Matthew 20:15).

"Oh that men would praise the LORD for his goodness, and for his wonderful works to the children of men!" (Psalm 107:8). Gratitude is the return justly required from the objects of His beneficence; yet is it often withheld from our great Benefactor simply because His goodness is so constant and so abundant. It is lightly esteemed because it is exercised toward us in the common course of events. It is not felt because we daily experience it. "Despisest thou the riches of his goodness?" (Romans 2:4). His goodness is despised when it is not improved as a means to lead men to repentance, but, on the contrary, serves to harden them from supposing that God entirely overlooks their sin.

The goodness of God is the life of the believer's trust. It is this excellency in God which most appeals to our hearts. Because His goodness endureth forever, we ought never to be discouraged: "The LORD is good, a strong hold in the day of trouble; and he knoweth them that trust in him" (Nahum 1:7).

> When others behave badly to us, it should only stir us up the more heartily to give thanks unto the Lord, because He is good; and when we ourselves are conscious that we are far from being good, we should only the more reverently bless Him that He is good. We must never tolerate an instant's unbelief as to the goodness of the Lord; whatever else may be questioned, this is absolutely certain, that Jehovah is good; His dispensations may vary, but His nature is always the same. (C. H. Spurgeon)

Chapter 13

THE PATIENCE OF GOD

ar less has been written on the patience of God than on the other excellencies of divine character. Not a few of those who have expatiated at length upon the divine attributes have passed over the patience of God without any comment. It is not easy to suggest a reason for this, for surely the long-suffering of God is as much one of the divine perfections as is His wisdom, power, or holiness—as much to be admired and revered by us. True, the actual term will not be found in a concordance so frequently as the others, but the glory of this grace shines on almost every page of Scripture. Certainly we lose much if we do not frequently meditate upon the patience of God and earnestly pray that our hearts and ways may be more completely conformed thereto.

Probably the principal reason why so many writers have failed to give us anything, separately, upon the patience of God is because of the difficulty of distinguishing this attribute from divine goodness and mercy, particularly the latter. God's long-suffering is mentioned in conjunction with His grace and mercy again and again (see Exodus 34:6; Numbers 14:18; Psalm 86:15). That the patience of God is really a display of His mercy is one way it is frequently manifested. But that they are one and the same excellency, and are not to be separated, we cannot concede. It may not be easy to discriminate between them. Nevertheless, Scripture fully warrants us in predicating some things of the one which we cannot of the other.

Stephen Charnock, the Puritan, defines God's patience, in part:

> It is a part of the Divine goodness and mercy, yet differs from both. God being the greatest goodness, hath the greatest mildness; mildness is always the companion of true goodness, and the greater the goodness, the greater the mildness. Who so holy as Christ, and who so meek? God's slowness to anger is a branch of His mercy: "The LORD is . . . full of compassion; slow to anger" (Psalm 145:8). It differs from mercy in the formal consideration of the subject: mercy respects the creature as miserable, patience respects the creature as criminal; mercy pities him in his misery, patience bears with the sin which engendered the misery, and giving birth to more.

Personally we define the divine patience as that power of control which God exercises over Himself, causing Him to bear with the wicked and forebear so long in punishing them. Nahum 1:3 reads, "The LORD is slow to anger, and great in power," upon which Mr. Charnock said:

> Men that are great in the world are quick in passion, and are not so ready to forgive an injury, or bear with an offender, as one of a meaner rank. It is a want of power over that man's self that makes him do unbecoming things upon a provocation. A prince that can bridle his passions is a king over himself as well as over his subjects. God is slow to anger because [he is] great in power. He has no less power over Himself than over His creatures.

At the above point, we think, God's *patience* is most clearly distinguished from His *mercy*. Though the creature is benefited, the patience of God chiefly respects Himself, a restraint placed upon His acts by His will; whereas His mercy terminates wholly upon the creature. The patience of God is that excellency which causes Him to sustain great injuries without immediately avenging Himself. Thus the Hebrew word for the divine long-suffering is rendered "slow to anger" in Nehemiah 9:17 and Psalm 103:8. Not that there are any passions in the divine nature, but God's wisdom and will is pleased to act with a stateliness and sobriety which becomes His exalted majesty.

In support of our definition we point out that it was to this excellency in the divine character that Moses appealed when Israel sinned so grievously at Kadesh-Barnea and there provoked Jehovah so sorely. Unto His servant the Lord said, "I will smite them with the pestilence, and disinherit them." Then the typical mediator pleaded, "I beseech thee, let the power of my Lord be great according as thou hast spoken, saying, The LORD is longsuffering" (Numbers 14:12, 17–18). Thus, His long-suffering is His power of self-restraint.

Again, in Romans 9:22 we read, "What if God, willing to shew his wrath, and to make his power known, endured with much longsuffering the vessels of wrath fitted to destruction." Were God to immediately break these reprobate vessels into pieces, His power of self-control would not so eminently appear; by bearing with their wickedness and forbearing punishment so long, the power of His patience is gloriously demonstrated. True, the wicked interpret His long-suffering quite differently—"Because sentence against an evil work is not executed speedily, therefore the heart of the sons of men is fully set in them to do evil" (Ecclesiastes 8:11)—but the anointed eye adores what they abuse.

"The God of patience" (Romans 15:5) is one of the divine titles. Deity is thus denominated, first, because God is both the author and object of the grace of patience in the creature. Second, because this is what He is in Himself: patience is one of His perfections. Third, as a pattern for us: "Put on therefore, as the elect of God, holy and beloved, bowels of mercies, kindness, humbleness of mind, meekness, longsuffering" (Colossians 3:12). And again, "Be ye therefore followers [emulators] of God, as dear children" (Ephesians 5:1). When tempted to be disgusted at the dullness of another, or to revenge one who has wronged you, remember God's infinite patience with you.

The patience of God is manifested in His dealings with sinners. How strikingly it was displayed toward the antediluvians. When mankind was universally degenerate, and all flesh had corrupted his way, God did not destroy them till He had forewarned them. He "waited" (1 Peter 3:20) probably no less than one hundred and twenty years (Genesis 6:3), during which time Noah was a "preacher of righteousness" (2 Peter 2:5). Later, when the Gentiles not only worshiped and served the creature more than the Creator, but also committed the vilest abominations contrary to even the dictates of nature (Romans 1:19–26), and hereby filled up the measure of their iniquity; yet, instead of drawing His sword to exterminate such rebels, God "suffered all nations to walk in their own ways" and gave them "rain from heaven, and fruitful seasons" (Acts 14:16–17).

Marvelously, God's patience was exercised and manifested toward Israel. First, He "suffered . . . their manners" for forty years in the wilderness (Acts 13:18). Later, they entered Canaan, but followed the evil customs of the nations around them and turned to idolatry; though God chastened them sorely, He did not utterly destroy them, but in their distress, raised up deliverers for them. When their iniquity rose to such a height that none but a God of infinite patience could have borne them, He, notwithstanding, spared them many years before He allowed them to be carried into Babylon. Finally, when their rebellion against Him reached its climax by crucifying His Son, He waited forty years before He sent the Romans against them; and that only after they had judged themselves "unworthy of everlasting life" (Acts 13:46).

How wondrous God's patience is with the world today. On every side people are sinning with a high hand. The divine law is trampled underfoot and God Himself openly despised. It is truly amazing that He does not instantly strike dead those who so brazenly defy Him. Why does He not suddenly cut off the haughty infidel and blatant blasphemer, as He did Ananias and Sapphira? Why does He not cause the earth to open and devour the persecutors of His people, so that, like Dathan and Abiram, they shall go down alive into the pit? And what of apostate Christendom, where every possible form of sin is now tolerated and practiced under cover of the holy name of Christ? Why does not the righteous wrath of heaven make an end of such abominations? Only one answer is possible: because God bears with "much longsuffering the vessels of wrath fitted to destruction."

What of the writer and the reader? Let us review our own lives. It is not long since we followed a multitude to do evil, had no concern for God's glory, and lived only to gratify self. How patiently He bore with our vile conduct! Now that grace has snatched us as brands from the burning, and given us a place in God's family, and begotten us unto an eternal inheritance in glory; how miserably we requite Him. How shallow our gratitude, how tardy our obedience, how frequent our backslidings! One reason why God suffers the flesh to remain in the believer is that He may exhibit His "longsuffering to us-ward" (2 Peter 3:9). Since this divine attribute is manifested only in this world, God takes advantage to display it toward "His own."

May our meditation upon this divine excellency soften our hearts and make our consciences tender; and may we learn in the school of experience the "patience of saints," namely, submission to the divine will and continuance in well doing. Let us seek grace to emulate this divine excellency. "Be ye therefore perfect, even as your Father which is in heaven is perfect" (Matthew 5:48). In the immediate context Christ exhorts us to love our enemies, bless them that curse us, do good to them that hate us. God bears long with the wicked notwithstanding the multitude of their sin. Shall we desire to be revenged because of a single injury?

Chapter 14

THE
GRACE
OF GOD

*T*his is a perfection of the divine character exercised only toward the elect. Neither in the Old Testament nor in the New is the grace of God ever mentioned in connection with mankind generally, still less with the lower orders of creatures. It is distinguished from *mercy*, for the mercy of God is "over all his works" (Psalm 145:9). Grace is the lone source from which flows the goodwill, love, and salvation of God unto His chosen people. This attribute of the divine character was defined by Abraham Booth in his helpful book, *The Reign of Grace*, thus: "It is the eternal and absolute free favor of God, manifested in the vouchsafement of spiritual and eternal blessings to the guilty and the unworthy."

Divine grace is the sovereign and saving favor of God exercised in bestowing blessings upon those who have no merit in them and for which no compensation is demanded. Nay, more; it is the favor of God to those who not only have no positive deserts of their own, but also who are thoroughly ill-deserving and hell-deserving. It is completely unmerited and unsought and is altogether unattracted by anything in or from or by the objects upon which it is bestowed.

Grace cannot be bought, earned, nor won by the creature. If it could be, it would cease to be grace. When a thing is said to be of "grace" we mean that the recipient has no claim upon it, that it was in no wise due him. It comes to him as pure charity, and, at first, unasked and undesired.

The fullest exposition of the amazing grace of God is found in the epistles of Paul. In his writings grace stands in direct opposition to works and worthiness—all works and worthiness, of whatever kind or degree. This is abundantly clear from Romans 11:6: "And if by grace, then is it no more of works: otherwise grace is no more grace. But if it be of works, then is it no more grace: otherwise work is no more work." Grace and works will no more unite than acid and alkali. "By grace are ye saved through faith; and that not of yourselves: it is the gift of God: not of works, lest any man should boast" (Ephesians 2:8–9). The absolute favor of God can no more consist with human merit than oil and water will fuse into one (see also Romans 4:4–5).

There are three principal characteristics of divine grace. First, *it is eternal*. Grace was planned before it was exercised, purposed before it was imparted: "Who hath saved us, and called us with an holy calling, not according to our works, but according to his own purpose and grace, which was given us in Christ Jesus before the world began" (2 Timothy 1:9). Second, *it is free,* for none ever purchased it: "Being justified freely by his grace" (Romans 3:24). Third, *it is sovereign,* because God exercises it toward and bestows it upon whom He pleases: "Even so might grace reign" (Romans 5:21). If grace reigns, then it is on the throne, and the occupant of the throne is sovereign. Hence, "the throne of grace" (Hebrews 4:16).

Just because grace is unmerited favor, it must be exercised in a sovereign manner. Therefore the Lord declares, "[I] will be gracious to whom I will be gracious" (Exodus 33:19). Were God to show grace to all of Adam's descendants, men would at once conclude that He was righteously compelled to take them to heaven as a compensation for allowing the human race to fall into sin. But God is under no obligation to any of His creatures, least of all to those who are rebels against Him.

Eternal life is a gift; therefore, it can neither be earned by good works, nor claimed as a right. Seeing that salvation is a gift, who has any right to tell God on whom He ought to bestow it? It is not that the Giver ever refuses this gift to any who seek it wholeheartedly and according to the rules which He has prescribed. No, He refuses none who come to Him empty-handed and in the way of His appointing. But if out of a world of impenitent and unbelieving, God is determined to exercise His sovereign right by choosing a limited number to be saved, who is wronged? Is God obliged to force His gift on those who do not value it? Is God compelled to save those who are determined to go their own way?

Nothing riles the natural man more and brings to the surface his innate, inveterate enmity against God than to press upon him the eternality, the freeness, and the absolute sovereignty of divine grace. That God should have formed His purpose from everlasting, without in anywise consulting the creature, is too abasing for the unbroken heart. That grace cannot be earned or won by any efforts of man is too self-emptying for self-righteousness. That grace singles out whom it pleases to be its favored objects arouses hot protests from haughty rebels. The clay rises up against the Potter and asks, "Why hast Thou made me thus?" A lawless insurrectionist dares to call into question the justice of divine sovereignty.

The distinguishing grace of God is seen in saving that people whom He has sovereignly singled out to be His high favorites. By *distinguishing* we mean that grace discriminates, makes differences, chooses some and passes by others. It was distinguishing grace which selected Abraham from the midst of his idolatrous neighbors and made him "the Friend of God" (James 2:23). Distinguishing grace saved "publicans and sinners" but said of the religious Pharisees, "Let them alone" (Matthew 15:14). Nowhere does the glory of God's free and sovereign grace shine more conspicuously than in the unworthiness and unlikeliness of its objects. Beautifully was this illustrated by James Hervey in 1751:

> Where sin has abounded, says the proclamation from the court of heaven, grace doth much more abound. Manasseh was a monster of barbarity, for he caused his own children to pass through the fire, and filled Jerusalem with innocent blood. Manasseh was an adept in iniquity, for he not only multiplied, and to an extravagant degree, his own sacrilegious impieties, but he poisoned the principles and perverted the manners of his subjects, making them do worse than the most detestable of the heathen idolators (see 2 Chronicles 33). Yet, through this superabundant grace he is humbled, he is reformed, and becomes a child of forgiving love, an heir of immortal glory.

> Behold that bitter and bloody persecutor, Saul; when breathing out

threatenings and bent upon slaughter, he worried the lambs and put to death the disciples of Jesus. The havoc he had committed, the inoffensive families he had already ruined, were not sufficient to assuage his vengeful spirit. They were only a taste, which, instead of glutting the bloodhound, made him more closely pursue the track, and more eagerly pant for destruction. He is still thirsty for violence and murder. So eager and insatiable is his thirst, that he even breathes out threatening and slaughter (Acts 9:1). His words are spears and arrows, and his tongue a sharp sword. 'Tis as natural for him to menace the Christians as to breathe the air. Nay, they bled every hour in the purposes of his rancorous heart. It is only owing to want of power that every syllable he utters, every breath he draws, does not deal out deaths, and cause some of the innocent disciples to fall. Who, upon the principles of human judgment, would not have pronounced him a vessel of wrath, destined to unavoidable damnation? Nay, who would not have been ready to conclude that, if there were heavier chains and a deeper dungeon in the world of woe, they must surely be reserved for such an implacable enemy of true godliness? Yes, admire and adore the inexhaustible treasures of grace—this Saul is admitted into the goodly fellowship of the prophets, is numbered with the noble army of martyrs and makes a distinguished figure among the glorious company of the apostles.

The Corinthians were flagitious even to a proverb. Some of them wallowing in such abominable vices, and habituated themselves to such outrageous acts of injustice, as were a reproach to human nature. Yet, even these sons of violence and slaves of sensuality were washed, sanctified, justified (1 Corinthians 6:9–11). "Washed," in the precious blood of a dying Redeemer; "sanctified," by the powerful operations of the blessed Spirit; "justified," through the infinitely tender mercies of a gracious God. Those who were once the burden of the earth, are now the joy of heaven, the delight of angels.

Now the grace of God is manifested in and by and through the Lord Jesus Christ. "The law was given by Moses, but grace and truth came by Jesus Christ" (John 1:17). This does not mean that God never exercised grace toward any before His Son became incarnate—Genesis 6:8 and Exodus 33:19 clearly show otherwise. But grace and truth were fully revealed and perfectly exemplified when the Redeemer came to this earth and died for His people upon the cross. It is through Christ the Mediator alone that the grace of God flows to His elect. "Much more the grace of God, and the gift by grace, which is by one man, Jesus Christ. . . . [Much] more they which receive abundance of grace and of the gift of righteousness shall reign in life by one, Jesus Christ. . . . [So] might grace reign through righteousness unto eternal life by Jesus Christ our Lord" (Romans 5:15, 17, 21).

The grace of God is proclaimed in the Gospel (Acts 20:24), which is to the self-righteous Jew a "stumblingblock," and to the conceited and philosophizing Greek "foolishness" (1 Corinthians 1:23). Why so? Because there is nothing whatever in it that is adapted to gratify the pride of man. It announces that unless we are saved by grace, we cannot be saved at all. It declares that apart from Christ, the unspeakable Gift of God's grace, the state of every man is desperate, irremediable, hopeless. The Gospel addresses men as guilty, condemned, perishing criminals. It declares that the most chaste moralist is in the same terrible plight as the most voluptuous profligate; that the zealous professor, with all his religious performances, is no better off than the most profane infidel.

The Gospel contemplates every descendant of Adam as a fallen, polluted, hell-deserving, and helpless sinner. The grace which the Gospel publishes is his only hope. All stand before God convicted as transgressors of His holy Law, as guilty and condemned criminals; awaiting not sentence, but the execution of sentence already passed on them (John 3:18; Romans 3:19). To complain against the partiality of grace is suicidal. If the sinner insists upon bare justice, then the lake of fire must be his eternal portion. His only hope lies in bowing to the sentence which divine justice has passed upon him, owning the absolute righteousness of it, casting himself on the mercy of God, and stretching forth empty hands to avail himself of the grace of God made known to him in the Gospel.

The third Person in the Godhead is the Communicator of grace; therefore, He is denominated "the spirit of grace" (Zechariah 12:10). God the Father is the Fountain of all grace, for He purposed in Himself the everlasting covenant of redemption. God the Son is the only Channel of grace. The Gospel is the publisher of grace. The Spirit is the Bestower. He is the One who applies the Gospel in saving power to the soul, quickens the elect while spiritually dead, conquers their rebellious wills, melts their hard hearts, opens their blind eyes, cleanses them from the leprosy of sin. Thus we say with the late G. S. Bishop, in *Grace in Galatians:*

Grace is a provision for men who are so fallen that they cannot lift the axe of justice, so corrupt that they cannot change their own natures, so averse to God that they cannot turn to Him, so blind that they cannot see Him, so deaf that they cannot hear Him, and so dead that He himself must open their graves and lift them into resurrection.

Chapter 15

THE
MERCY
OF GOD

"O give thanks unto the LORD; for he is good: for his mercy endureth for ever" (Psalm 136:1). For this perfection of the divine character God is greatly to be praised. Three times over in as many verses does the psalmist call upon the saints to give thanks unto the Lord for this adorable attribute. Surely this is the least that can be asked from those who have been such bounteous gainers. When we contemplate the characteristics of this divine excellency, we cannot do otherwise than bless God for it. His mercy is "great" (1 Kings 3:6); "plenteous" (Psalm 86:5); "tender" (Luke 1:78); "abundant" (1 Peter 1:3); it is "from everlasting to everlasting upon them that fear him" (Psalm 103:17). Well may we say with the psalmist, "I will sing aloud of thy mercy" (Psalm 59:16).

"I will make all my goodness pass before thee, and I will proclaim the name of the LORD before thee; and will be gracious to whom I will be gracious, and will shew mercy on whom I will shew mercy" (Exodus 33:19). Wherein differs the *mercy* of God from His *grace?* The mercy of God has its spring in the divine goodness. The first issue of God's goodness is His benignity or bounty, by which He gives liberally to His crea-

85

tures, as creatures; thus He has given being and life to all things. The second issue of God's goodness is His mercy, which denotes the ready inclination of God to relieve the misery of fallen creatures. Thus, mercy presupposes sin.

Though it may not be easy at the first consideration to see a real difference between the grace and the mercy of God, it helps us if we carefully ponder His dealings with unfallen angels. He has never exercised mercy toward them, for they have never stood in any need thereof, not having sinned or come beneath the effects of the curse. Yet, they certainly are the objects of God's free and sovereign grace. First, because of His election of them from out of the whole angelic race (1 Timothy 5:21). Second, and in consequence of their election, because of His preservation of them from apostasy, when Satan rebelled and dragged down with him one-third of the celestial hosts (Revelation 12:4). Third, in making Christ their Head (Colossians 2:10; 1 Peter 3:22), whereby they are eternally secured in the holy condition in which they were created. Fourth, because of the exalted position which has been assigned them: to live in God's immediate presence (Daniel 7:10), to serve Him constantly in His heavenly temple, to receive honorable commissions from Him (Hebrews 1:14). This is abundant *grace* toward them; but *mercy* it is not.

In endeavoring to study the mercy of God as set forth in Scripture, a threefold distinction needs to be made, if the Word is to be "rightly divided." First, there is a general mercy of God, extended not only to all men, believers and unbelievers alike, but also to the entire creation: "His tender mercies are over all his works" (Psalm 145:9); "he giveth to all life, and breath, and all things" (Acts 17:25). God has pity upon the brute creation in their needs, and supplies them with suitable provision.

Second, there is a special mercy of God, which is exercised toward the children of men, helping and succoring them, notwithstanding their sins. To them also He communicates all the necessities of life: "For he maketh his sun to rise on the evil and on the good, and sendeth rain on the just and on the unjust" (Matthew 5:45). Third, there is a sovereign mercy reserved for the heirs of salvation, which is communicated to them in a covenant way, through the Mediator.

Following out a little further the difference between the second and third distinctions pointed out above, it is important to note that the mercies which God bestows on the wicked are solely of a temporal nature; that is to say, they are confined strictly to this present life. There will be no mercy extended to them beyond the grave. "It is a people of no understanding: therefore he that made them will not have mercy on them, and he that formed them will shew them no favour" (Isaiah 27:11).

But at this point a difficulty may suggest itself to some of our readers, namely, does not Scripture affirm that "his mercy endureth for ever" (Psalm 136:1)? Two things need to be pointed out in that connection. God can never cease to be merciful, for this is a quality of the divine essence (Psalm 116:5); but the exercise of His mercy is regulated by His sovereign will. This must be so, for there is nothing outside Himself which obliges Him to act. If there were, that something would be supreme, and God would cease to be God.

It is pure, sovereign grace which alone determines the exercise of divine mercy. God expressly affirms this fact in Romans 9:15, "For he saith to Moses, I will have mercy on whom I will have mercy." It is not the wretchedness of the creature which causes Him to show mercy, for God is not influenced by things outside of Himself as we are. If God were influenced by the abject misery of leprous sinners, He would cleanse and save all of them. But He does not. Why? Simply because it is not His pleasure and purpose so to do. Still less is it the merits of the creature which causes Him to bestow mercies upon them, for it is a contradiction in terms to speak of meriting mercy. "Not by works of righteousness which we have done, but according to his mercy he saved us" (Titus 3:5) —the one standing in direct antithesis from the other. Nor is it the merits of Christ which move God to bestow mercies on His elect; that would be putting the effect for the cause. It is "through," or because of, "the tender mercy of our God" that Christ was sent here to His people (Luke 1:78). The merits of Christ make it possible for God to righteously bestow spiritual mercies on His elect, justice having been fully satisfied by the Surety! No, mercy arises solely from God's imperial pleasure.

Again, though it be true that God's mercy "endureth for ever," yet we must observe carefully the objects to whom His mercy is shown. Even the casting of the reprobate into the lake of fire is an act of mercy. Punishment of the wicked is to be contemplated from a threefold viewpoint. From God's side, it is an act of justice, vindicating His honor. The mercy of God is never shown to the prejudice of His holiness and righteousness. From their side, it is an act of equity, when they are made to suffer the due reward of their iniquities.

But from the standpoint of the redeemed, the punishment of the wicked is an act of unspeakable mercy. How dreadful would it be if the present order of things should continue forever, when the children of God are obliged to live in the midst of the children of the devil. Heaven would at once cease to be heaven if the ears of the saints still heard the blasphemous, filthy language of the reprobate. What a mercy that in the New Jerusalem "there shall in no wise enter into it any thing that de-fileth, neither whatsoever worketh abomination" (Revelation 21:27)!

Lest the reader think that in the last paragraph we have been draw-ing upon our imagination, let us appeal to Scripture in support of what has been said. In Psalm 143:12 David prays, "And of thy mercy cut off mine enemies, and destroy all them that afflict my soul: for I am thy ser-vant." Again, in Psalm 136:15, God "overthrew Pharaoh and his host in the Red sea: for his mercy endureth for ever." It was an act of vengeance upon Pharaoh and his hosts, but it was an act of mercy unto the Israelites. Again, in Revelation 19:1–3:

> I heard a great voice of much people in heaven, saying, Alleluia; Salvation, and glory, and honour, and power, unto the Lord our God: for true and righteous are his judgments: for he hath judged the great whore, which did corrupt the earth with her fornication, and hath avenged the blood of his servants at her hand. And again they said, Alleluia. And her smoke rose up for ever and ever.

From what has just been said, let us note how vain is the presumptu-ous hope of the wicked, who, notwithstanding their continued defiance of God, nevertheless count upon His being merciful to them. How many there are who say, I do not believe that God will ever cast me into hell; He is too merciful. Such a hope is a viper, which if cherished in their bosoms will sting them to death. God is a God of justice as well as mercy, and He has expressly declared that He will "by no means clear the guilty" (Exodus 34:7). He has said, "The wicked shall be turned into hell, and all the nations that forget God" (Psalm 9:17). As well might men reason: I do not believe that if filth be allowed to accumulate and sewerage become stagnant and people deprive themselves of fresh air, that a merciful God will let them fall a prey to a deadly fever. The fact is that those who neglect the laws of health are carried away by disease, notwithstanding God's mercy. It is equally true that those who neglect the laws of spiritual health shall forever suffer the second death.

Unspeakably solemn is it to see so many abuse this divine perfection. They continue to despise God's authority, trample upon His laws, continue in sin, and yet presume upon His mercy. But God will not be unjust to Himself. God shows mercy to the truly penitent, but not to the impenitent (Luke 13:3). To continue in sin and yet reckon upon divine mercy remitting punishment is diabolical. It is saying, "Let us do evil that good may come," and of all such it is written, "whose damnation is just" (Romans 3:8). Presumption shall most certainly be disappointed (read carefully Deuteronomy 29:18–20). Christ is the spiritual mercy seat, and all who despise and reject His Lordship shall "perish from the way, when his wrath is kindled but a little" (Psalm 2:12).

But let our final thought be of God's spiritual mercies unto His own people. "Thy mercy is great unto the heavens" (Psalm 57:10). The riches of it transcend our loftiest thought. "For as the heaven is high above the earth, so great is his mercy toward them that fear him" (103:11). None can measure it. The elect are designated "vessels of mercy" (Romans 9:23). It is mercy that quickened them when they were dead in sins (Ephesians 2:4–5). It is mercy that saves them (Titus 3:5). It is His abundant mercy which begat them unto an eternal inheritance (1 Peter 1:3). Time would fail us to tell of His preserving, sustaining, pardoning, supplying mercy. Unto His own, God is "the Father of mercies" (2 Corinthians 1:3).

> When all Thy mercies,
> O my God, my rising soul surveys,
> Transported with the view I'm lost,
> In wonder, love, and praise.

Chapter 16

THE
LOVE
OF GOD

Three things are told us in Scripture concerning the nature of God. First, "God is a Spirit" (John 4:24). In the Greek there is no indefinite article. To say God is *a* spirit is most objectionable, for it places Him in a class with others. God is spirit in the highest sense. Because He is spirit He is incorporeal, having no visible substance. Had God a tangible body, He would not be omnipresent but would be limited to one place; because He is spirit He fills heaven and earth.

Second, "God is light" (1 John 1:5), the opposite of darkness. In Scripture *darkness* stands for sin, evil, death; and *light* for holiness, goodness, life. "God is light" means that He is the sum of all excellency. Third, "God is love" (1 John 4:8). It is not simply that God loves, but that He is Love itself. Love is not merely one of His attributes, but His very nature.

There are many who talk about the love of God who are total strangers to the God of love. The divine love is commonly regarded as a species of amiable weakness, a sort of good-natured indulgence; it is reduced to a mere sickly sentiment, patterned after human emotion. The truth is that on this, as on everything else, our thoughts need to be formed and regulated by what is revealed in Scripture. That there is urgent need for this is apparent not only from the ignorance which so generally prevails, but also from the low state of spirituality which is now so sadly evident everywhere among professing Christians. How little real love there is for God. One chief reason for this is because our hearts are so little occupied with His wondrous love for His people. The better we are acquainted with His love—its character, fullness, blessedness—the more our hearts will be drawn out in love to Him.

1. The love of God is *uninfluenced*. By this we mean, there was nothing whatever in the objects of His love to call it into exercise, nothing in the creature to attract or prompt it. The love which one creature has for another is because of something in them; but the love of God is free, spontaneous, uncaused. The only reason God loves any is found in His own sovereign will: "The LORD did not set his love upon you, nor choose you, because ye were more in number than any people; for ye were the fewest of all people: but because the LORD loved you" (Deuteronomy 7:7–8). God has loved His people from everlasting, and therefore nothing of the creature can be the cause of what is found in God from eternity. He loves from Himself, "according to his own purpose" (2 Timothy 1:9).

"We love him, because he first loved us" (1 John 4:19). God did not love us because we loved Him, but He loved us before we had a particle of love for Him. Had God loved us in return for ours, then it would not be spontaneous on His part; but because He loved us when we were loveless, it is clear that His love was uninfluenced. It is highly important if God is to be honored and the heart of His child established, that we should be clear on this precious truth. God's love for me, and for each of "His own," was entirely unmoved by anything in them. What was there in me to attract the heart of God? Absolutely nothing. But, to the contrary, everything to repel Him, everything calculated to make Him loathe me—sinful, depraved, a mass of corruption, with "no good thing" in me. (Romans 7:18)

> What was there in me that could merit esteem,
> Or give the Creator delight?
> 'Twas even so, Father, I ever must sing,
> Because it seemed good in Thy sight.

2. It is *eternal.* This of necessity. God Himself is eternal, and God is love; therefore, as God Himself had no beginning, His love had none. Granted that such a concept far transcends the grasp of our finite minds; nevertheless, where we cannot comprehend, we can bow in adoring worship. How clear is the testimony of Jeremiah 31:3: "I have loved thee with an everlasting love: therefore with lovingkindness have I drawn thee." How blessed to know that the great and holy God loved His people before heaven and earth were called into existence, that He had set His heart upon them from all eternity. Clear proof is this: that His love is spontaneous, for He loved them endless ages before they had any being.

The same precious truth is set forth in Ephesians 1:4–5: "According as he hath chosen us in him before the foundation of the world, that we should be holy and without blame before him in love: having predestinated us." What praise should this evoke from each of His children! How quieting for the heart. Since God's love toward me had no beginning, it can have no ending! Since it is true that "from everlasting to everlasting" He is God, and since God is love, then it is equally true that "from everlasting to everlasting" He loves His people.

3. It is *sovereign.* This also is self-evident. God Himself is sovereign, under obligation to none, a law unto Himself, acting always according to His own imperial pleasure. Since God is sovereign, and since He is love, it necessarily follows that His love is sovereign. Because God is God, He does as He pleases; because God is love, He loves whom He pleases. Such is His own express affirmation: "Jacob have I loved, but Esau have I hated" (Romans 9:13). There was no more reason in Jacob why he should be the object of divine love than there was in Esau. They both had the same parents and were born at the same time, being twins, yet God loved the one and hated the other! Why? Because it pleased Him to do so.

The sovereignty of God's love necessarily follows from the fact that it is uninfluenced by anything in the creature. Thus, to affirm that the cause of His love lies in God Himself is only another way of saying that He loves whom He pleases. For a moment, assume the opposite. Suppose God's love were regulated by anything else than His will; in such a case He would love by rule, and loving by rule He would be under a law of love; and then so far from being free, God would Himself be ruled by law. "In love: having predestinated us unto the adoption of children by

Jesus Christ to himself, according to"—what? Some excellency which He foresaw in them? No. What then? "According to the good pleasure of his will" (Ephesians 1:4–5).

4. It is *infinite*. Everything about God is infinite. His essence fills heaven and earth. His wisdom is unlimitable, for He knows everything of the past, present, and future. His power is unbounded, for there is nothing too hard for Him. So His love is without limit. There is a depth to it which none can fathom; there is a height to it which none can scale; there is a length and breadth to it which defies measurement by any creature standard. Beautifully this is intimated in Ephesians 2:4, "But God, who is rich in mercy, for his great love wherewith he loved us." The word *great* there is parallel with the "God so loved" of John 3:16. It tells us that the love of God is so transcendent it cannot be estimated.

> No tongue can fully express the infinitude of God's love, or any mind comprehend it: it "passeth knowledge" (Ephesians 3:19). The most extensive ideas that a finite mind can frame about divine love are infinitely below its true nature. The heaven is not so far above the earth as the goodness of God is beyond the most raised conceptions which we are able to form of it. It is an ocean which swells higher than all the mountains of opposition in such as are the objects of it. It is a fountain from which flows all necessary good to all those who are interested in it. (John Brine, 1743)

5. It is *immutable*. As with God Himself there is "no variableness, neither shadow of turning" (James 1:17), so His love knows neither change or diminution. The worm Jacob supplies a forceful example of this: "Jacob have I loved," declared Jehovah, and despite all Jacob's unbelief and waywardness, He never ceased to love him. John 13:1 furnishes another beautiful illustration. That very night one of the apostles would say, "Shew us the Father" (John 14:8); another would deny Him with cursings (Matthew 26:69–75); all of them would be scandalized by and forsake Him (v. 56). Nevertheless, "having loved his own which were in the world, he loved them unto the end" (John 13:1). The divine love is subject to no vicissitudes. Divine love is "strong as death. . . . Many waters cannot quench" it (Song of Songs 8:6–7). Nothing can separate from it (Romans 8:35–39).

His love no end nor measure knows,
No change can turn its course,
Eternally the same it flows
From one eternal source.

6. It is *holy*. God's love is not regulated by caprice, passion, or sentiment, but by principle. Just as His grace reigns not at the expense of it, but "through righteousness" (Romans 5:21), so His love never conflicts with His holiness. "God is light" (1 John 1:5) is mentioned before "God is love" (4:8). God's love is no mere amiable weakness or effeminate softness. Scripture declares, "Whom the Lord loveth he chasteneth, and scourgeth every son whom he receiveth" (Hebrews 12:6). God will not wink at sin, even in His own people. His love is pure, unmixed with any maudlin sentimentality.

7. It is *gracious*. The love and favor of God are inseparable. This is clearly brought out in Romans 8:32–39. What that love is from which there can be no "separation" is easily perceived from the design and scope of the immediate context. It is that goodwill and grace of God which determined Him to give His Son for sinners. That love was the impulsive power of Christ's incarnation: "God so loved the world that he gave his only begotten Son" (John 3:16). Christ died not in order to make God love us, but because He did love His people. Calvary is the supreme demonstration of divine love. Whenever you are tempted to doubt the love of God, Christian reader, go back to Calvary.

Here then is abundant cause for trust and patience under divine affliction. Christ was beloved of the Father, yet He was not exempted from poverty, disgrace, and persecution. He hungered and thirsted. Thus, it was not incompatible with God's love for Christ when He permitted men to spit upon and smite Him. Then let no Christian call into question God's love when he is brought under painful afflictions and trials. God did not enrich Christ on earth with temporal prosperity, for "the Son of man hath not where to lay his head" (Matthew 8:20). But He did give Him the Spirit without measure (John 3:34). Learn that spiritual blessings are the principal gifts of divine love. How blessed to know that when the world hates us, God loves us!

Chapter 17

THE WRATH OF GOD

It is sad to find so many professing Christians who appear to regard the wrath of God as something for which they need to make an apology; or at least they wish there were no such thing. While some would not go so far as to openly admit that they consider it a blemish on the divine character, yet they are far from regarding it with delight. They like not to think about it, and they rarely hear it mentioned without a secret resentment rising up in their hearts against it. Even with those who are more sober in their judgment, not a few seem to imagine that there is a severity about the divine wrath which is too terrifying to form a theme for profitable contemplation. Others harbor the delusion that God's wrath is not consistent with His goodness, and so seek to banish it from their thoughts.

Yes, many turn away from a vision of God's wrath as though they were called to look upon some blotch in the divine character, or some blot upon the divine government. But what says the Scriptures? As we turn to them we find that God has made no attempt to conceal the fact of His wrath. He is not ashamed to make it known that vengeance and fury belong to Him. His own challenge is this:

> See now that I, even I, am he, and there is no god with me: I kill, and I make alive; I wound, and I heal: neither is there any that can deliver out of my hand. For I lift up my hand to heaven, and say, I live for ever. If I whet my glittering sword, and mine hand take hold on judgment; I will render vengeance to mine enemies, and will reward them that hate me. (Deuteronomy 32:39–41)

A study of the concordance shows that there are more references in Scripture to the anger, fury, and wrath of God than there are to His love and tenderness. Because God is holy, He hates all sin; because He hates all sin, His anger burns against the sinner (Psalm 7:11).

The wrath of God is as much a divine perfection as is His faithfulness, power, or mercy. It must be so, for there is no blemish whatever, not the slightest defect in the character of God. Yet there would be if "wrath" were absent from Him! Indifference to sin is a moral blemish, and he who does not hate it is a moral leper. How could He who is the sum of all excellency look with equal satisfaction upon virtue and vice, wisdom and folly? How could He who is infinitely holy disregard sin and refuse to manifest His "severity" (Romans 11:22) toward it? How could He who delights only in that which is pure and lovely, not loathe and hate that which is impure and vile? The very nature of God makes hell as real a necessity, as imperatively and eternally requisite, as heaven is. Not only is there no imperfection in God, but also there is no perfection in Him that is less perfect than another.

The wrath of God is eternal detestation of all unrighteousness. It is the displeasure and indignation of divine equity against evil. It is the holiness of God stirred into activity against sin. It is the moving cause of that just sentence which He passes upon evildoers. God is angry against sin because it is a rebelling against His authority, a wrong done to His inviolable sovereignty. Insurrectionists against God's government shall be made to know that God is the Lord. They shall be made to feel how great that Majesty is which they despise, and how dreadful is that threatened wrath which they so little regarded. Not that God's anger is a malignant and malicious retaliation, inflicting injury for the sake of it, or in return for injury received. No. While God will vindicate His dominion as the Governor of the universe, He will not be vindictive.

That divine wrath is one of the perfections of God is not only evident from the considerations presented above, but is also clearly established by the express declarations of His own Word.

"For the wrath of God is revealed from heaven" (Romans 1:18). It was revealed when the sentence of death was first pronounced, the earth cursed, and man driven out of the earthly paradise; and afterwards by such examples of punishment as those of the deluge and the destruction of the cities of the plain by fire from heaven; but especially by the reign of death throughout the world. It was proclaimed in the curse of the Law on every transgression, and was intimated in the institution of sacrifice. In the 8th [chapter] of Romans, the apostle calls the attention of believers to the fact that the whole creation has become subject to vanity, and groaneth and travaileth together in pain. The same creation which declares that there is a God, and publishes His glory, also proclaims that He is the enemy of sin and the avenger of the crimes of men. But above all, the wrath of God was revealed from heaven when the Son of God came down to manifest the divine character, and when that wrath was displayed in His sufferings and death, in a manner more awful than by all the tokens God had before given of His displeasure against sin. Besides this, the future and eternal punishment of the wicked is now declared in terms more solemn and explicit than formerly. Under the new dispensation there are two revelations given from heaven, one of wrath, the other of grace. (Robert Haldane)

Again, that the wrath of God is a divine perfection is plainly demonstrated by what we read in Psalm 95:11, "Unto whom I sware in my wrath." There are two occasions of God "swearing": in making promises (Genesis 22:16–18), and in denouncing threatening (Deuteronomy 1:34–36). In the former, He swears in mercy to His children; in the latter, He swears to terrify the wicked. An oath is for solemn confirmation (Hebrews 6:16). In Genesis 22:16, God said, "By myself have I sworn." In Psalm 89:35, He declares, "Once have I sworn by my holiness"; while in Psalm 95:11 He affirmed, "I sware in my wrath." Thus the great Jehovah Himself appeals to His wrath as a perfection equal to His holiness: He swears by the one as much as by the other. Again, as in Christ "dwelleth all the fulness of the Godhead bodily" (Colossians 2:9), and as all the divine perfections are illustriously displayed by Him (John 1:18), therefore we read of "the wrath of the Lamb" (Revelation 6:16).

The wrath of God is a perfection of the divine character upon which we need to frequently meditate. First, so that our hearts may be duly impressed by God's detestation of sin. We are prone to regard sin lightly, to gloss over its hideousness, to make excuses for it. But the more we study and ponder God's abhorrence of sin and His frightful vengeance upon it, the more likely we are to realize its heinousness.

Second, to beget a true fear in our souls for God: "Let us have grace, whereby we may serve God acceptably with reverence and godly fear: for our God is a consuming fire" (Hebrews 12:28–29). We cannot serve Him acceptably unless there is due reverence for His awful Majesty and godly fear of His righteous anger; these are best promoted by frequently calling to mind that "our God is a consuming fire." Third, to draw out our souls in fervent praise for having delivered us from "the wrath to come" (1 Thessalonians 1:10).

Our readiness or our reluctance to meditate upon the wrath of God becomes a sure test of how our hearts really are affected toward Him. If we do not truly rejoice in God, for what He is in Himself, and that because of all the perfections which are eternally resident in Him, then how dwelleth the love of God in us? Each of us needs to be most prayerfully on guard against devising an image of God in our thoughts which is patterned after our own evil inclinations. Of old, the Lord complained, "Thou thoughtest that I was altogether . . . as thyself" (Psalm 50:21). If we rejoice not "at the remembrance of his holiness" (97:12), if we rejoice not to know that in a soon-coming day God will make a glorious display of His wrath, by taking vengeance on all who now oppose Him, it is proof positive that our hearts are not in subjection to Him; that we are yet in our sins.

"Rejoice, O ye nations [Gentiles], with his people: for he will avenge the blood of his servants, and will render vengeance to his adversaries" (Deuteronomy 32:43). And again,

> I heard a great voice of much people in heaven, saying, Alleluia; Salvation, and glory, and honour, and power, unto the Lord our God: for true and righteous are his judgments: for he hath judged the great whore, which did corrupt the earth with her fornication, and hath avenged the blood of his servants at her hand. And again they said, Alleluia. (Revelation 19:1–3)

Great will be the rejoicing of saints in that day when the Lord shall vindicate His majesty, exercise His awful dominion, magnify His justice, and overthrow the proud rebels who dared to defy Him.

"If thou, LORD, shouldest mark [impute] iniquities, O Lord, who shall stand?" (Psalm 130:3). Well may each of us ask this question, for it is written, "The ungodly shall not stand in the judgment" (Psalm 1:5). How sorely was Christ's soul exercised with thoughts of God's marking the iniquities of His people when they were upon Him. He was "amazed, and . . . very heavy" (Mark 14:33). His awful agony, His bloody sweat, His strong cries and supplications (Hebrews 5:7), His repeated prayers, "If it be possible, let this cup pass from Me," His last dreadful cry, "My God, my God, why hast thou forsaken me?" all manifest what fearful apprehensions He had of what it was for God to "mark iniquities." Well may poor sinners cry out, "Lord who shall 'stand' when the Son of God Himself so trembled beneath the weight of His wrath?" If you, my reader, have not "fled for refuge" to Christ, the only Saviour, "how wilt thou do in the swelling of Jordan" (Jeremiah 12:5)?

> When I consider how the goodness of God is abused by the greatest part of mankind, l cannot but be of his mind that said, The greatest miracle in the world is God's patience and bounty to an ungrateful world. If a prince hath an enemy got into one of his towns, he doth not send them in provision, but lays close siege to the place, and doth what he can to starve them. But the great God, that could wink all His enemies into destruction, bears with them, and is at daily cost to maintain them. Well may He command us to bless them that curse us, who Himself does good to the evil and unthankful. But think not, sinners, that you shall escape thus; God's mill goes slow, but grinds small; the more admirable His patience and bounty now is, the more dreadful and unsupportable will that fury be which ariseth out of His abused goodness. Nothing smoother than the sea, yet when stirred into a tempest, nothing rageth more. Nothing so sweet as the patience and goodness of God, and nothing so terrible as His wrath when it takes fire. (William Gurnall, 1660)

Then flee, my reader, flee to Christ; "flee from the wrath to come" (Matthew 3:7) ere it is too late.

A word to preachers: Do we in our oral ministry preach on this solemn subject as much as we ought? The Old Testament prophets frequently told their hearers that their wicked lives provoked the Holy

One of Israel, and that they were treasuring up to themselves wrath against the day of wrath. Conditions in the world are no better now than they were then! Nothing is so calculated to arouse the careless and cause carnal professors to search their hearts as to enlarge upon the fact that "God is angry with the wicked every day" (Psalm 7:11).

The forerunner of Christ warned his hearers to "flee from the wrath to come" (Matthew 3:7). The Saviour bade His auditors, "Fear him, which after he hath killed hath power to cast into hell; yea, I say unto you, Fear him" (Luke 12:5). Paul said, "Knowing therefore the terror of the Lord, we persuade men" (2 Corinthians 5:11). Faithfulness demands that we speak as plainly about hell as about heaven.

Chapter 18

THE CONTEMPLATION OF GOD

e reviewed in previous chapters some of the wondrous and lovely perfections of the divine character. From this contemplation of His attributes, it should be evident to us all that God is, first, an incomprehensible Being; and, lost in wonder at His infinite greatness, we adopt the words of Zophar, "Canst thou by searching find out God? canst thou find out the Almighty unto perfection? It is as high as heaven; what canst thou do? deeper than hell; what canst thou know? The measure thereof is longer than the earth, and broader than the sea" (Job 11:7–9). When we turn our thoughts to God's eternity, His immateriality, His omnipresence, His almightiness, our minds are overwhelmed.

But the incomprehensibility of the divine nature is no reason why we should desist from reverent inquiry and prayerful striving to apprehend what He has so graciously revealed of Himself in His Word. Because we are unable to acquire perfect knowledge, it would be folly to say we will therefore make no efforts to attain to any degree of it. C. H. Spurgeon has well said:

Nothing will so enlarge the intellect, nothing so magnify the whole soul of man, as a devout, earnest, continued, investigation of the great subject of the Deity. The most excellent study for expanding the soul is the science of Christ and Him crucified and the knowledge of the Godhead in the glorious Trinity.

The proper study of the Christian is the Godhead. The highest science, the loftiest speculation, the mightiest philosophy, which can engage the attention of a child of God, is the name, the nature, the person, the doings, and the existence of the great God which he calls his Father. There is something exceedingly improving to the mind in a contemplation of the divinity. It is a subject so vast, that all our thoughts are lost in its immensity; so deep, that our pride is drowned in its infinity. Other subjects we can comprehend and grapple with; in them we feel a kind of self-content, and go on our way with the thought, "Behold I am wise." But when we come to this master science, finding that our plumbline cannot sound its depth, and that our eagle eye cannot see its height, we turn away with the thought "I am but of yesterday and know nothing." (Sermon on Malachi 3:6)

Yes, the incomprehensibility of the divine nature should teach us humility, caution, and reverence. After all our searchings and meditations we have to say with Job, "Lo, these are parts of his ways: but how little a portion is heard of him?" (26:14). When Moses besought Jehovah for a sight of His glory, He answered him, "I will proclaim the name of the LORD before thee" (Exodus 33:19); as another has said, "The name is the collection of His attributes." Rightly did the Puritan John Howe declare:

The notion therefore we can hence form of His glory, is only such as we may have of a large volume by a brief synopsis, or of a spacious country by a little landscape. He hath here given us a true report of Himself, but not a full; such as will secure our apprehensions—being guided thereby—from error, but not from ignorance. We can apply our minds to contemplate the several perfections whereby the blessed God discovers to us His being, and can in our thoughts attribute them all to Him, though we have still but low and defective conceptions of each one. Yet so far as our apprehensions can correspond to the discovery that He affords us of His several excellencies, we have a present view of His glory.

The difference is great between the knowledge of God which His saints have in this life and that which they shall have in heaven; yet, as the former should not be undervalued because it is imperfect, so the latter is not to be magnified above its reality. True, the Scripture declares that we shall see "face to face" and "know" even as we are known (1 Corinthians 13:12), but to infer from this that we shall then know God as fully as He knows us is to be misled by the mere sound of words and to disregard that restriction of the same which the subject necessarily requires. There is a vast difference between the saints being glorified and their being made divine. In their glorified state, Christians will still be finite creatures, and therefore, never able to fully comprehend the infinite God.

> The saints in heaven will see God with the eye of the mind, for He will be always invisible to the bodily eye; and will see Him more clearly than they could see Him by reason and faith, and more extensively than all His works and dispensations had hitherto revealed Him; but their minds will not be so enlarged as to be capable of contemplating at once, or in detail, the whole excellence of His nature. To comprehend infinite perfection, they must become infinite themselves. Even in heaven, their knowledge will be partial, but at the same time their happiness will be complete, because their knowledge will be perfect in this sense, that it will be adequate to the capacity of the subjects, although it will not exhaust the fulness of the object. We believe that it will be progressive, and that as their views expand, their blessedness will increase; but it will never reach a limit beyond which there is nothing to be discovered; and when ages after ages have passed away, He will still be the incomprehensible God. (John Dick, 1840)

Second, from a review of the perfections of God, it appears that He is an all-sufficient Being. He is all-sufficient in Himself and to Himself. As the First of beings, He could receive nothing from another, nor be limited by the power of another. Being infinite, He is possessed of all possible perfection. When the Triune God existed all alone, He was all to Himself. His understanding, His love, His energies, found an adequate object in Himself. Had He stood in need of anything external, He had not been independent, and therefore would not have been God.

He created all things, and that for himself (Colossians 1:16), yet it was not in order to supply a lack, but that He might communicate life and happiness to angels and men and admit them to the vision of His glory. True, He demands the allegiance and services of His intelligent creatures, yet He derives no benefit from their offices; all the advantage redounds to themselves (Job 22:2–3). He makes use of means and instruments to accomplish His ends, yet not from a deficiency of power, but oftentimes to more strikingly display His power through the feebleness of the instruments.

The all-sufficiency of God makes Him the Supreme Object which is ever to be sought. True happiness consists only in the enjoyment of God. His favor is life, and His loving-kindness is better than life. "The LORD is my portion, saith my soul; therefore will I hope in him" (Lamentations 3:24); our perceptions of His love, His grace, His glory, are the chief objects of the saints' desire and the springs of their highest satisfaction. "There be many that say, Who will shew us any good? LORD, lift thou up the light of thy countenance upon us. Thou hast put gladness in my heart, more than in the time that their corn and their wine increased" (Psalm 4:6–7). Yes, the Christian, when in his right mind, is able to say, "Although the fig tree shall not blossom, neither shall fruit be in the vines; the labour of the olive shall fail, and the fields shall yield no meat; the flock shall be cut off from the fold, and there shall be no herd in the stalls: Yet I will rejoice in the LORD, I will joy in the God of my salvation" (Habakkuk 3:17–18).

Third, from a review of the perfections of God, it appears that He is the Sovereign of the universe. John Dick said:

> No dominion is so absolute as that which is founded on creation. He who might not have made any thing, had a right to make all things according to His own pleasure. In the exercise of His uncontrolled power, He has made some parts of the creation mere inanimate matter, of grosser or more refined texture, and distinguished by different qualities, but all inert and unconscious. He has given organization to other parts, and made them susceptible of growth and expansion, but still without life in the proper sense of the term. To others He has given not only organization, but conscious existence, organs of sense and self-motive power. To these He has added in man the gift of reason, and an immortal spirit, by which he is allied to a higher order of beings who are placed in the superior regions. Over the world which He has created, He sways the scepter of omnipotence. "I praised and honoured him that liveth forever, whose dominion is an everlasting dominion, and his kingdom is from generation to generation: and all the inhabitants of the earth are reputed as nothing: and he doeth according to his will in the army of heaven, and among the inhabitants of the earth: and none can stay his hand, or say unto him, What doeth thou?" (Daniel 4:34–35).

A creature, considered as such, has no rights. He can demand nothing from his Maker; and in whatever manner he may be treated, has no title to complain. Yet, when thinking of the absolute dominion of God over all, we ought never to lose sight of His moral perfections. God is just and good, and ever does that which is right. Nevertheless, He exercises His sovereignty according to His own imperial and righteous pleasure.

He assigns each creature his place as seems good in His own sight. He orders the varied circumstances of each according to His own counsels. He molds each vessel according to His own uninfluenced determination. He has mercy on whom He will; and whom He will, He hardens. Wherever we are, His eye is upon us. Whoever we are, our life and everything is held at His disposal. To the Christian, He is a tender Father; to the rebellious sinner He will yet be a consuming fire. "Now unto the King eternal, immortal, invisible, the only wise God, be honour and glory for ever and ever. Amen" (1 Timothy 1:17).

Chapter 19

THE BOUNTIES OF GOD

*E*ye hath not seen, nor ear heard, neither have entered into the heart of man, the things which God hath prepared for them that love him" (1 Corinthians 2:9). How often this passage is quoted only that far; how rarely are the words added, "But God hath revealed them unto us by his Spirit" (v. 10). Why is this? Is it because so few of God's people search out and enjoy what the Spirit has revealed in the Word about those things God has prepared for them that love Him? If we were more occupied with God's riches than with our poverty, Christ's fulness than our emptiness, the divine bounties than our leanness, on what a different plane of experience we would live!

We are much impressed by noting some of "the riches of his grace" (Ephesians 1:7). It is striking to note that our Christian life starts at a marriage feast (Luke 14:16–24; see also Matthew 22:1–10), just as Christ's first miracle was wrought at one (John 2). The word to us is "Come; for all things are now ready" (Luke 14:17); "behold, I have prepared my dinner: my oxen and my fatlings are killed, and all things are ready: come unto the marriage" (Matthew 22:4). Observe the "I have prepared," agreeing with "the things which God hath prepared for them that love him" (1 Corinthians 2:9). Notice the "*are* ready," confirming "God *hath* revealed them unto us" (v. 10). Mark the "my dinner: my oxen and my fatlings," for "all things are of God" (2 Corinthians 5:18). The creature contributes nothing; all is provided for him. Finally, weigh the "come unto *the marriage.*" The figure is very blessed; it speaks of joy, festivity, feasting.

> He spread the banquet, made me eat.
> Bid all my fears remove,
> Yea, o'er my guilty, rebel head
> He placed His banner—Love.

Practically the same figure is employed by Christ again in Luke 15. There He pictures the penitent prodigal welcomed home by the father. No sooner is he clothed and fitted for the house than the words go forth, "Bring hither the fatted calf, and kill it; and let us eat, and be merry" (v. 23); and we are told, "They began to be merry" (v. 24). In the parable, that merriment met with no reverse, since it is portrayed without a break and without a bound. Then we may conclude that this newborn joy ought to characterize all this festive scene—as truly so now, as soon it will be in glory.

A beautiful type of the lavish manner in which God bestows His bounties upon His people is found in Genesis 9:3: "Every moving thing that liveth shall be meat for you; even as the green herb have I given you all things." This was Jehovah's response to the "sweet savour" which He had just smelled (8:21). It is most important that we should note the connection and perceive the ground on which God so freely bestowed "all things" upon the patriarch. At the close of Genesis 8 Noah built an altar unto the Lord and presented burnt offerings. At the beginning of Genesis 9 we learn God's answer, which blessedly foreshadowed the unmeasured portion bestowed upon the new creation, the members of which have been blessed "with all spiritual blessings in heavenly places in Christ" (Ephesians 1:3).

These blessings are based upon God's estimate of the value of Christ's sacrifice of Himself. The abiding worth of that sacrifice is immeasurable and illimitable; as immeasurable as the personal excellency of the Son, as illimitable as the Father's delight in Him. The nature and extent of those blessings, which accrue to God's elect on the ground of Christ's finished work, are intimated by the substantives and adjectives employed by the Holy Spirit when He describes the profuseness of the divine bounties already bestowed upon us, and which we shall enjoy forever!

Take first God's *grace*. Not only are we told of the "riches of his grace" (Ephesians 1:7) and of the "exceeding riches of his grace" (2:7); but also we read that it has "abounded unto many," and that we receive "abundance of grace," yes, that grace has superabounded (Greek, Romans 5:15, 17, 20)—the limitless wealth of divine grace flowing forth and multiplying itself in its objects. The foundation or moving cause of this is found in John 1. When the only begotten Son became flesh and tabernacled here for a season, it was as One who was "full of grace and truth" (v. 14). Because we have been made joint heirs with Him it is written, "And of his fulness have all we received, and grace for grace" (v. 16).

Take again God's *love*. There has been neither reserve nor restraint in the outflow of His love to its loveless, unlovely objects. He has loved His people "with an everlasting love" (Jeremiah 31:3). Wondrously He manifested it, for when the fulness of time was come, He sent forth His Son, born of a woman. Yes, He "so loved the world" as to give "his only begotten Son, that whosoever believeth in him should not perish, but have everlasting life" (John 3:16); therefore we read of His "great love wherewith he loved us" (Ephesians 2:4). The Greek word translated *great* is rendered *plenteous* (Matthew 9:37) and *abundant* (1 Peter 1:3). Love unmeasured, that passes knowledge, fills our lives with its unceasing ministrations, ever active in priesthood and advocacy on high, how truly it is love abundant.

Our present theme is inexhaustible. Our Lord came here that His people "might have life, and that they might have it more abundantly" (John 10:10). This was first made good when Christ, as the Head of the new creation and the "beginning of the creation of God" (Revelation 3:14), breathed on His disciples, "Receive ye the Holy Ghost" (John 20:22). It was the risen Saviour communicating His resurrection life to His own (compare Genesis 2:7 for the beginning of the old creation). So, too, when that same One, who down here received the Spirit without measure (John 3:34), ascended on high as the glorified Man, He baptized His people in the Holy Spirit (Acts 2). As the apostle Paul assures Gentile saints, "He shed on us abundantly" (Titus 3:6). Once more, he emphasized the profuseness of God's bounties.

Consider now His *confidences.* The Lord Jesus said to His disciples, "Henceforth I call you not servants; for the servant knoweth not what his lord doeth: but I have called you friends; for all things that I have heard of my Father I have made known unto you" (John 15:15). There are things which the angels "desire to look into" (1 Peter 1:12), yet they have been made known to us by God's Spirit. What a word in Ephesians, "Wherein he hath abounded toward us in all wisdom and prudence; having made known unto us the mystery of his will" (1:8–9). This may be termed the abundance of His counsels.

Once more, consider the exercise and display of His *power.* Paul prayed that we might know "what is the exceeding greatness of his power to us-ward who believe, according to the working of his mighty power, which he wrought in Christ, when he raised him from the dead, and set him at his own right hand in the heavenly places" (Ephesians 1:19–20). Here was the might of God working transcendently in an objective way; its correlative is recorded in Ephesians 3:20: "Now unto him that is able to do exceeding abundantly above all that we ask or think, according to the power that worketh in us." Clearly this is the highest putting forth of energy, working subjectively.

In such lavish measure then God has blessed His people. As the apostle wrote to the Colossians concerning Him, "For in him dwelleth all the fulness of the Godhead bodily. And ye are complete [filled full] in him" (Colossians 2:9–10). But it is one thing to know, intellectually, of these bounties of God; it is quite another, by faith, to make them our own. It is one thing to be familiar with the letter of them; it is another to live in their power and be the personal expression of them.

What shall our response be to such divine munificence? Surely it is that "the abundant grace might through the thanksgiving of many redound to the glory of God" (2 Corinthians 4:15). Surely it is that we should "abound in hope, through the power of the Holy Ghost" (Romans 15:13). It is only here that hope finds its sphere of exercise, since only in the saints will it receive full fruition. If God speaks so uniformly of the varied character of our blessing—whether it be His grace, His love, His life imparted to us, His confidences, His power, His mercy (1 Peter 1:3–5)—as being so abundant, it must be because He wants to impress our hearts with the exuberance of the bounties He has bestowed on us. The practical effect of this on our souls should cause us to "joy in God through our Lord Jesus Christ" (Romans 5:11), to draw out all that is within us in true worship, to fit us for a closer and deeper fellowship with Him. "And God is able to make all grace abound toward you; that ye, always having all sufficiency in all things, may abound to every good work" (2 Corinthians 9:8).

Chapter 20

THE
GIFTS
OF GOD

A giving God! What a concept! To our regret, our familiarity with it often dulls our sense of wonderment at it. There is nothing that resembles such a concept in the religions of heathendom. Very much to the contrary; their deities are portrayed as monsters of cruelty and greed, always exacting painful sacrifices from deluded devotees. But the God of Scripture is portrayed as the Father of mercies, "who giveth us richly all things to enjoy" (1 Timothy 6:17). It is true that He has His own rights—the rights of His holiness and proprietorship. Nor does He rescind them, but rather enforces them. But what we would contemplate here is something which transcends reason and had never entered our minds to conceive. The Divine Claimer is at once the Divine Meeter. He required satisfaction of His broken Law, and Himself supplied it. His just claims are met by His own grace. He who asks for sacrifices from us made the supreme sacrifice for us! God is both the Demander and the Donor, the Requirer and the Provider.

1. *The gift of His Son.* Of old the language of prophecy announced:

"For unto us a child is born, unto us a son is given" (Isaiah 9:6). Accordingly, the angels announced to the shepherds at the time of His advent: "Unto you is born this day . . . a Saviour" (Luke 2:11). That gift was the supreme exemplification of the divine benignity. "In this was manifested the love of God toward us, because that God sent his only begotten Son into the world, that we might live through him. Herein is love, not that we loved God, but that he loved us, and sent his Son to be the propitiation for our sins" (1 John 4:9–10). That was the guaranty of all other blessings. As the apostle argued from the greater to the less, assuring us that Christ is at once the pledge and channel of every other mercy: "He that spared not his own Son, but delivered him up for us all, how shall he not with him also freely give us all things?" (Romans 8:32). God did not withhold His choicest treasure, the darling of His bosom, but freely yielded Him up; and the love that spared not Him will not begrudge anything that is for the good of His people.

2. *The gift of His Spirit.* The Son is God's all-inclusive gift. As Manton said, "Christ cometh not to us empty handed: His person and His benefits are not divided. He came to purchase all manner of blessings for us." The greatest of these is the Holy Spirit, who applies and communicates what the Lord Jesus obtained for His people. God pardoned and justified His elect in Old Testament times on the ground of the atonement, which His Son should make at the appointed time. On the same basis He communicated to them the Spirit (Numbers 11:25; Nehemiah 9:20); otherwise, none would have been regenerated, fitted for communion with God, or enabled to bring forth spiritual fruit. But He then wrought more secretly, rather than "in demonstration and in power"; came as "the dew," rather than was "poured out" copiously; was restricted to Israel, rather than communicated to Gentiles also. The Spirit in His fullness was God's ascension gift to Christ (Acts 2:33) and Christ's coronation gift to His Church (John 16:7). The gift of the Spirit was purchased for His people by Christ (see Galatians 3:13–14 and note carefully the second *that* in v. 14). Every blessing we receive is through the merits and mediation of Christ.

3. *The gift of life.* "For the wages of sin is death; but the gift of God is eternal life through Jesus Christ our Lord" (Romans 6:23). There is a double antithesis between those two things. First, the justice of God will

render unto the wicked what is due them for their sins, but His mercy bestows upon His people what they do not deserve. Second, eternal death follows as a natural and inevitable consequence from what is in and done by its objects. Not so eternal life, for it is bestowed without any consideration of something in or from its subjects. It is communicated and sustained gratuitously. Eternal life is a free bounty, not only unmerited but also unsolicited by us, for in every instance God has reason to say, "I am sought of them that asked not for me" (Isaiah 65:1; cf. Romans 3:11). The recipient is wholly passive. He does not act, but is acted upon when he is brought from death unto life. Eternal life—a spiritual life now, a life of glory hereafter—is sovereignly and freely bestowed by God. Yet it is also a blessing communicated by Him unto His elect because the Lord Jesus Christ paid the price of redemption. Yes, it is actually dispensed by Christ. "I give unto them [not merely "offer"] eternal life" (John 10:28; see also 17:2–3).

4. *The gift of spiritual understanding.* "And we know that the Son of God is come, and hath given us an understanding, that we may know him that is true" (1 John 5:20). What is communicated to the saint when he is born again is wholly spiritual and exactly suited for taking in the scriptural knowledge of Christ. It is not an entirely new faculty which is then imparted, but rather the renewing of the original one, fitting it for the apprehension of new objects. It consists of an internal illumination, a divine light that shines in our hearts, enabling us to discern the glory of God shining in the face of Jesus Christ (2 Corinthians 4:6). Though we are not now admitted into a corporeal sight of Christ, yet He is made a living reality to those who have been quickened into newness of life. By this divine renewing of the understanding we can now perceive the peerless excellency and perfect suitability of Christ. The knowledge we have of Him is seated in the understanding. That fires the affections, sanctifies the will, and raises the mind into being fixed upon Him. Such a spiritual understanding is not attained by any efforts of ours, but is a supernatural bestowment, a divine gift conferred upon the elect, which admits them into the secrets of the Most High.

5. *The gift of faith.* The salvation of God does not actually become ours until we believe in, rest upon, and receive Christ as a personal Saviour. But as we cannot see without both sight and light, neither can we

believe until life and faith are divinely communicated to us. Accordingly, "For by grace are ye saved through faith; and that not of yourselves: it is the gift of God: not of works, lest any man should boast" (Ephesians 2:8–9). Arminians would make the second clause of verse 8 a mere repetition of the first, and in less expressive and emphatic language. Since salvation is by grace, it is superfluous to add that it is "not of yourselves." But because "faith" is our act, it was necessary—so that the excellency of it should not be arrogated by the creature, but ascribed unto God—to point out that it is not of ourselves. The very faith which receives a gratuitous salvation is not the unassisted act of man's own will. As God must give me breath before I can breathe, so faith ere I believe. Compare also "faith which is by him" (Acts 3:16); "who believe, according to the working of his mighty power" (Ephesians 1:19); "through the faith of the operation of God" (Colossians 2:12); "who by him do believe in God" (1 Peter 1:21).

6. *The gift of repentance.* While it is the bound duty of every sinner to repent (Acts 17:30)—for ought he not to cease from and abhor his rebellion against God?—yet he is so completely under the blinding power of sin that a miracle of grace is necessary before he will do so. A broken and a contrite spirit are of God's providing. It is the Holy Spirit who illuminates the understanding to perceive the heinousness of sin, the heart to loathe it, and the will to repudiate it. Faith and repentance are the first evidence of spiritual life. For when God quickens a sinner He convicts him of the evil of sin, causes him to hate it, moves him to sorrow over and turn from it. "Surely after that I was turned, I repented; and after that I was instructed, I smote upon my thigh: I was ashamed, yea, even confounded" (Jeremiah 31:19). "All His grace in us" (Matthew Henry). Compare "a Prince and a Saviour, for to give repentance to Israel" (Acts 5:31); "then hath God also to the Gentiles granted repentance unto life" (11:18); "if God peradventure will give them repentance" (2 Timothy 2:25).

7. *The gift of grace.* "I thank my God always on your behalf, for the grace of God which is given you by Jesus Christ" (1 Corinthians 1:4). Grace is used there in its widest sense, including all the benefits of Christ's merits and mediation, providential or spiritual, temporal or eternal. It includes regenerating, sanctifying, preserving grace, as well as

every particular grace of the new nature—faith, hope, love. "But unto every one of us is given grace according to the measure of the gift of Christ" (Ephesians 4:7), that is, according as He is pleased to bestow, and not according to our ability or asking. Therefore we have no cause to be proud or boastful. Whatever grace we have to resist the devil, patiently bear affliction, or overcome the world is from Him. Whatever obedience we perform, or devotion we render Him, or sacrifice we make is of His grace. Therefore must we confess, "For all things come of thee, and of thine own have we given thee" (1 Chronicles 29:14).

Chapter 21

THE
GUIDANCE
OF GOD

There is a need to amplify the positive aspect of divine guidance. There are few subjects which bear on the practical side of the Christian life, and that believers are more exercised about, than that they may be "led of the Lord" in all their ways. Yet when some important decision has to be made, they are often puzzled to know *how* "the Lord's mind" is obtained. Great numbers of tracts and booklets on this subject have been written, but they are so vague that they offer little help. There certainly exists a real need today for some clear, definitive treatment of the subject.

For some years I have been convinced that one thing which contributes much to shrouding this subject in mystery is the loose, misleading terms generally employed by those who refer to it. While such expressions are used—"Is this according to God's will?" "Do I have the prompting of the Holy Spirit?" "Were you led of the Lord in that?"—sincere minds will continue to be perplexed and never arrive at any certainty. These expressions are so commonly used in religious circles that probably quite a few readers will be surprised at our challenging them.

We certainly do not condemn these expressions as erroneous, but rather we wish to point out that they are too intangible for most people until more definitely defined.

What alternative, then, have we to suggest? In connection with every decision we make, every plan we form, every action we execute, let the question be, "Is this in harmony with God's Word?" Is it what the Scriptures enjoin? Does it square with the rule God has given us to walk by? Is it in accord with the example which Christ left us to follow? If it is in harmony with God's Word, then it must be "according to God's will," for His will is revealed *in* His Word. If I do what the Scriptures enjoin, then I *must* be "prompted by the Holy Spirit," for He never moves anyone to act contrary thereto. If my conduct squares with the rule of righteousness (the precepts and commands of the Word), then I *must be* "led of the Lord," for He leads only into the "paths of righteousness" (Psalm 23:3). A great deal of mystical vagueness and puzzling uncertainty will be removed if the reader substitutes for, "Is this according to God's will?" the simpler and more tangible, "Is this according to God's Word?"

God, in His infinite condescension and transcendent grace, has given us His Word for this very purpose, so that we need not stumble along blindly, ignorant of what pleases or displeases Him but that we might *know* His mind. That divine Word is given to us not simply for information, but to regulate our conduct, to enlighten our minds, and to mold our hearts. The Word supplies us with an unerring chart by which to steer through the dangerous sea of life. If we sincerely and diligently follow, it will deliver us from disastrous rocks and submerged reefs and direct us safely to the heavenly harbor. That Word has all the instructions we need for every problem, every emergency we may be called upon to face. That Word has been given to us "that the man of God may be perfect, thoroughly furnished unto all good works" (2 Timothy 3:17). How thankful we should be that the Triune God has favored us with such a Word.

"Thy word is a lamp unto my feet, and a light unto my path" (Psalm 119:105). The metaphor used here is taken from a man walking along a dangerous road on a dark night, in urgent need of a lantern to show him where to walk safely and comfortably, to avoid injury and destruction. The same figure is used again in the New Testament. "We have also a more sure word of prophecy; whereunto ye do well that ye take heed, as unto a light that shineth in a dark place" (2 Peter 1:19). The dark place is this world, and it is only as we take heed to the Word, to the light God has given us, that we shall be able to perceive and avoid "the broad [road] that leadeth to destruction," and discern the narrow way which alone "leadeth unto life" (Matthew 7:13–14).

It should be observed that this verse plainly intimates that God has placed His Word in our hands for an intensely practical purpose, namely, to direct our walk and to regulate our deportment. At once this shows us what is the first and principal use we are to make of this divine gift. It would do a traveler little good to diligently scrutinize the mechanism of a lamp, or to admire its beautiful design. Rather, he is to take it up and make a practical use of it. Many are zealous in reading "the letter of Scripture," and many are charmed with the evidences of its divine Authorship. But how few realize the primary purpose for which God gave the Scriptures; how few make *a practical use* of them—ordering the details of their lives by its rules and regulations. They eulogize the lamp, but they do not walk by its light.

Our first need as little children was to learn to walk. The mother's milk was only a means to an end: to nourish the infant's life, to strengthen its limbs so that they should be put to a practical use. So it is spiritually. When we have been born again and fed by the Spirit on the pure milk of the Word, our first need is to learn to walk, to walk as the children of God. This can be learned only as we ascertain our Father's will as revealed in Holy Writ. By nature we are totally ignorant of His will for us and of what promotes our highest interests. It is solemn and humbling that man is the only creature born into this world devoid of intelligence as to how to act and who needs to be taught what is evil and what is good for him.

All the lower orders of creation are endowed with an instinct which moves them to act discreetly, to avoid what is harmful, and to follow what is good. But not so man. Animals and birds do not have to be taught which herbs and berries are poisonous; they need no curbs upon them not to overeat or overdrink—you cannot even force a horse or a cow to gorge and make itself sick. Even plants turn their faces to the light and open their mouths to catch the falling rain. But fallen man has not even the instinct of the brutes. Usually he has to learn by painful experience what is harmful and injurious. And, as it has been well said, "Experience keeps an expensive school"—her fees are high. Too bad that so many only discover this when it is too late, when they have wrecked their constitutions beyond repair.

Some may answer to this, "But man is endowed with a conscience." True, but how well does it serve him until he is enlightened by the Word and convicted by the Spirit? Man's understanding has been so darkened by sin, and folly is so bound up in his heart from childhood (Proverbs 22:15), that until he is instructed he does not know what God requires of him, nor what is for his highest good. That is why God gave us His Word: to make known what He justly demands of us; to inform us of those things which destroy the soul; to reveal the baits which Satan uses to capture and slay so many; to point out the highway of holiness which alone leads to heaven (Hebrews 12:14); and to acquaint us with the rules which must be observed if we are to walk that highway.

Our first duty, and our first aim, must be to take up the Scriptures to ascertain what is God's revealed will for us, what are the paths He forbids us to walk, what are the ways pleasing in His sight. Many things are prohibited in the Word which neither our reason nor our conscience would discover. For example, we learn "that which is highly esteemed among men is abomination in the sight of God" (Luke 16:15); "the friendship of the world is enmity with God" (James 4:4); "he that hasteth with his feet sinneth" (Proverbs 19:2). Many things are also commanded which can only be known if we acquaint ourselves with its contents. For example, "Lean not unto thine own understanding" (Proverbs 3:5); "put not your trust in princes, nor in the son of man, in whom there is no help" (Psalm 146:3); "love your enemies, bless them that curse you, do good to them that hate you, and pray for them which despitefully use you, and persecute you" (Matthew 5:44).

The above are but samples of hundreds of others. It is obvious that God's Word cannot be a lamp unto our feet and a light unto our path unless we are familiar with its contents, particularly until we are informed on the practical rules God has given us to walk by. Hence it should be obvious that the first need of the Christian is not to delve into the intricacies and mysteries of Scripture, study the prophecies, nor entertain himself with the wonderful types therein. Rather he needs to concentrate on what will instruct him as to the kind of conduct which will be pleasing to the Lord. The Scriptures are given us, primarily, not for our intellectual gratification, nor for emotional admiration, but for life's regulation. Nor are the precepts and commands, the warnings and encouragements contained therein simply for our information. They are to be reduced to practice; they require unqualified obedience.

"This book of the law shall not depart out of thy mouth; but thou shalt meditate therein day and night, that thou mayest observe to do according to all that is written therein: for then thou shalt make thy way prosperous, and then thou shalt have good success" (Joshua 1:8). God will be no man's debtor. In keeping His commands there is "great reward" (Psalm 19:11) Part of that reward is deliverance from being deceived by the false appearances of things, from forming erroneous estimates, from pursuing a foolish policy. Part of that reward is acquiring wisdom so that we choose what is good, act prudently, and follow those paths which lead to righteousness, peace, and joy. He who treasures in his heart the divine precepts and diligently seeks to walk by their rule will escape those evils which destroy his fellows.

"If any man walk in the day, he stumbleth not, because he seeth the light of this world" (John 11:9). To walk "in the day" means to be in communion with One who is Light, to conduct ourselves according to His revealed will. Just so far as the Christian walks in the path of duty, as defined for him in the Word, will he walk surely and comfortably. The light of that Word makes the way plain before him, and he is preserved from falling over the obstacles with which Satan seeks to trip him. "But if a man walk in the night, he stumbleth, because there is no light in him" (v. 10). Here is the solemn contrast: He who walks according to the dictates of his lusts and follows the counsel and example of the ungodly falls into the snares of the devil and perishes. There is no light in such a one, for he is not regulated by the Sun of righteousness.

"I am the light of the world: he that followeth me shall not walk in darkness, but shall have the light of life" (John 8:12). It is one thing to have "life"; it is another to enjoy the "light of life" that is only obtained by following Christ. Notice the tense of the verb: It is "he that *followeth* me," which signifies a steady, continuous course of action. The promise to such a one is he "shall not walk in darkness." But what does it mean to follow Christ? First and foremost, to be emptied of self-will, for "even Christ pleased not himself" (Romans 15:3). It is absolutely essential that self-will and self-pleasing be mortified if we are to be delivered from walking in darkness.

The unchanging order is made known by Christ: "If any man will come after me, let him deny himself, and take up his cross, and follow me" (Matthew 16:24). Christ cannot be followed until self is denied and the cross accepted as the distinguishing mark of discipleship. What does it mean to deny self? It means to repudiate our own goodness, to renounce our own wisdom, to have no confidence in our own strength, to completely set aside our own will and wishes, that we "should not henceforth live unto [ourselves], but unto him [who] died for [us]" (2 Corinthians 5:15). What does it mean to "take up our cross"? It signifies a readiness to endure the world's hatred and scorn, to voluntarily surrender our lives to God, to use all our faculties for His glory. The cross stands for unreserved and loving obedience to the Lord, for of Him it is written, "He . . . became obedient unto death, even the death of the cross" (Philippians 2:8). It is only as self with all its lustings and interests is denied, and as the heart is dominated by the spirit of Calvary, that we are prepared to follow Christ.

And what is signified by "follow" Christ? It means to take His yoke upon us (Matthew 11:29) and live in complete subjection to Him; to yield fully to His Lordship, to obey His commands, and thus truly serve Him. It is seeking to do only those things which are pleasing in His sight; to emulate the example which He left us: and He was in all things subject to the Scriptures. As we follow Him, we "shall not walk in darkness" (John 8:12). We will be in happy fellowship with Him who is the true light. For our encouragement—for they were men of like passions—it is recorded of Caleb and Joshua, "They have wholly followed the LORD" (Numbers 32:12). Having put their hand to the plow, they did not look back. Consequently, instead of perishing in the wilderness with their disobedient fellows, they entered the Promised Land.

Thus the great business, the task of the Christian, is to regulate his life by and conform his conduct to the precepts of the written Word and the example left us by the Incarnate Word. As he does so, and in proportion as he does so, he is emancipated from the darkness of his natural mind, freed from the follies of his corrupt heart, delivered from the mad course of this world, and escapes the snares of the devil. "Through knowledge shall the just be delivered" (Proverbs 11:9). Yes, great is the reward of keeping God's commandments. "Then shalt thou understand righteousness, and judgment, and equity; yea, every good path. When wisdom entereth into thine heart, and knowledge is pleasant unto thy soul; discretion shall preserve thee, understanding shall keep thee" (2:9–11).

It is well for those who are sensitive to both their own weakness and fallibility, and the difficulties with which they are surrounded in life, that the Lord has promised to guide His people with His eye, to cause them to hear, "This is the way, walk ye in it," when they are in danger of turning aside (Isaiah 30:21). For this purpose He has given to us the written Word as a lamp to our feet and encourages us to pray for the teaching of His Holy Spirit so that we may rightly understand and apply it. However, too often many widely deviate from the path of duty and commit gross, perplexing mistakes, while they profess a sincere desire to know the will of God and think they have His warrant and authority. This must certainly be due to misapplication of the rule by which they judge, since the rule itself is infallible. The Scriptures cannot deceive us, if rightly understood; but they may, if perverted, confirm us in a mistake. The Holy Spirit cannot mislead those under His influence; but we may suppose that we are so, when we are not.

Many have been deceived as to what they ought to do, or into forming a judgment beforehand of events in which they are closely concerned, by expecting direction in ways which the Lord has not warranted. Here are some of the principal ones:

Some, when two or more things were in view, and they could not immediately determine which to prefer, committed their case to the Lord in prayer. Then they have proceeded to cast lots, taking it for granted, after such a solemn appeal, that the turning up of the lot might be safely rested on as an answer from God. It is true, the Scripture (and right reason) assures us that the Lord disposes the lot. Several cases are recorded in the Old Testament where lots were used by divine appointment. But I think neither these, nor the choosing of Matthias to the apostleship by lot, are proper precedents for our conduct. In the division of the land of Canaan, in the affair of Achan, and in the nomination of Saul to the kingdom, recourse to lots was by God's express command. The instance of Matthias likewise was singular, since it can never happen again (namely, the choice of an apostle).

All these were before the canon of Scripture was completed and before the full descent and communication of the Holy Spirit, who was promised to dwell with the Church to the end of time. Under the New Testament dispensation, we are invited to come boldly to the throne of grace, to make our requests known to the Lord, and to cast our cares upon Him (see Hebrews 4:16; Philippians 4:6; 1 Peter 5:7). But we have neither precept nor promise respecting the use of lots. To have recourse to them without His appointment seems to be tempting Him rather than honoring Him, and it savors more of presumption than dependence. Effects of this expedient have often been unhappy and hurtful, a sufficient proof of how little it is to be trusted as a guide of our conduct.

Others, when in doubt, have opened the Bible and expected to find something to direct them to the first verse they should cast their eye upon. It is no small discredit to this practice that the heathens used some of their favorite books in the same way. They based their persuasions of what they ought to do, or what should befall them, according to the passage they happened upon. Among the Romans, the writings of Virgil were frequently consulted on these occasions, which gave rise to the well-known expression of the *Sortes Virgilinae*. Indeed, Virgil is as well adapted to satisfy inquiries in this way as the Bible itself. For if people will be governed by the occurrence of a single text of Scripture without regarding the context, or comparing it with the general tenor of the Word and with their own circumstances, they may commit the greatest extravagances. They may expect the greatest impossibilities, and contradict the plainest dictates of common sense, and all the while they think they have the Word of God on their side. Can opening to 2 Samuel 7:3, when Nathan said unto David, "Do all that is in thine heart; for the LORD is with thee," be sufficient to determine the lawfulness or expediency of actions? Or can a glance of the eye upon our Lord's words to the woman of Canaan, "Be it unto thee even as thou wilt" (Matthew 15:28), amount to proof that the present earnest desire of the mind (whatever it may be) shall be surely accomplished? Yet it is certain that big matters with important consequences have been engaged in, and the most sanguine expectations formed, upon no better warrant than dipping (as it is called) upon a text of Scripture.

A sudden strong impression of a text that seems to have some resemblance to the concern on the mind has been accepted by many as an infallible token that they were right, and that things would go just as they would have them. Or, on the other hand, if the passage bore a threatening aspect, it has filled them with fears which they have found afterwards were groundless. These impressions have been more generally regarded and trusted to, but have frequently proved no less delusive. It is true that such impressions of a precept or a promise that humble, animate, or comfort the soul, by giving it a lively sense of the truth contained in the words, are both profitable and pleasant. Many of the Lord's people have been instructed and supported (especially in a time of trouble) by some seasonable word of grace applied and sealed by His Spirit to their hearts. But if impressions or impulses are received as a voice from heaven, directing to particular actions that could not be proved to be duties without them, a person may be inwardly misled into great evils and gross delusions. Many have been so. There is no doubt that the enemy of our souls, if permitted, can furnish us with Scriptures in abundance for these purposes.

Some persons judge of the nature and event of their designs by the freedom they find in prayer. They say that they commit their ways to God, seek His direction, and are favored with much enlargement of spirit. Therefore they cannot doubt but what they have in view is acceptable in the Lord's sight. I would not absolutely reject every plea of this kind, yet without other corroborating evidence I could not admit it as proof. It is not always easy to determine when we have spiritual freedom in prayer. Self is deceitful. When our hearts are much fixed upon a thing, this may put words and earnestness into our mouths. Too often we first determine secretly for ourselves, and then ask counsel of God. In such a disposition we are ready to grasp at everything that may seem to favor our darling scheme. And the Lord, for the detecting and chastisement of our hypocrisy (for hypocrisy it is, though perhaps hardly perceptible to ourselves), may answer us according to our idols (see Ezekiel 14:3–4). Besides, the grace of prayer may be in exercise when the subject matter of the prayer may be founded upon a mistake, from the intervention of circumstances with which we are unacquainted. Thus, I may have a friend in a distant country. I hope he is alive, I pray for him, and it is my duty to do so. The Lord, by His Spirit, assists His people in their present duty. If I can pray with much liberty for my distant friend, it may be a proof that the Spirit is pleased to assist my infirmities, but it is no proof my friend is alive at the time I pray for him. If the next time I pray for him I should find my spirit straitened, I am not to conclude that my friend is dead, and therefore the Lord will not assist me in praying for him any longer.

Once more, a remarkable dream has often been thought as decisive as any of these methods of knowing the will of God. True, many wholesome and seasonable admonitions have been received in dreams. But to pay great attention to dreams, or especially to be guided by them, to form our sentiments, or conduct our expectations upon them is superstitious and dangerous. The promises are not made to those who *dream,* but to those who *watch.*

The Lord may give to some upon occasion a hint or encouragement out of the common way. But to seek His direction in such things as just mentioned is unscriptural and ensnaring. Some presumed they were doing God's service while acting in contradiction to His express commands. Others were infatuated to believe a lie, declaring themselves assured beyond the shadow of a doubt of things which never came to pass. When they were disappointed, Satan improved the occasion to make them doubt the plainest and most important truths and to count their whole former experience as a delusion. These things have caused weak believers to stumble, offenses against the Gospel have multiplied, and evil spoken of the way of truth.

How, then, may the Lord's guidance be expected? After all these negative premises, the question may be answered in a few words. In general, He directs His people by affording them, in answer to prayer, the light of His Holy Spirit, which enables them to understand and love the Scriptures. The Word of God is not to be used as a lottery, nor is it designed to instruct us by shreds and scraps, which detached from their proper places have no determined import. But it is to furnish us with just principles and right apprehensions to regulate our judgments and affections and thereby to influence and regulate our conduct. Those who study the Scriptures in humble dependence upon divine teaching are convinced of their own weakness. They are taught to make a true estimate of everything around them and are gradually formed into a spirit of submission to the will of God. They discover the nature and duties of their situations and relations in life, and the snares and temptations to which they are exposed. The Word of God dwelling in them is a preservative from error, a light to their feet, and a spring of strength and consolation. By treasuring up the doctrines, precepts, promises, examples, and exhortations of Scripture in their minds—and daily comparing them with the rule by which they walk—they grow into an habitual frame of spiritual wisdom. They acquire a gracious taste which enables them to judge right and wrong with a degree of certainty, as a musical ear judges sounds. They are seldom mistaken, because they are influenced by the love of Christ which rules in their hearts, and a regard for the glory of God.

In particular cases, the Lord opens and shuts for them, breaks down walls of difficulty which obstruct their path, or hedges up their way with thorns when they are in danger of going wrong. They know their concerns are in His hands; they are willing to follow where and when He leads but are afraid of running before Him. They are not impatient. Because they *believe,* they will not be hasty, but wait daily upon Him in prayer, especially when they find their hearts engaged in any pursuit. They are jealous of being deceived by appearances and dare not move farther or faster than they can see His light shining upon their paths. They express at least their desire, if not their attainment. Though there are seasons when faith languishes and self prevails too much, this is their general disposition. And the Lord does not disappoint their expectations. He leads them on a right way, preserves them from a thousand snares, and satisfies them that He is and will be their Guide even unto death.

The positive side of the subject probably needs some amplification. The general rule may be stated thus: If we are daily concerned in seeking to please God in all the details, great and small, of our lives, He will not leave us in ignorance of His will concerning us. But if we are accustomed to gratify self and only turn up to God for help in times of difficulty and emergency, then we must not be surprised if He mocks us and allows us to reap the fruits of our folly. Our business is to walk in obedient subjection to Christ, and His sure promise is "He that followeth me shall not walk in darkness" (John 8:12). Make sure you sincerely endeavor to follow the example Christ left us, and He will not leave you in uncertainty as to which step you should take when you come to the place of decision.

"Wherefore be ye not unwise, but understanding what the will of the Lord is" (Ephesians 5:17). From this verse it is clear that it is both the right and the duty of the Christian to know the Lord's will for him. God can neither be pleased nor glorified by His children walking in ignorance or proceeding blindly. Did not Christ say to His beloved disciples, "Henceforth I call you not servants; for the servant knoweth not what His lord doeth: but I have called you friends; for all things that I have heard of my Father I have made known unto you" (John 15:15). If we are in the dark as to how we ought to proceed in anything, it is clear that we are living far below our privileges. No doubt the majority of our readers will give hearty assent to these statements, but the question which concerns most of them is, How are we to ascertain the Lord's will concerning the varied details of our lives?

First, notice this exhortation, that we should be understanding "what the will of the Lord is," is preceded by "Wherefore be ye not unwise." That word *unwise* does not signify bare ignorance or lack of knowledge; otherwise, the two halves of the verse would merely express the same thought in its negative and positive forms. No, the word *unwise* there means "lacking in common sense" (or "be not ye foolish" [RV]). Nor does the word *foolish* signify no more than it now does in common speech. In Scripture the fool is not simply one who is mentally deficient, but is the man who leaves God out of his life, who acts independently of Him. This must be borne in mind as we arrive at the meaning of the second half of Ephesians 5:17.

Observe that Ephesians 5:17 opens with the word *Wherefore,* which points back to what immediately precedes: "See then that ye walk circumspectly, not as fools, but as wise, redeeming the time, because the days are evil" (vv. 15–16). Unless those exhortations are prayerfully and diligently heeded, it is impossible that we "understand what the will of the Lord is." Unless our walk be right, there can be no spiritual discernment of God's will for us. This brings us back to a central thought. Our daily walk is to be ordered by God's Word. In proportion as it is, so we will be kept in His will and preserved from folly and sin.

"A good understanding have all they that do his commandments" (Psalm 111:10). A "good understanding" may be defined as spiritual instinct. We all know what is meant by the instinct with which the Creator has endowed animals and birds. It is an inward faculty which prompts them to avoid danger and moves them to seek what is for their well-being. Man was endowed originally with a similar instinct, though of a far superior order to that of lower creatures. But at the Fall, he, to a large extent, lost it. As one generation of depraved beings followed another, their instinct has become more and more weakened, until now we see many conducting themselves with far less intelligence than the beasts of the field. They rush madly to destruction, which the instinct of the brutes would avoid. They act foolishly, yes, madly, contrary even to common sense, in conducting their affairs and concerns without discretion.

At regeneration, God gives His elect "the spirit . . . of a sound mind" (2 Timothy 1:7), but that spirit has to be cultivated. It needs training and direction. The necessary instruction is found in the Word. From that

Word we learn what things will prove beneficial to us, and what will be injurious; what things to seek after, and what to avoid. As the precepts of Scripture are reduced to practice by us, and as its prohibitions and warnings are heeded, we are able to judge things in their true light. We are delivered from being deceived by false appearances; we are kept from making foolish mistakes. The closer we walk by the Word, the more fully this will prove to be the case with us: A good judgment or spiritual instinct will form in us, so that we conduct our affairs discreetly and adorn the doctrine we profess.

So highly does the saint prize this spiritual instinct or sound mind, that he prays, "Teach me good judgment and knowledge: for I have believed thy commandments" (Psalm 119:66). He realizes it can only be increased as he is divinely taught by the Spirit applying the Word to his heart, opening to him its meaning, bringing it to his remembrance when needed, and enabling him to make a proper use of it. But note that in this prayer the petition is backed up with a plea, "for I have believed thy commandments." *Believed* is not merely an intellectual assent, but is approved with the affections. Only when that is the case is such a petition sincere. There is an inseparable connection between these two things. Where God's commandments are loved by us, we can count upon Him to teach us good judgment.

As we said, the *fool* is not the mentally deficient, but the one who leaves God out of his thoughts and plans, who cares not whether his conduct pleases or displeases Him. The fool is a godless person. Contrariwise, the *wise* (in Scripture) are not the highly intellectual or the brilliantly educated, but those who honestly seek to put God first in their lives. God "honors" those who honor Him (1 Samuel 2:30). He gives them "good judgment" (Psalm 119:66). True, it is not acquired all in a day, but "here a little, and there a little" (see Isaiah 28:10, 13). Yet the more completely we surrender to God, the more the principles of His Word regulate our conduct, the swifter will be our growth in spiritual wisdom. In saying that this good judgment is not acquired all at once, we do not mean that a whole lifetime has to be lived before it becomes ours, though this is often the case with many. Some who have been converted but a few years are often more spiritual, godly, and possess more spiritual wisdom than those who were converted years before.

By treasuring up in his mind the doctrines, precepts, promises, exhortations, and warnings of Scripture; and by diligently comparing himself with the rule by which he is to walk; the Christian grows into a habitual frame of spiritual wisdom. He acquires a gracious taste which enables him to judge of right and wrong with a degree of readiness and certainty, as a musical ear judges sounds, so that he is rarely mistaken. He who has the Word ruling in his heart is influenced by it in all his actions. Because the glory of God is the great aim before him, he is not permitted to go far wrong. Moreover, God has promised to show Himself strong on behalf of the one whose heart is perfect toward Him. He does this by regulating His providences and causing all things to work together for his good.

"The light of the body is the eye: if therefore thine eye be single, thy whole body shall be full of light" (Matthew 6:22). The language is figurative, yet its meaning is not difficult to ascertain. What the eye is to the body, the heart is to the soul, for out of the heart are "the issues of life" (Proverbs 4:23). The actions of the body are directed by the light received from the eye. If the eye is single, that is, sound and clear, perceiving objects as they really are, then the whole body has light to direct its members, and the man moves with safety and comfort. In like manner, if the heart is undivided, set on pleasing God in all things, then the soul has clear vision, discerning the true nature of things, forming a sound judgment of their worth, choosing wisely, and directing itself prudently. When the heart is right with God, the soul is endowed with spiritual wisdom so that there is full light for our path.

"But if thine eye be evil, thy whole body shall be full of darkness. If therefore the light that is in thee be darkness, how great is that darkness!" (Matthew 6:23). Here is the solemn contrast. If the vision of our bodily eye is defective, a cataract dimming it, then nothing is seen clearly. All is confusion, the man stumbles as if in the dark, as if continually liable to lose his way and run into danger. In like manner, where the heart be not right with God, where sin and self dominate, the whole soul is under the reign of darkness. In consequence, the judgment is blinded so that it cannot rightly discern between good and evil, cannot see through the gild of Satan's baits, and thus is fatally deceived by them. The very light which is in fallen man, namely his reason, is controlled by his lusts; thus great is his darkness.

The verses we have just considered were spoken by Christ immediately after what He had been saying about the right laying up of treasures (Matthew 6:19–21). It was as though He both anticipated and answered a question from His disciples. If it is so important for us not to lay up treasures on earth, but rather treasures in heaven, why is it that the men commonly regarded as the shrewdest, and considered to be the most successful, seek after earthly treasures, rather than heavenly? To this Christ replied: Marvel not at this—they cannot see what they are doing: they are like blind men gathering pebbles supposing that they are valuable diamonds.

Christ casts much light on what we now see on every side. They who have set their hearts on things of time and sense are but spending their energies for that which will stand them in no stead when they come to their deathbeds. They labor for that which "satisfieth not" (Isaiah 55:2). The reason they conduct themselves so insanely—pursuing so eagerly the pleasures of this world, which will bear nothing but bitter regrets in the world to come—is because their hearts are evil. God has no real place in their thoughts, and so He gives them up to the spirit of madness. There must be the single eye—the heart set upon pleasing God—if the soul is to be filled with heavenly wisdom, which loves, seeks, and lays up heavenly things. That wisdom is something which no university can impart. It is "from above" (James 3:17).

It should be noted that our Lord's teaching upon the "single eye," with the whole body "full of light," and the "evil eye" with the whole body "full of darkness," is immediately followed with, "No man can serve two masters: for either he will hate the one, and love the other; or else he will hold to the one, and despise the other. Ye cannot serve God and mammon" (Matthew 6:24). This at once establishes the meaning of the preceding verses. Christ had been speaking (in a figure) of setting the Lord supremely before the heart, which necessarily involves casting out worldly things and fleshly considerations. Men think to compound with God and their lusts, God and mammon, God and worldly pleasures. No, says Christ. God will have all or nothing. He that serveth Him must serve Him singly and supremely. Are you willing to pay the price to have divine light on your path?

We have not attempted to enter into specific details and state how a person is to act when some difficult or sudden emergency confronts him. Rather we have sought to treat of basic principles and thoroughly establish them. Though it might satisfy curiosity, it would serve no good purpose for a teacher to explain an intricate problem in higher mathematics to a student who had not already mastered the elementary rules of arithmetic. So it would be out of place to explain how particular cases or circumstances are to be handled before we have presented those rules which must guide our general walk.

Thus far we have dealt with two main things: the absolute necessity of being controlled by the Word of God *without,* and the having a heart *within* which is single to God's glory and set upon pleasing Him—if we are to have the light of heaven on our earthly path. A third consideration must now engage our attention: the help of the Holy Spirit. But at this point we most need to be on our guard, lest we lapse into a vague mysticism on the one hand, or become guilty of wild fanaticism on the other. Many have plunged into the most foolish and evil courses under the plea they were "prompted by the Spirit." No doubt they were prompted by some spirit, but most certainly not by the Holy Spirit. He never prompts anything contrary to the Word. Our only safety is to impartially bring our inward impulses to the test of Holy Writ.

"For as many as are led by the Spirit of God, they are the sons of God" (Romans 8:14). This divine Guide is perfectly acquainted with the path God has ordained for each celestial traveler. He is fully conversant with all its windings and narrowness, its intricacies and dangers. To be led by the Spirit is to be under His government. He perceives our temptations and weakness, knows our aspirations, hears our groans, and marks our strugglings after holiness. He knows when to supply a check, administer a rebuke, apply a promise, sympathize with a sorrow, strengthen a wavering purpose, confirm a fluctuating hope. The sure promise is "He will guide you into all truth" (John 16:13). He does so by regulating our thoughts, affections, and conduct; by opening our understandings to perceive the meaning of Scripture, applying it in power to the heart, enabling us to appropriate and reduce it to practice. Each time we open the sacred volume, let us humbly and earnestly seek the aid of Him who inspired it.

Note that Romans 8:14 opens with *for.* The apostle introduces a confirmation of what he had affirmed in the previous verses. They who "walk not after the flesh, but after the Spirit" (v. 4); they who mind "the things of the Spirit" (v. 5); they who "through the Spirit do mortify the deeds of the body" (v. 13), are the ones who are "led by the Spirit" (v. 14). As the Spirit of holiness, His aim is to deepen the imprint of the restored image of God in the soul, to increase our happiness by making us more holy. Thus He leads to nothing but what is sanctifying. The

Spirit guides by subduing the power of indwelling sin, by weaning us from the world, by maintaining a tender conscience in us, by drawing out the heart to Christ, by causing us to live for eternity.

"Trust in the LORD with all thine heart; and lean not unto thine own understanding. In all thy ways acknowledge him, and he shall direct thy paths" (Proverbs 3:5–6). Note the order: The promise at the close of the passage is conditional upon our meeting three requirements. First, we are to have full confidence in the Lord. The Hebrew verb for "trust" here literally means "to lean upon." It conveys the idea of one who is conscious of feebleness turning unto and resting upon a stronger one for support. To "trust in the Lord" signifies to count upon Him in every emergency, to look to Him for the supply of every need, to say with the psalmist, "The LORD is my shepherd; I shall not want" (Psalm 23:1). It means that we cast all our cares upon Him, draw from Him strength hour by hour and thus prove the sufficiency of His grace. It means for the Christian to continue as he began. When we first cast ourselves upon Him as lost sinners, we abandoned all our own doings and relied upon His abounding mercy.

But what is meant by "trust in the Lord with all thine heart"? First, the giving to God our undivided confidence, not looking to any other for help and relief. Second, turning to Him with childlike simplicity. When a little one trusts, there is no reasoning, but a simple taking of the parent's words at face value, fully assured that he will make good what he said; the child does not dwell on the difficulties in the way, but expects a fulfillment of what is promised. So it should be with us and our heavenly Father's words. Third, it means with our affections going out to Him: Love "believeth all things, hopeth all things" (1 Corinthians 13:7). Thus, to trust in the Lord "with all our heart" is love's reliance in believing dependence and expectation.

The second requirement is "And lean not unto thine own understanding," which means we are not to trust in our own wisdom or rely upon the dictates of human reason. The highest act of human reason is to disown its sufficiency and bow before the wisdom of God. To lean unto our own understanding is to rest upon a broken reed, for it has been deranged by sin. Yet many find it harder to repudiate their own wisdom than they do to abandon their own righteousness. Many of God's ways are "past finding out" (Romans 11:33). To seek to solve the mysteries of Providence is the finite attempting to comprehend the Infinite. Philosophizing about our lot or reasoning about our circumstances is fatal to rest of soul and peace of heart.

Third, "in all thy ways acknowledge him." This means, first, we must ask God's permission for all that we do, and not act without His leave. Only then do we conduct ourselves as dutiful children and respectful servants. It means, second, that we seek God's guidance in every undertaking, acknowledging our ignorance and owning our complete dependence upon Him. "In every thing by prayer and supplication" (Philippians 4:6). Only so is God's lordship over us owned in a practical way. It means, third, seeking God's glory in all our ways, "Whatsoever ye do, do all to the glory of God" (1 Corinthians 10:31). If we only did so, how very different many of our ways would be! If more frequently we paused and inquired, "Will this be for God's glory?" we would be withheld from much sinning and folly, with all its painful consequences. It means, fourth, to seek God's *blessing* upon everything. Here is another simple and sufficient rule: Anything on which I cannot ask God's blessing is wrong.

Fourth, "And he shall direct thy paths." Meet the three conditions just mentioned and this is the sure consequence. The need to be directed by God is real and pressing. Left to ourselves we are no better off than a rudderless ship or an auto without a steering wheel. It is not without reason that the Lord's people are so often termed *sheep,* for no other creature is so apt to stray or has such a propensity to wander. The Hebrew word for "direct" means "to make straight." We live in a world where everything is crooked. Sin has thrown everything out of joint, and in consequence confusion abounds all around us. A deceitful heart, a wicked world, and a subtle devil ever seek to lead us astray and compass our destruction. How necessary it is, then, for God to "direct my paths."

What is meant by "He shall direct thy paths"? It means, He will make clear to me the course of duty. God's "will" always lies in the path of duty and never runs counter to it. Much needless uncertainty would be spared if only this principle were recognized. When you feel a strong desire or prompting to shirk a plain duty, you may be assured it is a temptation from Satan and not the leading of the Holy Spirit. For example, it is contrary to God's revealed will for a woman to be constantly attending meetings to the neglect of her children and home. It is shirking his responsibility for a husband to get off alone in the evenings, even in religious exercises, and leave his tired wife to wash the dishes and put the children to bed. It is a sin for a Christian employee to read the Scriptures or "speak to people about their souls" during business hours.

The difficulty arises when it appears we have to choose between two or more duties, or when some important change has to be made in our circumstances. There are many people who think they want to be guided by God when some crisis arrives or some important decision has to be made. But few of them are prepared to meet the requirements intimated in the Scriptures. The fact is that God was rarely in their thoughts before the emergency arose. Pleasing Him did not exercise them while things were going smoothly. But when difficulty confronts them, when they are at their wits' end on how to act, they suddenly become very pious, turn to the Lord, earnestly ask Him to direct them and make His way plain.

But God cannot be imposed upon in any such manner. Usually such people make a rash decision and bring themselves into still greater difficulties. Then they attempt to console themselves with, "Well, I sought God's guidance." God is not to be mocked like that. If we ignore His claims on us when the sailing is pleasant, we cannot count upon Him to deliver us when the storm comes. The One we have to do with is holy, and He will not set a premium upon godlessness (called by many "carelessness"), even though we howl like beasts when in anguish (Hosea 7:14). On the other hand, if we diligently seek grace to walk with God day by day, regulating our ways by His commandments, then we may rightfully count upon His aid in every emergency that arises.

But how is the conscientious Christian to act when some emergency confronts him? Suppose he stands at the dividing of the ways. Two paths, two alternatives, are before him, and he does not know which to choose. What must he do? First, let him heed that most necessary word, which as a rule of general application is ever binding upon us, "He that believeth shall not make haste" (Isaiah 28:16). To act from a sudden impulse never becomes a child of God, and to rush ahead of the Lord is sure to involve us in painful consequences. "The LORD is good unto them that wait for him, to the soul that seeketh him. It is good that a man should both hope and quietly wait for the salvation [deliverance] of the LORD" (Lamentations 3:25–26). To act in haste generally means that afterward we repent at leisure. How much each of us needs to beg the Lord to daily lay His quieting hand upon our feverish flesh!

Second, ask the Lord for Him to empty your heart of every wish of your own. It is impossible for us to sincerely pray, "Thy will be done" until our own will has, by the power of the Holy Spirit, been brought into complete subjection to God. Just so long as there is a secret (but real) preference in my heart, my judgment will be biased. While my heart is really set upon the attainment of a certain object, then I only mock God when I ask Him to make His way plain; and I am sure to misinterpret all His providences, twisting them to fit my own desire. If an obstacle is in my path, I then regard it as a "testing of faith"; if a barrier is removed, I at once jump to the conclusion that God is undertaking for me, when instead He may be testing, on the eve of giving me up to my own "heart's lust" (see Psalm 81:12).

This point is of supreme importance for those who desire their steps to be truly ordered of the Lord. We cannot discern His best for us while the heart has its own preference. Thus it is imperative to ask God to empty our hearts of all personal preferences, to remove any secret, set desire of our own. But often it is not easy to take this attitude before God, the more so if we are not in the habit of seeking grace to mortify the flesh. By nature each of us wants his own way and chafes against every curb placed upon us. Just as a photographic plate must be blank if it is to receive a picture upon it, so our hearts must be free from personal bias if God is to work in us "both to will and to do of his good pleasure" (Philippians 2:13).

If you find that as you continue to wait upon God, the inward struggle between the flesh and the spirit continues, and you have not reached the point where you can honestly say, "Have Thine own way, Lord," then a season of fasting is in order. Ezra 8:21 reads, "Then I proclaimed a fast there . . . that we might afflict ourselves before our God, to seek of him a right way for us, and for our little ones." This is written for our instruction, and even a glance at it shows it is pertinent. Nor is fasting a religious exercise peculiar to Old Testament times. Acts 13:3 records that before Barnabas and Saul were sent forth on their missionary journey by the church at Antioch, "When they had fasted and prayed, and laid their hands on them, they sent them away." There is nothing meritorious in fasting, but it expresses humility of soul and earnestness of heart.

The next thing is to humbly and sincerely acknowledge to God our ignorance, and request Him not to leave us to ourselves. Tell Him frankly you are perplexed and do not know what to do. But plead before Him His own promise and ask Him for Christ's sake to make it good to you. "If any of you lack wisdom, let him ask of God, that giveth to all men liberally, and upbraideth not; and it shall be given him. But let him ask in faith, nothing wavering" (James 1:5–6). Ask Him to grant the wisdom you need so much, that you may judge rightly, that you may discern clearly what will promote your spiritual welfare, and therefore be most for His glory.

"Commit thy way unto the LORD, trust also in him; and he shall bring it to pass" (Psalm 37:5). In the interval, if you go to fellow Christians for advice, most probably no two will agree and their discordant counsel will only confuse. Instead of looking to man for help, "continue in prayer, and watch in the same with thanksgiving" (Colossians 4:2). Be on the lookout for God's answer. Mark attentively each movement of His providence, for as a straw in the air indicates which way the wind is blowing, so the hand of God may often be discerned by a spiritual eye in what are trifling incidents to others. "And let it be, when thou hearest the sound of a going in the tops of the mulberry trees, that then thou shalt bestir thyself: for then shall the LORD go out before thee" (2 Samuel 5:24).

Finally remember that we need not only light from the Lord to discover our duty in particular cases, but when that has been obtained, we need His presence to accompany us, so that we may be enabled to rightly follow the path He bids us go. Moses realized this when he said to the Lord, "If thy presence go not with me, carry us not up hence" (Exodus 33:15). If we do not have the presence of God with us in an undertaking —His approval upon it, His assistance in it, His blessing upon it—then we find it a snare if not a curse to us.

As a general rule it is better for us to trouble our minds very little about guidance. That is God's work. Our business is to walk in obedience to Him day by day. As we do so, there works within us a prudence which will preserve us from all serious mistakes. "I understand more than the ancients, because I keep thy precepts" (Psalm 119:100). The man who keeps God's precepts is endowed with a wisdom which far surpasses that possessed by the sages or the learned philosophers. "Unto the upright there ariseth light in the darkness" (112:4). The upright man may experience his days of darkness, but when the hour of emergency arrives light will be given him by God. Serve God with all your might today, and you may calmly and safely leave the future with Him. A duteous conformity to what is right will be followed by luminous discernment of what would be wrong.

Seek earnestly to get the fear of God fixed in your heart so that you tremble at His Word (Isaiah 66:2) and are really afraid to displease Him. "What man is he which feareth the Lord? him shall he teach in the way that he shall choose" (Psalm 25:12). "Behold, the fear of the Lord, that is wisdom; and to depart from evil is understanding" (Job 28:28). "Then shall we know, if we follow on to know the LORD" (Hosea 6:3). The more we grow in grace the fuller our knowledge will be of God's revealed will. The more we cultivate the practice of seeking to please God in all things, the more light we will have for our path. The "pure in heart . . . shall see God" (Matthew 5:8). If our motive is right, our vision will be clear.

"The integrity of the upright shall guide them: but the perverseness of transgressors shall destroy them" (Proverbs 11:3). The upright man will not willingly and knowingly go aside into crooked paths. The honest heart is not bewildered by domineering lusts nor blinded by corrupt motives. Having a tender conscience, he possesses keen spiritual discernment; but the crooked policy of the wicked involves them in increasing trouble and ends in their eternal ruin. "The righteousness of the perfect [sincere] shall direct his way: but the wicked shall fall by his own wickedness" (v. 5). An eye single to God's glory delivers from those snares in which the ungodly are taken. "Evil men understand not judgment: but they that seek the LORD understand all things" (28:5). Unbridled passions becloud the understanding and pervert the judgment until men call good "evil" and evil "good" (Isaiah 5:20); but he who seeks to be subject to the Lord shall be given discretion.

The Lord "shall direct thy paths" (Proverbs 3:6). First, by His *Word:* not in some magical way so as to encourage laziness, nor like consulting a cookbook full of recipes for all occasions, but by warning us of the by-ways of sin and making known the paths of righteousness and blessing. Second, by his *Spirit:* giving us strength to obey the precepts of God, causing us to wait patiently on the Lord for directions, enabling us to apply the rules of Holy Writ to the varied duties of our lives, bringing to our remembrance a word in due season. Third, by His *providences:* causing friends to fail us so that we are delivered from leaning upon the arm of flesh, thwarting our carnal plans so that we are preserved from shipwreck, shutting doors which it would not be good for us to enter, and opening doors before us which none can shut.

Chapter 22

THE
BLESSINGS
OF GOD

he blessing of the LORD, it maketh rich, and he addeth no sorrow with it" (Proverbs 10:22). Temporal blessing, as well as spiritual, comes from Him. "The LORD maketh poor, and maketh rich" (1 Samuel 2:7). God is the sovereign disposer of material wealth. If it is received by birth or inheritance, it is by His providence. If it comes by gift, He moved the donors to bestow. If it accumulates as the result of hard work, skill, or thrift, He bestowed the talent, directed its use, and granted the success. This is abundantly clear in the Scriptures. "The LORD hath blessed my master greatly; and . . . hath given him flocks, and herds, and silver, and gold" (Genesis 24:35). "Isaac sowed in that land, and received in the same year an hundredfold: and the LORD blessed him" (26:12). So it is with us. Say not in your heart, "The might of my hand or brains has gotten me this temporal prosperity." Rather, "thou shalt remember the LORD thy God: for it is he that giveth thee power to get wealth" (Deuteronomy 8:18). When riches are acquired by God's blessing by honest industry, there is no accusing conscience to sour the same. If sorrow attend the use or enjoyment of them, it is due entirely to our own folly.

"Blessed is the man whom thou choosest, and causest to approach unto thee, that he may dwell in thy courts" (Psalm 65:4). There is no doubt that the primary reference there (though not the exclusive one) is to "the man Christ Jesus" (1 Timothy 2:5), for as God-man He is what He is by the grace of election, when His humanity was chosen and foreordained to union with one of the Persons in the Godhead. None other than Jehovah proclaimed Him "mine elect, in whom my soul delighteth" (Isaiah 42:1). As such He is "the man that is my fellow, saith the LORD of hosts" (Zechariah 13:7), the "heir of all things " (Hebrews 1:2). Christ was not chosen for us, but for God; and we were chosen for Christ, to be His bride. "Christ is My first elect," He said, then chose our souls in Christ the Head. The essence of all blessings is to be in Christ, and those who partake of it do so by the act of God, as the fruit of His everlasting love unto them. "Blessed be the God and Father of our Lord Jesus Christ, who hath blessed us with all spiritual blessings in heavenly places in Christ: according as he hath chosen us in him before the foundation of the world" (Ephesians 1:3–4). In that initial blessing of election all others are wrapped up, and in due course we are partakers of them.

"As the dew that descended upon the mountains of Zion: for there the LORD commanded the blessing, even life for evermore" (Psalm 133:3). It is both the duty and privilege of every sin-laden soul to come to Christ for rest; nevertheless, it is equally true that no man can come to Him except the Father draw him (John 6:44). Likewise it falls upon all who hear the Gospel to respond to that call. "Incline your ear, and come unto me: hear, and your soul shall live" (Isaiah 55:3), yet how can those who are "dead in trespasses and sins" (Ephesians 2:1) do so? They cannot. They must first be divinely quickened into newness of life. A beautiful figure of that divine operation is here before us. In eastern lands the earth is hard, dry, barren. So are our natural hearts. The dew descends from above silently, mysteriously, imperceptibly and moistens the ground, imparting vitality to vegetation, making the mountainside fruitful. Such is the miracle of the new birth. Life is communicated by divine fiat; not a probationary or conditional one, not a fleeting or temporal one, but spiritual and endless, for the stream of regeneration can never dry up. When God commands, He communicates (see Psalms 42:8; 68:28; 111:9). As the blessing is a divine favor, so the manner of bestowing it is sovereign. That is solely His prerogative, for man can do nothing but beg. Zion (Sion) is the place of all spiritual blessings (Hebrews 12:22–24).

"Blessed is the people that know the joyful sound: they shall walk, O LORD, in the light of thy countenance" (Psalm 89:15). This is one of the blessed effects of divine quickening. When one has been born of the Spirit, the eyes and ears of his soul are opened to recognize spiritual things. It is not merely that they hear "the joyful sound," for many do that without any experiential knowledge of its charm; but they know from its message being brought home in power to their hearts. That joyful sound is the "glad tidings of good things" (Romans 10:15), namely, "that Christ Jesus came into the world to save sinners" (1 Timothy 1:15). Such souls as inwardly know that heavenly music are indeed blessed. As they are assured of free access unto God through the blood of Christ, the beneficent light of the divine countenance is now beheld by them. There is probably an allusion in Psalm 89:15, first to the sound made by Aaron as he went into the holy place and came out (Exodus 28:33–35), which was indeed a "joyful sound" unto the people of God. It gave evidence that their high priest was engaged before the Lord on their behalf. Second, a general reference to the sound of the sacred trumpets which called Israel to their solemn feasts (Numbers 10:10). Third, a more specific one to the trumpet of jubilee (Leviticus 25:9–10), which proclaimed liberty to bondmen and restoration of their inheritance to them who had forfeited it. So the announcement of the Gospel of liberty to sin's captives is music to those who have ears to hear.

"Blessed are all they that put their trust in him" (Psalm 2:12). The critical reader observes that we follow a strictly logical order. First, election is the foundation blessing, being "[unto] salvation" and including all the means thereof (2 Thessalonians 2:13); second, the bestowal of eternal life which capacitates the favored recipient to welcome experientially the joyful sound of the Gospel. Now there is a personal and saving embracing thereof. Note that the last sentence of Psalm 2:12 is preceded by the statement, "Kiss the Son," which signifies, "Bow in submission before His sceptre, yield to His Kingly rule, render allegiance to Him" (see 1 Samuel 10:1; 1 Kings 19:18). It is most important to note that order, and still more so to put it into practice. Christ must be received as *Lord* (Colossians 2:6) before He can be received as *Saviour*. Note the order in 2 Peter 1:11; 2:20; 3:18. The "put their trust in Him" signifies to take refuge in. They repudiate their own righteousness and evince their confidence in Him by committing themselves to His keeping for time and eternity. His Gospel is their warrant for doing so, His veracity their security.

"Blessed is he whose transgression is forgiven, whose sin is covered" (Psalm 32:1). This is an intrinsic part of the blessedness of putting our trust in Him. The joyful sound has assured them that "Christ died for the ungodly" (Romans 5:6), and that He will by no means cast out anyone who comes unto Him. Therefore do they express their faith in Christ by fleeing to Him for refuge. Blessed indeed are such, for, having surrendered to His lordship and placed their reliance in His atoning blood, they now enter into the benefits of His righteous and benevolent government. More specifically, their "iniquities are forgiven and their sins are covered"—"covered *by God,* as the ark was covered with the mercy seat; as Noah was covered from the flood; as the Egyptians were covered by the depths of the sea. What a cover that must be which hides forever from the sight of the all-seeing God all the filthiness of the flesh and of the spirit" (Charles Spurgeon). Paul quotes those precious words of Psalm 32:1 in Romans 4:7, as proof of the grand truth of justification by faith. While the sins of believers were all atoned for at the cross and an everlasting righteousness procured for them, they do not become actual participants until they believe (Acts 13:39; Galatians 2:16).

"Blessed is the man whose strength is in thee; in whose heart are the ways of them" (Psalm 84:5). This is another accompaniment of the new birth. The regenerated receives the spirit of "a sound mind" (2 Timothy 1:7) so that he now sees himself to be not only without any righteousness of his own but also is conscious of his weakness and insufficiency. He has made the name of the Lord his strong tower, having run into it for safety (Proverbs 18:10). Now he declares, "In the LORD have I righteousness and strength" (Isaiah 45:24), strength to fight the good fight of faith, to resist temptations, to endure persecution, to perform duty. While he keeps in his right mind, he will continue to go forth not in his own strength, but in complete dependence upon the strength in Christ Jesus. Those ways of God's strength are the divinely appointed means of grace to maintain communion: feeding on the Word, living on Christ, adhering to the path of His precepts.

"Blessed is every one that feareth the LORD; that walketh in his ways" (Psalm 128:1). Here is another mark of those under divine benediction: to have such a deep reverence of the Spirit as results in regular obedience to Him. The fear of the Lord is a holy awe of His majesty, a filial dread of displeasing Him. It is not so much an emotional thing as practical, for it is idle to talk about fearing God if we have no deep concern for His will. It is the fear of love which shrinks from dishonoring Him, a dread of forgetting His goodness and abusing His mercy. Where such fear is, all other graces are found.

Chapter 23

THE CURSINGS OF GOD

It is solemn to learn that these blessings and cursings proceed from the same mouth. Yet a little reflection will convince the reader that such must be the case. God is light as well as love, holy as well as gracious, righteous as well as merciful. Therefore He expresses His abhorrence of and visits His judgments upon the wicked, as truly as He blesses and manifests His approval on those who are pleasing in His sight. An eternal heaven and an eternal hell are the inevitable and ultimate pair of opposites. This awesome duality is displayed in the natural world. On one hand our senses are charmed by the golden sunsets, the flowering gardens, the gentle showers, and the fertile fields. On the other hand, we are shocked and terrified by the fearful tornado, the devouring blights, the devastating flood, and the destructive earthquake. "Behold therefore the goodness and severity of God" (Romans 11:22). From Mount Ebal were announced the divine curses (Deuteronomy 27), and from Mount Gerizim the divine blessings (Deuteronomy 28). The one could not be without the other. Thus too it will be in the last day, or while Christ will say unto His brethren, "Come, ye blessed of my

Father, inherit the kingdom prepared for you from the foundation of the world," yet to those who despised and rejected Him shall He say, "Depart from me, ye cursed, into everlasting fire" (Matthew 25:34, 41).

"Cursed is the ground for thy sake; in sorrow shalt thou eat of it all the days of thy life" (Genesis 3:17). That was one of the consequences that attended Adam's apostasy from God, a part of the divine vengeance which fell upon him. Because the first man stood as the covenant head and legal representative of his race, the judgment which came upon him is shared by all his descendants. Adam was the vice-regent of God in this scene. He was given dominion over all things mundane, and when he fell the effects of his awful sin were evident on every hand. His fair inheritance was blasted. The very ground on which he trod was cursed, so that henceforth it brought forth thorns and thistles, compelling him to toil for his daily bread in the sweat of his face. Every time we cultivate a plot of land, the numerous weeds it produces hinder our efforts and supply very real proof of the divine sentence pronounced in Genesis 3 and evince that we belong to a fallen race.

"Thus saith the LORD; Cursed be the man that trusteth in man, and maketh flesh his arm, and whose heart departeth from the LORD" (Jeremiah 17:5). A thorough acquaintance with ourselves ought to render the warning of this solemn passage unnecessary, yet sad experience proves otherwise. Have we not sufficient knowledge of ourselves—our changeableness and utter unreliability—to discover that "he that trusteth in his own heart is a fool" (Proverbs 28:26)? Then why should we suppose that any of our fellows are more stable and dependable? The best of Adam's race, when left to themselves, are spectacles of fickleness and frailty. "Surely men of low degree are vanity, and men of high degree are a lie: to be laid in the balance, they are altogether lighter than vanity" (Psalm 62:9). To seek either the patronage or protection of man is an affront to the Most High, for it puts that confidence in the creature to which the Creator alone is entitled. The folly of such wickedness is emphasized in "and maketh flesh his arm" (Jeremiah 17:5), leaning upon that which is frail and helpless (2 Chronicles 32:8; Matthew 26:41; Romans 8:3). The Christian needs to turn this awful malediction into prayer for deliverance from the temptation to look to man for help or relief! Indirectly, yet powerfully, Jeremiah 17:5 proves that Christ is far more than man; for if it calls down a divine curse for one to put his trust in man for any temporal advantage, how much more so if he trusts in a mere creature for eternal salvation!

"If ye will not hear, and ye will not lay it to heart, to give glory unto my name, saith the LORD of hosts, I will even send a curse upon you, and I will curse your blessings: yea, I have cursed them already, because ye do not lay it to heart" (Malachi 2:2). The Lord is very tender of His honor and will not share His glory with another (Isaiah 48:11), and those who do not take that fact to heart are certain to call down divine wrath upon themselves. Those words (Malachi 2:2) were addressed in the first instance to the priests of Israel. The prophet had reproved them for their sins. Now he declared that if they would not seriously attend to his warnings and glorify God by repentance and reformation of conduct, then He would blight their temporal mercies. It is a signal favor for man to be called to minister publicly in the name of the Lord. But infidelity entails the most dreadful consequences. Often they are given up to blindness of mind, hardness of heart, seared consciences. The principle of this malediction has a much wider bearing and applies both to those who hear the Gospel and a nation blessed with its light.

"But though we, or an angel from heaven, preach any other gospel unto you than that which we have preached unto you, let him be accursed" (Galatians 1:8). God is very jealous of His Gospel, and this verse should also convince His servants and people of the solemn responsibility resting upon them to preserve it in its purity. The Gospel of God makes known the only true way of salvation, and therefore any corrupting of it is not only dishonoring to its Author, but also most dangerous and disastrous to the souls of men. The apostle was censuring those who were repeating an impossible mixture of Law and Gospel, insisting that circumcision and compliance with the ceremonial rites of Judaism were as necessary as faith in Christ for justification. His was not the language of intemperate zeal, for he repeats the same in the next verse, but a holy fidelity which expressed his detestation of an error which not only insulted the Saviour but also would prove fatal to those who embraced it. The single foundation of a sinner's hope is the merits of Christ, His finished work of redemption. Those who would add to the same by any doings of their own are headed for eternal destruction. Therefore any who teach men to do so are cursed of God and should be abhorred by His people.

"For as many as are of the works of the law are under the curse: for it is written, Cursed is every one that continueth not in all things which are written in the book of the law to do them" (Galatians 3:10). The first part of this verse means: All who count on being saved by their own performances, or rely upon their own obedience for acceptance by God, are under the curse of His Law and exposed to His wrath. Justification by keeping the Law is an utter impossibility for any fallen creature. Why so? Because God's Law requires flawless and perpetual conformity, sinless perfection in thought and word and deed, and because it makes no provision for failure to comply with its holy and righteous terms. It is not sufficient to hear about or know the requirements of God's Law. They must be met. Thus it is obvious that a Law which already condemns cannot justify, that any who hope to merit God's favor by their faulty attempts to obey it are badly deceived. "To expect to be warmed by the keen northern blast, or to have our thirst quenched by a draught of liquid fire, were not more, were not so, incongruous" (J. Brown). This statement (Galatians 3:10) was made by the apostle to show that every man is under divine condemnation until he flees to Christ for refuge.

"Christ hath redeemed us from the curse of the law, being made a curse for us" (Galatians 3:13). Here is the glorious Gospel summed up in a brief sentence. The curse has been borne for all those who believe, visited upon the Saviour. A way has been opened where guilty sinners may not only escape from the curse of the Law, but actually be received into the favor of God. Amazing grace! Matchless mercy! All who put their trust in Christ are delivered from the Law's sentence of doom so that they shall never fall under it. We are righteously delivered, for as the Surety of His people Christ was born under the Law, stood in their place, had all their sins imputed to Him, and made Himself answerable for them. The Law, so finding Him, charged Him with the same, cursed Him, and demanded satisfaction. Accordingly He was dealt with by the supreme Judge, for God "spared not his own Son" (Romans 8:32), but called upon the sword of justice to "smite the shepherd" (Zechariah 13:7). By His own consent the Lord Jesus was "made a curse" by God Himself. Because He paid the ransom price all believers are "redeemed"—delivered from God's wrath and inducted into His blessing.

"But that which beareth thorns and briers is rejected, and is nigh unto cursing; whose end is to be burned" (Hebrews 6:8). This is in sharp contrast with the previous verse. The good-ground hearer "bringeth forth"—the Greek signifying a production of what is normal and in due season. The graceless professor "beareth thorns"—the Greek word connoting an unnatural and monstrous production. There, "herbs meet for them by whom it is dressed" (v. 7) ; here, worthless "thorns and briers" (v. 8). The one "receiveth blessing from God" (v. 7); the other is "nigh unto cursing" (v. 8)—about to be visited with divine judgment.

Chapter 24

THE LOVE OF GOD TO US

By "us" we mean His people. Although we read of the love "which is in Christ Jesus our Lord" (Romans 8:39), Holy Writ knows nothing of a love of God outside of Christ. "The LORD is good to all: and his tender mercies are over all his works" (Psalm 145:9), so that He provides the ravens with food. "He is kind unto the unthankful and to the evil" (Luke 6:35), and His providence ministers unto the just and the unjust (Matthew 5:45). But His love is reserved for His elect. That is unequivocally established by its characteristics, for the attributes of His love are identical with Himself. Necessarily so, for "God is love." In making that postulate it is but another way to say God's love is like Himself, from everlasting to everlasting, immutable. Nothing is more absurd than to imagine that anyone beloved of God can eternally perish or shall ever experience His everlasting vengeance. Since the love of God is "in Christ Jesus," it was attracted by nothing in its objects, nor can it be repelled by anything in, of, or by them. "Having loved his own which were in the world, he loved them unto the end" (John 13:1). The *world* in John 3:16 is a general term used in contrast with the Jews, and the verse must be interpreted so as not to contradict Psalm 5:5; 6:7; John 3:36; and Romans 9:13.

The chief design of God is to commend the love of God in Christ, for He is the sole channel through which it flows. The Son has not induced the Father to love His people, but rather was it His love for them which moved Him to give His Son for them. Ralph Erskine said:

> God hath taken a marvelous way to manifest His love. When He would show His power, He makes a world. When He would display His wisdom, He puts it in a frame and form that discovers its vastness. When He would manifest the grandeur and glory of His name, He makes a heaven, and puts angels and archangels, principalities and powers therein. And when He would manifest His love, what will He not do? God hath taken a great and marvelous way of manifesting it in Christ: His person, His blood, His death, His righteousness.

"All the promises of God in him [Christ] are yea, and in him Amen, unto the glory of God" (2 Corinthians 1:20). As we were chosen in Christ (Ephesians 1:4), as we were accepted in Him (v. 6), as our life is hid in Him (Colossians 3:3), so are we beloved in Him—"the love of God, which is in Christ Jesus" (Romans 8:39)—as our Head and Husband, which is why nothing can separate us therefrom, for that union is indissoluble.

Nothing so warms the heart of the saint as a spiritual contemplation of God's love. As he is occupied with it, he is lifted outside of and above his wretched self. A believing apprehension fills the renewed soul with holy satisfaction and makes him as happy as it is possible for one to be this side of heaven. To know and believe the love which God has toward me is both an earnest and a foretaste of heaven itself. Since God loves His people in Christ, it is not for any amiableness in or attraction about them: "Jacob have I loved." Yes, the naturally unattractive, yes, despicable, Jacob—"thou worm Jacob." Since God loves His people in Christ, it is not regulated by their fruitfulness, but is the same at all times. Because He loves them in Christ, the Father loves them as Christ. The time will come when His prayer will be answered: "That the world may know that thou hast sent me, and hast loved them, as thou hast loved me" (John 17:23). Only faith can grasp those marvelous things, for neither reasoning nor feelings can do so. God loves us in Christ: What infinite delight the Father has as He beholds His people in His dear Son! All our blessings flow from that precious fountain.

God's love to His people is not of yesterday. It did not begin with their love to Him. No, "we love him, because he first loved us" (1 John 4:19). We do not first give to Him, that He may return to us again. Our regeneration is not the motive of His love; rather, His love is the reason why He renews us after His image. This is often made to appear in the first manifestation of it, when so far from its objects being engaged in seeking Him, they are at their worst. "Now when I passed by thee, and looked upon thee, behold, thy time was the time of love; and I spread my skirt over thee, and covered thy nakedness: yea, I sware unto thee, and entered into a covenant with thee, saith the Lord GOD, and thou becamest [manifestly] mine" (Ezekiel 16:8).

Not only are its objects often at their worst when God's love is first revealed to them, but actually doing their worst, as in the case of Saul of Tarsus. Not only is God's love antecedent to ours, but also it was borne in His heart toward us long before we were delivered from the power of darkness and translated into the Kingdom of His dear Son. It began not in time, but bears the date of eternity. "I have loved thee with an everlasting love" (Jeremiah 31:3).

"Herein is love, not that we loved God, but that he loved us, and sent his Son to be the propitiation for our sins" (1 John 4:10). It is clear from those words that God loved His people while they were in a state of nature, destitute of all grace, without a particle of love towards Him or faith in Him; yes, while they were His enemies (Romans 5:8, 10). Clearly that lays me under a thousand times greater obligation to love, serve, and glorify Him than had He loved me for the first time when my heart was won. All the acts of God to His people in time are the expressions of the love He bore them from eternity. It is because God loves us in Christ, and has done so from everlasting, that the gifts of His love are irrevocable. They are the bestowal of "the Father of lights, with whom is no variableness, neither shadow of turning" (James 1:17). The love of God indeed makes a change in us when it is "shed abroad in our hearts" (Romans 5:5), but it makes none in Him. He sometimes varies the dispensations of His providence toward us, but that is not because His affection has altered. Even when He chastens us, it is in love (Hebrews 12:6), since He has our good in view.

Let us look more closely at some of the operations of God's love.

First, in *election*. "We are bound to give thanks alway to God for you, brethren beloved of the Lord, because God hath from the beginning chosen you to salvation through sanctification of the Spirit [His quickening] and belief of the truth" (2 Thessalonians 2:13). There is an infallible connection between God's love and His selection of those who were to be saved. That election is the consequence of His love is clear again from Deuteronomy: "The LORD did not [1] set His love upon you, nor [2] choose you, because ye were more in number than any people" (7:7). So again in Ephesians: "In love: having predestinated us unto the adoption of children by Jesus Christ to himself, according to the good pleasure of his will" (1:4–5).

Second, in *redeeming*. As we have seen from 1 John 4:10, out of His sovereign love God made provision for Christ to render satisfaction for their sins, though prior to their conversion He was angry with them in respect to His violated Law. And "how shall he not with him also freely give us all things?" (Romans 8:32)—another clear proof that His Son was not "delivered up" to the cross for all mankind. For He gives them neither the Holy Spirit, a new nature, nor repentance and faith.

Third, *effectual calling*. From the enthroned Saviour the Father sends forth the Holy Spirit (Acts 2:33). Having loved His elect with an everlasting love, with loving-kindness He draws them (Jeremiah 31:3), quickens them into newness of life, calls them out of darkness into His marvelous light, makes them His children. "Behold, what manner of love the Father hath bestowed upon us, that we should be called the sons of God" (1 John 3:1). If filiation does not issue from God's love as a sure effect, to what purpose are those words?

Fourth, *healing of backslidings:* "I will heal their backsliding, I will love them freely" (Hosea 14:4), without reluctance or hesitation. "Many waters cannot quench love, neither can the floods drown it" (Song of Songs 8:7). Such is God's love to His people—invincible, unquenchable. Not only is there no possibility of its expiring, but also the waters of backslidings cannot extinguish it, nor the floods of unbelief put it out.

Nothing is more irresistible than death in the natural world, nothing so invincible as the love of God in the realm of grace. Goodwin remarked:

> What difficulties does the love of God overcome! For God to overcome His own heart! Do you think it was nothing for Him to put His Son to

death? . . . When He came to call us, had He no difficulties which love overcame? We were dead in trespasses and sins, yet from the great love wherewith He loved us, He quickened us in the grave of our corruption: "Lo, he stinketh"—even then did God come and conquer us. After our calling, how sadly do we provoke God! Such temptations that if it were possible the elect should be deceived. It is so with all Christians. No righteous man but he is "scarcely saved" (1 Peter 4:18), and yet saved he *is*, because the love of God invincible: it overcomes all difficulties.

An application is hardly necessary for such a theme. Let God's love daily engage your mind by devout meditations on it so that the affections of your heart may be drawn out to Him. When cast down in spirit, or in sore straits, plead His love in prayer, assured that it cannot deny anything good for you. Make God's wondrous love to you the incentive of your obedience to Him—gratitude requires nothing less.

Chapter 25

THE GOSPEL OF THE GRACE OF GOD

"To testify the gospel of the grace of God" (Acts 20:24) formed part of the farewell address of the apostle Paul to the leaders of the church at Ephesus. After he reminded them of his manner of life among them (vv. 18–21), he told them of his forthcoming trip to Jerusalem, which was to culminate in his being carried prisoner to Rome. He says, "And now, behold, I go bound in the spirit unto Jerusalem, not knowing the things that shall befall me there: save that the Holy Ghost witnesseth in every city, saying that bonds and afflictions abide me" (vv. 22–23). And, then, in a truly characteristic word, he says, "But none of these things move me, neither count I my life dear unto myself, so that I might finish my course with joy, and the ministry, which I have received of the Lord Jesus, to testify the gospel of the grace of God" (v. 24). Wherever the providence of God might take him, whatever his circumstances might be, whether in bonds or in freedom, this should be his mission and message. It is to this same ministry that the Lord of the harvest still appoints His servants: to "testify the gospel of the grace of God."

There is a continual need to return to the great fundamental of the faith. As long as the age lasts the Gospel of God's grace must be preached. The need arises out of the natural state of the human heart, which is essentially legalistic. The cardinal error against which the Gospel has to contend is the inveterate tendency of men to rely on their own performances. The great antagonist to the truth is the pride of man, which causes him to imagine that he can be, in part at least, his own Saviour. This error is the prolific mother of a multitude of heresies. It is by this falsehood that the pure stream of God's truth, passing through human channels, has been polluted.

Now the Gospel of God's grace is epitomized in Ephesians 2:8–9: "For by grace are ye saved through faith; and that not of yourselves: it is the gift of God: not of works, lest any man should boast." All genuine reforms or revivals in the churches of God must have as their basis a plain declaration of this doctrine. The tendency of Christians is like that of the world, to shy away from this truth which is the very sum and substance of the Gospel. Those with any acquaintance with Church history know how sadly true this is. Within fifty years of the death of the last of the apostles, so far as we can now learn, the Gospel of God's grace almost ceased to be preached. Instead of evangelizing, the preachers of the second and third centuries gave themselves to philosophizing. Metaphysics took the place of the simplicity of the Gospel.

Then, in the fourth century, God mercifully raised up a man, Augustine, who faithfully and fearlessly proclaimed the Gospel. So mightily did God empower both his voice and pen that more than half of Christendom was shaken by him. Through his instrumentality came a heaven-sent revival. His influence for good staved off the great Romish heresy for another century. Had the churches heeded his teaching, popery would never have been born. But they turned back to vain philosophy and science, falsely so-called.

Then came the Dark Ages, when for centuries the Gospel ceased to be generally preached. Here and there feeble voices were raised, but most of them were soon silenced by the Italian priests. It was not until the fifteenth century that the great Reformation came. God raised up Martin Luther, who taught in no uncertain terms that sinners are justified by faith and not by works.

After Luther came a still more distinguished teacher, John Calvin. He was much more deeply taught in the truth of the Gospel and pushed its central doctrine of grace to its logical conclusions. As Charles Spurgeon said, "Luther had, as it were, undamped the stream of truth, by breaking down the barriers which had kept back its living waters as in a great reservoir. But the stream was turbid and carried down with it much which ought to have been left behind. Then Calvin came, and cast salt into the waters, and purged them, so that there flowed on a purer stream to gladden and refresh souls and quench the thirst of poor lost sinners."

The great center of all Calvin's preaching was the grace of God. It has been the custom ever since to designate as "Calvinists" those who emphasize what he emphasized. We do not accept that title without qualification, but we certainly are not ashamed of it. The truth Calvin thundered forth was identical with the truth Paul had preached and set down in writing centuries before. This was also the substance of Whitefield's preaching, which God honored so extensively as to produce the great revival in his day.

Let us now consider:

THE GOSPEL IS A REVELATION OF THE GRACE OF GOD

The "gospel of the grace of God" (Acts 20:24) is one of the Holy Spirit's titles of that Good News which the ambassadors of Christ are called upon to preach. Various names are given to it in the Scriptures. Romans 1:1 calls it the "gospel of God," for He is its Author. Romans 1:16 terms it the "gospel of Christ," for He is its theme. Ephesians 6:15 designates it the "gospel of peace," for this is its bestowment. Our text speaks of it as the "gospel of the grace of God," for this is its Source.

Grace is a truth peculiar to divine revelation. It is a concept to which the unaided powers of man's mind never rises. Proof of this is in the fact that where the Bible has not gone "grace" is unknown. Very often missionaries have found, when translating the Scriptures into native tongues of the heathen, they were unable to discover a word which in any way corresponded to the Bible word *grace*. Grace is absent from all the great heathen religions—Brahmanism, Buddhism, Islam, Confucianism, Zoroastrianism. Even nature does not teach grace: break her laws and you must suffer the penalty.

What then is *grace?* First, it is evidently something blessed and joyous, for our text speaks of the "good news" (to paraphrase *gospel*) "of the grace of God." Second, it is the opposite of Law: *Law* and *Gospel* are antithetical terms: "The law was given by Moses, but grace and truth came by Jesus Christ" (John 1:17). It is significant that the word *gospel* is never found in the Old Testament. Consider a few contrasts between them.

The Law manifested what was in man—sin; grace manifests what is in God—love and mercy. The Law speaks of what man must do for God; grace tells of what Christ has done for men. The Law demanded righteousness from men; grace brings righteousness to men. The Law brought out God to men; grace brings in men to God. The Law sentenced a living man to death; grace brings a dead man to life. The Law never had a missionary; the Gospel is to be preached to every creature. The Law makes known the will of God; grace reveals the heart of God!

In the third place, grace, then, is the very opposite of justice. Justice shows no favor and knows no mercy. Grace is the reverse of this. Justice requires that everyone should receive his due; grace bestows on sinners what they are not entitled to—pure charity. Grace is "something for nothing."

Now the Gospel is a *revelation* of this wondrous grace of God. It tells us that Christ has done for sinners what they could not do for themselves—it satisfied the demands of God's Law. Christ has fully and perfectly met all the requirements of God's holiness so that He can righteously receive every poor sinner who comes to Him. The Gospel tells us that Christ died not for good people, who never did anything very bad, but for lost and godless sinners, who never did anything good. The Gospel reveals to every sinner, for his acceptance, a Saviour all-sufficient, "able to also save . . . to the uttermost [them] that come unto God by him" (Hebrews 7:25).

THE GOSPEL IS A PROCLAMATION
OF THE GRACE OF GOD

The word *gospel* is a technical one, employed in the New Testament in a double sense: in a narrower, and in a wider one. In its narrower sense, it refers to heralding the glorious fact that the grace of God has provided a Saviour for every poor sinner who feels his need and by faith receives Him. In its wider sense, it comprehends the whole revelation which God made of Himself in and through Christ. In this sense it includes the whole of the New Testament.

Proof of this double application of the term *gospel* is found in

1 Corinthians 15:1–4, a definition of the Gospel in its narrower sense: "that Christ died for our sins, . . . was buried, and . . . rose again." Then Romans 1:1 uses the term *gospel* in its wider sense: there it includes the whole doctrinal exposition of that epistle: "the gospel of God." When Christ bade His disciples, "Preach the gospel to every creature" (Mark 16:15), I do not think He had reference to all that is in the New Testament, but simply to the fact that the grace of God has provided a Saviour for sinners. Therefore, we say that the Gospel is a proclamation of the grace of God.

The Gospel affirms that grace is the sinner's only hope. Unless we are saved by grace we cannot be saved at all. To reject a gratuitous salvation is to spurn the only one that is available for lost sinners. Grace is God's provision for those who are so corrupt that they cannot change their own natures; so averse to God, they cannot turn to Him; so blind, they cannot see Him; so deaf, they cannot hear Him; in a word, so dead in sin that He must open their graves and bring them on to resurrection-ground, if ever they are to be saved. Grace, then, implies that the sinner's case is desperate, but that God is merciful.

The Gospel of God's grace is for sinners in whom there is no help. It is exercised by God "without respect of persons" (1 Peter 1:17), without regard to merit, without requirement of any return. The Gospel is not good advice, but Good News. It does not speak of what man is to do, but tells what Christ has done. It is not sent to good men, but to bad. Grace, then, is something that is worthy of God.

THE GOSPEL IS A MANIFESTATION OF THE GRACE OF GOD

The Gospel is the "power of God unto salvation to every one that believeth" (Romans 1:16). It is the chosen instrument God uses in freeing and delivering His people from error, ignorance, darkness, and the power of Satan. It is by and through the Gospel, applied by the Holy Spirit, that His elect are emancipated from the guilt and power of sin. "For the preaching of the cross is to them that perish foolishness; but unto us which are saved it is the power of God. . . . But we preach Christ crucified, unto the Jews a stumblingblock, and unto the Greeks foolishness; but unto them which are called, both Jews and Greeks, Christ the power of God, and the wisdom of God" (1 Corinthians 1:18, 23–24). Where evolution is substituted for the new birth, the cultivation of character for faith in the blood of Christ, development of willpower for humble dependence on God, the carnal mind may be attracted and poor human reason appealed to, but it is all destitute of power and brings no salvation to the perishing. There is no Gospel in a system of ethics, and no dynamic in the exactions of law.

But grace *works*. It is something more than a good-natured smile or a sentiment of pity. It redeems, conquers, saves. The New Testament interprets grace as power. By it redemption comes, for it was by "the grace of God" that Christ tasted death "for every [one]" of the sons (Hebrews 2:9). Forgiveness of sins is proclaimed through His blood "according to the riches of his grace" (Ephesians 1:7). Grace not only makes salvation possible but also effectual. Grace is all-powerful. "My grace is sufficient for thee" (2 Corinthians 12:9)—sufficient to overcome unbelief, the infirmities of the flesh, the oppositions of men, and the attacks of Satan.

This is the glory of the Gospel: It is the power of God unto salvation. In one of his books, Dr. J. H. Jowett says:

> A little while ago I was speaking to a New York doctor, a man of long and varied experience with diseases that afflict both the body and mind. I asked him how many cases he had known of the slaves of drink having been delivered by medical treatment into health and freedom. How many he had been able to "doctor" into liberty and self-control. He immediately replied, "Not one." He further assured me that he believed his experience would be corroborated by the testimony of the faculty of medicine.

Doctors might afford a temporary escape, but the real bonds are not broken. At the end of the apparent but brief deliverance, it will be found that the chains remain. Medicine might address itself to effects, but the cause is as real and dominant as ever. The doctor has no cure for the drunkard. Medical skill cannot save him. But grace can! Without doctors, drugs, priests, penance, works, money or price, grace actually saves. Hallelujah! Yes, grace saves. It snaps the fetters of a lifetime and makes a poor sinner a partaker of the divine nature and a rejoicing saint. It saves not only from the bondage of fleshly habits, but also from the curse of the Fall, from the captivity of Satan, from the wrath to come.

What effect has this message on your heart? Does it fill you with praise to God? Are you thankful to know that salvation is by grace? Can you see and appreciate the infinite difference between all of man's schemes for self-betterment and the "gospel of the grace of God"?

Part 2

EXCELLENCIES WHICH PERTAIN TO GOD THE SON AS CHRIST

Chapter 26

THE
FULLNESS
OF CHRIST

It is fitting that we should contemplate the excellencies of Christ the Mediator, for "the light of the knowledge of the glory of God" is to be seen "in the face of Jesus Christ" (2 Corinthians 4:6). The fullest revelation that God is and what He is, is made in the person of Christ. "No man hath seen God at any time; the only begotten Son, which is in the bosom of the Father, he hath declared him" (John 1:18). But this knowledge of God is not a mere matter of intellectual apprehension, which one man can communicate to another. It is a spiritual discernment, imparted by the Holy Spirit. God must shine in our hearts to give us that knowledge.

When the materialistic Philip said, "Lord, show us the Father," the Lord Jesus replied, "He that hath seen me hath seen the Father" (John 14:9). Yes, He was "the brightness of his glory, and the express image of his person" (Hebrews 1:3). In the eternal, incarnate Word "dwelleth all the fulness of the Godhead bodily" (Colossians 2:9). Amazing and glorious fact, it is in the perfection of manhood that the fulness of the Godhead is in Christ revealed to our faith. We could not ascend to God, so

He descended to us. All that men can ever know of God is presented to them in the person of His incarnate Son. Hence, "That I may know him" (Philippians 3:10) is the constant longing of the most mature Christian.

It is our design to declare some part of that glory of our Lord Jesus Christ which is revealed in Scripture, and proposed as the object of our faith, love, delight, admiration, and adoration. But after our utmost endeavors and most diligent inquiries, we have to say, "How little a portion" (Job 26:14) of Him we understand. His glory is incomprehensible, His praises unutterable. Some things a divinely illuminated mind can conceive of, but what we express, in comparison to what the glory is in itself, is less than nothing. Nevertheless, that view which the Spirit grants from the Scriptures concerning Christ and His glory is to be preferred above all other knowledge or understanding. So it was declared, by him who was favored to know Him, "Yea doubtless, and I count all things but loss for the excellency of the knowledge of Christ Jesus my Lord" (Philippians 3:8).

John Owen has well said:

> The revelation made of Christ in the blessed Gospel is far more excellent, more glorious, more filled with rays of Divine wisdom and goodness than the whole creation, and the just comprehension of it, if attainable, can contain or apprehend. Without the knowledge hereof, the mind of man, however priding itself in other inventions and discoveries, is wrapped up in darkness and confusion. This therefore deserves the severest of our thoughts, the best of our meditations, and our utmost diligence in them. For if our future blessedness shall consist in living where He is, and beholding of His glory; what better preparation can there be for it, than in a constant previous contemplation of that glory, in the revelation that is made in the Gospel unto this very end, that by a view of it we may be gradually transformed into the same glory.

The grandest of all privileges which believers are capable of, either in this world or the next, is to behold the glory (the personal and official excellencies) of Christ; now by faith, then by sight. Equally certain, no man will ever behold the glory of Christ by sight in heaven, who does not now behold it by faith. Where the soul has not been previously purified by grace and faith, it is incapable of glory and the open vision. Those who pretend to be greatly enamored by or to ardently desire that which they never saw or experienced, only dote on their imaginations. The pretended desires of many (especially on deathbeds) to behold the glory of Christ in heaven, but who had no vision of it by faith while they were in this world, are nothing but self-deceiving delusions.

There is no true rest for the mind nor satisfaction for the heart until we rest in Christ (Matthew 11:28–30). God has proposed to us the "mystery of godliness" (1 Timothy 3:16), that is, the person of His incarnate Son and His mediatorial work, as the supreme object of our faith and meditation. In this "mystery" we are called upon to behold the highest exhibition of the divine wisdom, goodness, and condescension. The Son of God assumed manhood by union with Himself, thereby constituting the same person in two natures, yet infinitely distinct as those of God and man. Thereby the Infinite became finite, the Eternal temporal, and the Immortal mortal, yet continued still infinite, eternal, and immortal.

It cannot be expected that those who are drowned in the love of the world will have any true apprehension of Christ, or any real desire for it. But for those who have "tasted that the Lord is gracious" (1 Peter 2:3), how foolish we would be if we gave all our time and strength to other things, to the neglect of diligent searching of Scripture to obtain a fuller knowledge of Him.

Man is "born unto trouble, as the sparks fly upward" (Job 5:7), but the same Scriptures reveal a divinely appointed relief from all the evils to which fallen man is heir—so that we may not faint under them, but gain the victory over them.

Listen to the testimony of one who passed through a far deeper sea of trial than the great majority of men:

> We are troubled on every side, yet not distressed; we are perplexed, but not in despair; persecuted, but not forsaken; cast down, but not destroyed. . . . For which cause we faint not; but though our outward man perish, yet the inward is renewed day by day. For our light affliction, which is but for a moment, worketh for us a far more exceeding and eternal weight of glory; while we look not at the things which are seen, . . . but the things which are not seen are eternal. (2 Corinthians 4:8–9, 16–18)

It is beholding by faith things which "are not seen" by the eye (which the spiritually poverty-stricken occupants of palaces and millionaire mansions know nothing of), the things that are spiritual and eternal, which alleviates the Christian's afflictions. Of these unseen, eternal things the supernal glories of Christ are the principal. He who can contemplate Him who is "the Lord of glory," will, when "all around gives way," be lifted out of himself and delivered from the prevailing power of evil.

Not until the mind arrives at a fixed judgment that all things here are transitory and reach only to outward man—that everything under the sun is but "vanity and vexation of spirit" (Ecclesiastes 4:16), and there are other things incalculably better to comfort and satisfy the heart—not till then will we ever be delivered from spending our lives in fear, distress, and sorrow. Christ alone can satisfy the heart. And when He does truly satisfy, the language of the soul is "Whom have I in heaven but thee? and there is none upon earth that I desire beside thee" (Psalm 73:25).

How slight and shadowy, how petty and puerile are those things from which the trials of men arise! They all grow from the one root of the overvaluation of temporal things. Money cannot purchase joy of soul. Health does not insure happiness. A beautiful home will not satisfy the heart. Earthly friends, no matter how loyal and loving, cannot speak peace to a sin-burdened conscience, nor impart eternal life. Envy, covetousness, discontent, receive their death wound when Christ, in all His loveliness, is revealed as the "chiefest among ten thousand" (Song of Songs 5:10).

Chapter 27
THE RADIANCE OF CHRIST

*T*he law had "a shadow of good things to come" (Hebrews 10:1). A beautiful illustration of this is in the closing verses of Exodus 34, where Moses descends from the mount with a radiant face (vv. 29–35). The key to the passage is found in noting the exact position it occupies in this book of redemption. It comes after the legal covenant which Jehovah made with Israel; it comes before the actual setting up of the tabernacle and the Shekinah glory filling it. This passage is interpreted in 2 Corinthians 3. Exodus 34 supplies both a comparison and a contrast with the new dispensation of the Spirit, of grace, of life more abundant. But before that dispensation was inaugurated, God saw fit for man to be tested under Law, to demonstrate what he is as a fallen and sinful creature.

Man's trial under the Mosaic economy demonstrated two things: first, that he is "ungodly"; second, that he is "without strength" (Romans 5:6). But these are negative things. Romans 8:7 mentions a third feature of man's terrible state, namely, that he is "enmity against God." This was manifest when God's Son tabernacled for thirty-three years on this earth. "He came unto his own, and his own received him not" (John

1:11). Not only so, but also He was "despised and rejected of men" (Isaiah 53:3). Nay, more, they hated Him "without a cause" (John 15:25). Nor could their hatred be appeased until they had condemned Him to a malefactor's death and nailed Him to the cross. Remember it was not only the Jews who put to death the Lord of glory, but also the Gentiles. Therefore the Lord said, when looking forward to His death, "Now is the judgment of this world" (12:31), not of Israel only. There the probation or testing of man ended.

Man is not now under probation; he is under condemnation: "As it is written, There is none righteous, no, not one: there is none that understandeth, there is none that seeketh after God. They are all gone out of the way, they are together become unprofitable; there is none that doeth good, no, not one" (Romans 3:10–12). Man is not on trial; he is a culprit under sentence. No pleading will avail; no excuses will be accepted. The present issue between God and the sinner is, Will man bow to God's righteous verdict?

This is where the Gospel meets us. It comes to us as to those who are already lost, to those who are "ungodly," "without strength," and "enmity against God." It announces to us the amazing grace of God, the only hope for poor sinners. But grace will not be welcomed until the sinner bows to the sentence of God against him. That is why both repentance and faith are demanded from the sinner. These two must not be separated. Paul preached "repentance toward God, and faith toward our Lord Jesus Christ" (Acts 20:21). Repentance is the sinner's acknowledgment of that sentence of condemnation under which he lives. Faith is acceptance of the grace and mercy extended to him through Christ. Repentance is not turning over a new leaf and vowing to mend our ways. Rather it is personally affirming God is true when He tells me I am "without strength," that in myself my case is hopeless, that I am no more able to "do better next time" than I am to create a world. Not until this is really believed (not as the result of experience, but on the authority of God's Word) shall we really turn to Christ and welcome Him—not as a Helper, but as a Saviour.

As it was dispensationally, so it is experimentally. There must be "a ministration of death" (2 Corinthians 3:7) before there is a "ministration of the spirit," or life (v. 8); there must be "the ministration of condemnation" before "the ministration of righteousness" (v. 9). A "ministration of condemnation and death" falls strangely on our ears, does it not? A "ministration of grace" we can understand, but a "ministration of condemnation" is not so easy to grasp. But this latter was man's first need. He must be shown what he is in himself—a hopeless wreck, utterly incapable of meeting the righteous requirements of a holy God—before he is ready to be a debtor to mercy alone. We repeat: As it was dispensationally, so it is experimentally. It was to his own experience that the apostle Paul referred when he said, "For I was alive without the law once: but when the commandment came, sin revived, and I died" (Romans 7:9). In his unregenerate days he was, in his own estimation, "alive," yet it was "without the law," that is, apart from meeting its demands. "But when the commandment came," when the Holy Spirit wrought within him, when the Word of God came in power to his heart, then "sin revived." He was made aware of his awful condition, and then he "died" to his self-righteous complacency. He saw that, in himself, his case was hopeless. Yes, the appearing of the glorified Mediator comes not before, but after, the legal covenant.

"And he was there with the LORD forty days and forty nights; he did neither eat bread, nor drink water. And he wrote upon the tables the words of the covenant, the ten commandments" (Exodus 34:28). Our passage abounds in comparisons and contrasts. The "forty days" here at once recalls the "forty days" in Matthew 4. Here it was Moses; there it was Christ. Here it was Moses on the mount; there it was Christ in the wilderness. Here it was Moses favored with a glorious revelation from God; there it was Christ being tempted of the devil. Here it was Moses receiving the Law at the mouth of Jehovah; there it was Christ being assailed by the devil to repudiate that Law. We scarcely know which is the greater wonder of the two: that a sinful man was raised to such a height of honor as to spend a season in the presence of the great Jehovah, or that the Lord of glory should stoop so low as to be for *six weeks* with the foul fiend.

"And it came to pass, when Moses came down from mount Sinai with the two tables of testimony in Moses' hand, when he came down from the mount, that Moses wist not that the skin of his face shone while he talked with him" (Exodus 34:29). Blessed it is to compare and contrast this second descent of Moses from the mount with what is before us in Exodus 32:19. There the face of Moses was diffused with anger; here he comes down with countenance radiant. There he beheld a people engaged in idolatry; here he returns to a people abashed. There we behold him dashing the tables of stone to the ground; here he deposits them in the ark (Deuteronomy 10:5).

This event also reminds us of a New Testament episode, very similar, yet dissimilar. It was on the mount that the face of Moses was made radiant, and it was on the mount that our Lord was transfigured. But the glory of Moses was only a reflected one, whereas that of Christ was inherent. The shining of Moses' face was the consequence of his being brought into the immediate presence of the glory of Jehovah; the transfiguration of Christ was the outshining of His own personal glory. The radiance of Moses was confined to his face, but of Christ we read, "His raiment was white as the light" (Matthew 17:2). Moses knew not ("wist not," KJV) that the skin of his face shone; Christ did, evident from His words, "Tell the vision to no man" (v. 9).

Exodus 34:29 brings out what is the certain consequence of intimate communion with the Lord, and in a twofold way. First, no soul can enjoy real fellowship with God without being affected by it to a marked degree. Moses had been absorbed in the communications received and in contemplating His glory. His own person caught and retained some of the beams of that glory. So it is still: "Look to him, and be radiant" (Psalm 34:5 RSV). It is communion with the Lord that conforms us to His image. We shall not be more Christlike until we walk more frequently and more closely with Him. "But we all, with open face beholding as in a glass the glory of the Lord, are changed into the same image from glory to glory, even as by the Spirit of the Lord" (2 Corinthians 3:18).

The second consequence of real communion with God is that we will be less occupied with ourselves. Though Moses' face shone with "a light not seen on land or sea," he did not know it. This illustrates a vital difference between self-righteous Pharisaism and true godliness; the former produces complacency and pride, the latter leads to self-abnegation and humility. The Pharisee (there are many of his tribe still on earth) boasts of his attainments, advertises his imaginary spirituality, and thanks God he is not as other men. But the one who, by grace, enjoys much fellowship with the Lord learns of Him who was "meek and lowly in heart," and says, "Not unto us, O LORD, not unto us, but unto thy name give glory" (Psalm 115:1). Engaged with the beauty of the Lord, he is delivered from self-occupation, and is therefore unconscious of the very fruit of the Spirit being brought forth in him. But though *he* is not aware of his increasing conformity to Christ, *others* are.

"And when Aaron and all the children of Israel saw Moses, behold, the skin of his face shone; and they were afraid to come nigh him" (Exodus 34:30). This shows us the third effect of communion with God. Though the individual himself is unconscious of the glory manifested through him, others recognize it. Thus it was when two of Christ's apostles stood before the Jewish Sanhedrin: "Now when they saw the boldness of Peter and John, and perceived that they were unlearned and ignorant men, they marvelled; and they took knowledge of them, *that they had been with Jesus*" (Acts 4:13, italics added). We cannot keep company very long with the Holy One without His imprint being left upon us. The man who is thoroughly devoted to the Lord does not need to wear some badge in his coat lapel, nor to proclaim that he is "living a life of victory." It is still true that actions speak louder than words.

"And when Aaron and all the children of Israel saw Moses, behold, the skin of his face shone; and they were afraid to come nigh him." The typical meaning of this is given in 2 Corinthians 3:7, "But if the ministration of death, written and engraven in stones, was glorious, so that the children of Israel could not stedfastly behold the face of Moses for the glory of his countenance." Concerning this, Ed Dennett has said:

> Why, then, were they afraid to come near him? Because the very glory that shone upon his face searched their hearts and consciences—being what they were, sinners, and unable of themselves to meet even the smallest requirements of the covenant which had now been inaugurated. It was of necessity a "ministration" of condemnation and death, for it required a righteousness from them which they could not render, and inasmuch as they must fail in the rendering it, would pronounce their condemnation, and bring them under the penalty of transgression, which was death. The glory which they thus beheld upon the face of Moses was the expression to them of the holiness of God—that holiness which sought from them conformity to its own standards, and which would vindicate the breaches of that covenant which had now been established. They were therefore afraid because they knew in their inmost souls that they could not stand before Him from whose presence Moses had come.

Typically the covenant Jehovah made with Moses and Israel at Sinai, and the tables of stone on which the Ten Commandments were engraved, foreshadowed a new covenant.

For I will take you from among the heathen, and gather you out of all countries, and will bring you into your own land. Then will I sprinkle clean water upon you, and ye shall be clean: from all your filthiness, and from all your idols, will I cleanse you. A new heart also will I give you, and a new spirit will I put within you: and I will take away the stony heart out of your flesh, and I will give you an heart of flesh. And I will put my spirit within you, and cause you to walk in my statutes, and ye shall keep my judgments, and do them. And ye shall dwell in the land that I gave to your fathers; and ye shall be my people, and I will be your God. (Ezekiel 36:24–28)

Behold, the days come, saith the LORD, that I will make a new covenant with the house of Israel, and with the house of Judah. . . . After those days, saith the LORD, I will put my law in their inward parts, and write in their hearts. . . . And they shall teach no more every man his neighbour, and every man his brother, saying, Know the LORD: for they shall all know me, from the least of them unto the greatest of them, saith the LORD. (Jeremiah 31:31, 33–34)

Spiritually, this is made good for Christians even now. Under the gracious operations of the Spirit of God our hearts have been made plastic and receptive. Paul refers to this at the beginning of 2 Corinthians 3.

The saints at Corinth had been manifested to be Christ's epistle ministered by us, written not with ink, but with the Spirit of the living God, not on stone tables, but on fleshy tables of the heart. Their hearts being made impressionable by Divine working, Christ could write upon them, using Paul as a pen, and making every mark in the power of the Spirit of God. But what is written is the knowledge of God as revealed through the Mediator in the grace of the new covenant, so that it might be true in the hearts of the saints—"They shall all know Me." Then Paul goes on to speak of himself as made competent by God to be a new covenant ministry, "not of the letter, but of the spirit." (C. A. Coates)

"And Moses called unto them; and Aaron and all the rulers of the congregation returned unto him: and Moses talked with them. And afterward all the children of Israel came nigh: and he gave them in commandment all that the LORD had spoken with him in mount Sinai. And till Moses had done speaking with them, he put a vail on his face" (Exodus 34:31–33). Does not this explain their fear as they beheld the shine of Moses' face? Note what was in his hands! He carried the two tables of stone on which were written the ten words of the Law, the "ministration of condemnation." The nearer the light of the glory came, while it was connected with the righteous claims of God upon them, the more cause they had to fear. That holy Law condemned them, for man in the flesh could not meet its claims. "However blessed it was *typically,* it was *literally* a ministry of death, for Moses was not a quickening spirit, nor could he give his spirit to the people, nor could the glory of his face bring them into conformity with himself as the mediator. Hence the veil had to be on his face" (C. A. Coates).

The dispensational interpretation of this is given in 2 Corinthians 3:13: "And not as Moses, which put a vail over his face, that the children of Israel could not stedfastly look to the end of that which is abolished." Here the apostle treats of Judaism as an economy. Owing to their spiritual blindness Israel was unable to discern the deep significance of the ministry of Moses, or the purpose of God behind it, that to which all the types and shadows pointed. The "end" of 2 Corinthians 3:13 is parallel with Romans 10:4: "For Christ is the end of the law for righteousness to every one that believeth."

> The veil on Israel's heart is self-sufficiency, which makes them still refuse to submit to God's righteousness. But when Israel's heart turns to the Lord the veil will be taken away. What a wonderful chapter Exodus 34 will be to them then! For they will see that *Christ* is the spirit of it all. What they will see, we are privileged to see now. All this had an "end" on which *we* can, through infinite grace, fix our eyes. The "end" was the glory of the Lord as the Mediator of the new covenant. He has come out of death and gone up on high, and the glory of all that God is in grace is shining in His face. (C. A. Coates)

"But when Moses went in before the LORD to speak with him, he took the vail off, until he came out. And he came out, and spake unto the children of Israel that which he was commanded. And the children of Israel saw the face of Moses, that the skin of Moses' face shone: and Moses put the vail upon his face again, until he went in to speak with him" (Exodus 34:34–35). Moses unveiled in the presence of the Lord is a beautiful type of the believer of this dispensation. The Christian beholds the glory of God shining in the face of Jesus Christ (2 Corinthians 4:6). Therefore, instead of being stricken with fear, he approaches with boldness. God's Law cannot condemn him, for its every demand has been fully met and satisfied by his Substitute. Hence, instead of trembling before the glory of God, we "rejoice in hope of the glory of God" (Romans 5:2).

> There is no veil now either on His face or our hearts. He makes those who believe on Him to live in the knowledge of God, and in response to God, for He is the quickening Spirit. And He gives His Spirit to those who believe. We have the Spirit of the glorious Man in whose face the glory of God shines. Is it not wonderful? One has to ask, Do we really believe it? But we all, looking on the glory of the Lord with unveiled face, are transformed according to the same image from glory to glory, even as by the Lord the Spirit (2 Corinthians 3:18). If we had not His Spirit we should have no liberty to look on the glory of the Lord, or to see Him as the Spirit of these marvelous types. But we have liberty to look on it all, and there is transforming power in it. Saints under the new covenant ministry are transfigured.
>
> This is the "surpassing glory" which could not be seen or known until it shone in the face of Him of whom Moses in Exodus 34 is so distinctly a type. The whole typical system was temporary, but its "spirit" abides, for Christ was the Spirit of it all. Now [today] we have to do with the ministry of the new covenant [which], subsists and abounds in glory. (C. A. Coates)

The authority of Paul's apostleship had been called into question by certain Judaizers. In the first verses of 2 Corinthians 3 he appeals to the Christians there as the proof of his God-commissioned ministry. He defines the character of his ministry to show its superiority over that of his enemies: He and his fellow gospelers were "ministers of the new testament," or covenant (v. 6). He then draws a series of contrasts between the two covenants, Judaism and Christianity. What pertained to the old is called "the letter," and that relating to the new "the spirit." One was mainly concerned with what was external, the other was largely internal; the one slew, the other gave life—one of the leading differences between the Law and the Gospel.

In what follows, the apostle, while allowing the Law was glorious, shows that the Gospel is still more glorious. The old covenant was a "ministration of death," for the Law could only condemn (v. 7). Therefore, though a glory was connected with it, yet it was such that man in the flesh could not behold (v. 7). Then how much more excellent would be, must be, the glory of the new covenant, seeing it was "a ministration of the spirit" (v. 8). Compare verse 3 for proof of this. If there were a glory connected with what "concluded all under sin" (Galatians 3:22), much more glorious that ministration must be which announced a righteousness "unto all and upon all them that believe" (Romans 3:22). It is more glorious to pardon than to condemn; to give life than to destroy (2 Corinthians 3:9). The glory of the former covenant therefore pales into nothingness before the latter (v. 10), further seen from the fact Judaism is "done away," whereas Christianity "remaineth" (v. 11). Compare Hebrews 8:7–8.

The apostle draws still another contrast in 2 Corinthians 3 between the two economies, namely the plainness or perspicuity over against the obscurity and ambiguity of their respective ministries (vv. 12–15). The apostle used "great plainness of speech," while the teaching of the ceremonial law was by shadows and symbols. Moreover, the minds of the Israelites were blinded, so that there was a veil over their eyes. Therefore, when the writings of Moses were read they were incapable of looking beyond the type to the Antitype. This veil remains upon them to this day, and will continue until they turn to the Lord (vv. 15–16). Literally the covenant of Sinai was a ministration of condemnation and death, and the glory of it had to be veiled. But it had an "end" (v. 13) which Israel could not see. They will see that end in a coming day.

But in the meantime we are permitted to read the old covenant without a veil, and to see that Christ is the "spirit" of it all.

The language of verse 17 is somewhat obscure: "Now the Lord is that Spirit," which does not mean that Christ is the Holy Spirit. The "spirit" here is the same as in verse 6, "not of the letter, but of the spirit" (compare Romans 7:6). The Mosaic system is called "the letter" because it was purely objective and possessed no inward principle or power. But the Gospel deals with the heart, and supplies the spiritual power (Romans 1:16). Moreover, Christ is the spirit, the life, the heart and center of all the ritual and ceremonialism of Judaism. He is the key to the Old Testament, for "in the volume of the book" it is written of Him (Psalm 40:7; Hebrews 10:7). So also Christ is the spirit and life of Christianity. He is "a quickening spirit" (1 Corinthians 15:45). And "where the Spirit of the Lord is, there is liberty" (2 Corinthians 3:17). Apart from Christ, the sinner, be he Jew or Gentile, is in bondage; he is the slave of sin and the captive of the devil. But where the Son makes free, He frees indeed (John 8:36).

Finally, the apostle contrasts the two glories, the glory connected with the old covenant—the shining on Moses' face at the giving of the Law with the glory of the new covenant, in the person of Christ. "But we all, with open [unveiled] face beholding as in a glass the glory of the Lord, are changed into the same image from glory to glory, even as by the Spirit of the Lord" (2 Corinthians 3:18). Note here, first, "we all." Moses alone beheld the glory of the Lord in the mount; every Christian now beholds it. Second, "with open face," with freedom and with confidence; whereas Israel was afraid to gaze on the radiant and majestical face of Moses. Third, we are "changed into the same image." The Law had no power to convert or purify; but the ministry of the Gospel, under the operation of the Spirit, has a transforming power. Those who are saved by it and who are occupied with Christ as set forth in the Word (the "mirror"), are, little by little, conformed to His image. Ultimately, when we "see him as he is" (1 John 3:2), we shall be "like him"—fully, perfectly, eternally.

Chapter 28

THE CONDESCENSION OF CHRIST

*F*or the sake of accuracy, a distinction should be drawn between the condescension and the humiliation of Christ, though most writers confound them. This distinction is made by the Holy Spirit (Philippians 2:7–8). First, He "made himself of no reputation"; second, He "humbled himself." The condescension of God the Son consisted in His assuming our nature, the Word becoming flesh. His humiliation lay in the consequent abasement and sufferings He endured in our nature. The assumption of human nature was not, of itself, a part of Christ's humiliation, for He still retained it in His glorious exaltation. But for God the Son to take into union with Himself a created nature, animated dust, was an act of infinite condescension.

> Who, being in the form of God, thought it not robbery to be equal with God: but made himself of no reputation, and took upon him the form of a servant, and was made in the likeness of men: and being found in fashion as a man, he humbled himself, and became obedient unto death, even the death of the cross. Wherefore God also hath highly exalted him, and given him a name which is above every name. (Philippians 2:6–9)

These verses trace the path of the Mediator from highest glory to deepest humiliation and back again to His supreme honor. What a wondrous path was His! And how terrible that this divine description of His path should have become the battleground of theological contention. At few points has the awful depravity of man's heart been more horribly displayed than by the blasphemies vented upon these verses.

A glance at the context (Philippians 2:1–5) at once shows the practical design of the apostle was to exhort Christians to spiritual fellowship among themselves—to be like-minded, to love one another, to be humble and lowly, to esteem others better than themselves. To enforce this, the example of our Lord is proposed in the verses we now consider. We are to have the same mind in us that was in Him; the mind, spirit, and habit, of self-abnegation; the mind of self-sacrifice and of obedience to God. We must humble ourselves beneath the mighty hand of God, if we are to be exalted by Him in due time (1 Peter 5:6). To set before us the example of Christ in its most vivid colors, the Holy Spirit takes us back to the position which our Mediator occupied in eternity. He shows us that supreme dignity and glory was His, then reminds us of those unfathomable depths of condescension and humiliation into which He descended for our sakes.

"Who, being in the form of God." First of all, this affirms the absolute Deity of the Son, for no mere creature, no matter how high in the scale of being, could ever be "in the form of God." Three words are used concerning the Son's relation to the Godhead. First, He subsists in the "form" of God, seen in Him alone. Second, He is "the image of the invisible God" (Colossians 1:15), which expression tells of His manifestation of God to us (compare 2 Corinthians 4:6). Third, He is the "brightness of his glory, and the express image of his person" (Hebrews 1:3), or more exactly, the "effulgency (outshining) of His glory and the exact Expression of His substance" (Bagster *InterlinearGreek-English New Testament*). These perhaps combine both concepts suggested by form and image, namely, that the whole nature of God is in Christ, that *by* Him God is declared and expressed to us.

"Who being," or subsisting (it is hardly correct to speak of a divine person "existing"): He is self-existent; He always was in "the form of God." "Form" (the Greek word is only found elsewhere in the New Testament in Mark 16:12 and Philippians 2:6) is what is apparent. "The form of God" is an expression which seems to denote His visible glory,

His displayed majesty, His manifested sovereignty. From eternity the Son was clothed with all the insignia of deity, adorned with all divine splendor. "The Word was God" (John 1:1).

"Thought it not robbery to be equal with God." Almost every word in this verse has been the occasion of contention. But we have sufficient confidence in the superintending providence of God to be satisfied the translators of our authorized version were preserved from any serious mistake on a subject so vitally important. As the first clause of our verse refers to an objective delineation of the divine dignity of the Son, so this second clause affirms His subjective consciousness. The word *thought* is used (here in the aorist tense) to indicate a definite point in time past. The Greek word rendered "robbery" denotes not the spoil or prize, but the act of taking the spoil. The Son did not reckon equality with the Father and the Holy Spirit an act of usurping.

"Thought it not robbery to be equal with God." This is only a negative way to say that Christ considered equality with God as what justly and essentially belonged to Him. It was His by indisputable right. Christ esteemed such equality as no invasion of Another's prerogative, but regarded Himself as being entitled to all divine honors. Because He held the rank of one of the Three coeternal, coessential, and co-glorious Persons of the Godhead, the Son reckoned His full and perfect equality with the other two was His unchallengeable portion. In verse 6 is no doubt a latent reference to Satan's fall. He, though "the anointed cherub" (Ezekiel 28:14), was infinitely below God, yet he grasped at equality with Him. "I will ascend above the heights of the clouds; I will be like the most High" (Isaiah 14:14).

However the Greek word for "robbery" is translated, it is evident the emphatic term of this clause is the word *equal*. For if it signifies a real and proper equality, then the proof for the absolute deity of the Saviour is irrefutable. How, then, is the exact significance of this term to be determined? Not by having recourse to Homer, nor any other heathen writer, but by discovering the meaning of its cognate. If we can fix the precise rendering of the adjective, then we may be sure of the adverb. The Greek adjective is found in several passages (Matthew 20:12; Luke 6:34: "as *much* again"; John 5:18; Acts 11:17: "the *like* gift"; Revelation 21:16). In each passage the reference is not to a likeness only, but to a real and proper equality! Thus the force of this clause is parallel with "I and my Father are one" (John 10:30).

"My Father is greater than I" (John 14:28) must not be allowed to negate John 10:30. There are no contradictions in Holy Writ. Each of these passages may be given its full force without there being any conflict between them. The simple way to discover their perfect consistency is to remember that Scripture exhibits our Saviour in two chief characters: as God the Son, the second Person of the Trinity; and as Mediator, the God-man, the Word become flesh. In the former, He is described as possessing all the perfections of deity; in the latter, as the Servant of the Godhead. Speaking of Himself according to His essential Being, He could unqualifiedly say, "I and my Father are one"—one in essence or nature. Speaking of Himself according to His mediatorial office, He could say, "My Father is greater than I," not essentially, but economically.

Each expression used (Philippians 2:6) is expressly designed by the Holy Spirit to magnify the divine dignity of Christ's person. He is the Possesser of a glory equal with God's, with an unquestioned right to that glory, deeming it no robbery to challenge it. His glory is not an accidental or phenomenal one, but a substantial and essential one, subsisting in the very "form of God." Between what is Infinite and what is finite, what is Eternal and what is temporal, He who is the Creator and what is the creature, it is utterly impossible there should be any equality. "To whom then will ye liken me, or shall I be equal? saith the Holy One" (Isaiah 40:25), is God's own challenge. Thus, for any creature to deem himself "equal with God" would be the highest robbery and supremest blasphemy.

"But made himself of no reputation." The meaning of the words is explained in those which immediately follow. So far was the Son from tenaciously insisting upon His personal rights as a member of the blessed Trinity, He voluntarily relinquished them. He willingly set aside the magnificent distinctions of the Creator, to appear in the form of a creature, yes, in the likeness of a fallen man. He abdicated His position of supremacy and entered one of servitude. Though equal in majesty and glory with God, He joyfully resigned Himself to the Father's will (John 6:38). Incomparable condescension was this. He who was by inherent right in the form of God, suffered His glory to be eclipsed, His honor to be laid in the dust, and Himself to be humbled to a most shameful death.

"And took upon him the form of a servant." In so doing, He did not cease to be all that He was before, but He assumed something He had not been previously. There was no change in His divine nature, but the uniting to His divine person of a human nature. "He who is God, can no more be not God, than he who is not God, can be God" (John Owen). None of Christ's divine attributes were relinquished, for they are as inseparable from His person as heat is from fire, or weight from substance. But His majestic glory was, for a season, obscured by the interposing veil of human flesh. Nor is this statement negated by John 1:14: "We beheld his glory" (explained by Matthew 16:17), in contrast from the unregenerate masses before whom He appeared as "a root out of a dry ground," having "no form nor comeliness" (Isaiah 53:2).

It was God Himself who was "manifest in the flesh" (1 Timothy 3:16). The One born in Bethlehem's manger was "The mighty God" (Isaiah 9:6), and heralded as "Christ the Lord" (Luke 2:11). Let there be no uncertainty on this point. Had He been "emptied" of any of His personal excellency, had His divine attributes been laid aside, then His satisfaction or sacrifice would not have possessed infinite value. The glory of His person was not in the slightest degree diminished when He became incarnate, though it was (in measure) concealed by the lowly form of the servant He assumed. Christ was still "equal with God" when He descended to earth. It was "the Lord of glory" (1 Corinthians 2:8) whom men crucified.

"And took upon him the form of a servant." That was the great condescension, yet is it not possible for us to fully grasp the infinity of the Son's stoop. If God "humbleth himself to behold the things that are in heaven, and in the earth" (Psalm 113:6), how much more so to actually become "flesh" and be amongst the most lowly. He entered into an office which placed Him below God (John 14:28; 1 Corinthians 11:3). He was, for a season, made "a little lower than the angels" (Hebrews 2:7); He was "made under the law" (Galatians 4:4). He was made lower than the ordinary condition of man, for He was "a reproach of men, and despised of the people" (Psalm 22:6).

What point all this gives to "Let this mind be in you, which was also in Christ Jesus" (Philippians 2:5). How earnestly the Christian needs to seek grace to be content with the lowest place God and men assign him; to be ready to perform the meanest service; to be and do anything which brings glory to God.

Chapter 29

THE HUMANITY OF CHRIST

It has been truly said:

> Right views concerning Christ are indispensable to a right faith, and a right faith is indispensable to salvation. To stumble at the foundation, is, concerning faith, to make shipwreck altogether; for as Immanuel, God with us, is the grand Object of faith, to err in views of His eternal Deity, or to err in views of His sacred humanity, is alike destructive. There are points of truth which are not fundamental, though erroneous views on any one point must lead to God-dishonoring consequences in strict proportion to its importance and magnitude; but there are certain foundation truths to err concerning which is to insure for the erroneous and the unbelieving, the blackness of darkness forever. (J. C. Philpot, 1859)

To know Christ as God, to know Him as man, to know Him as God-man, and this by a divine revelation of His person, is indeed to have eternal life in our hearts. Nor can He be known in any other way than by divine and special revelation. "But when it pleased God, who separated me from my mother's womb, and called me by his grace, to reveal his Son in me" (Galatians 1:15–16). An imaginary conception of His person may be obtained by diligently studying the Scriptures, but a vital knowledge of Him must be communicated from on high (Matthew 16:17). A theoretical and theological knowledge of Christ is what the natural man may acquire, but a saving, soul-transforming view of Him (2 Corinthians 3:18) is only given by the Spirit to the regenerate (1 John 5:20).

"But made himself of no reputation, and took upon him the form of a servant, and was made in the likeness of men" (Philippians 2:7). The first clause (and the preceding verse) was before us in the last two chapters. The two expressions we consider here balance with (and thus serve to explain) those in verse 6. The last clause of verse 7 is an exegesis of the one immediately preceding. "Made in the likeness of men" refers to the human nature Christ assumed. The "form of a servant" denotes the position or state which He entered. Thus "equal with God" refers to the divine nature; the "form of God" signifies His manifested glory in His position of Lord over all.

The humanity of Christ was unique. History supplies no analogy, nor can His humanity be illustrated by anything in nature. It is incomparable, not only to our fallen human nature, but also to unfallen Adam's. The Lord Jesus was born into circumstances totally different from those in which Adam first found himself, but the sins and griefs of His people were on Him from the first. His humanity was produced neither by natural generation (as is ours), nor by special creation, as was Adam's. The humanity of Christ was, under the immediate agency of the Holy Spirit, supernaturally "conceived" (Isaiah 7:14) of the virgin. It was "prepared" of God (Hebrews 10:5); yet "made of a woman" (Galatians 4:4).

The uniqueness of Christ's humanity also appears in that it never had a separate existence of its own. The eternal Son assumed (at the moment of Mary's conception) a human nature, but not a human person. This important distinction calls for careful consideration. By a "person" is meant an intelligent being subsisting by himself. The second Person of the Trinity assumed a human nature and gave it subsistence by union with His divine personality. It would have been a human person, if it had not been united to the Son of God. But being united to Him, it cannot be called a person, because it never subsisted by itself, as other men do. Hence the force of "that holy thing which shall be born of thee" (Luke 1:35). It was not possible for a divine person to assume another person, subsisting of itself, into union with Himself. For two persons, remaining two, to become one person is a contradiction. "A body hast thou prepared me" (Hebrews 10:5). The "me" denotes the Divine Person, the "body," the nature He took unto Himself.

The humanity of Christ was real. "Forasmuch then as the children are partakers of flesh and blood, he also himself likewise took part of the same. . . . Wherefore in all things it behoved him to be made like unto his brethren" (Hebrews 2:14, 17). He assumed a complete human nature, spirit, soul, and body. Christ did not bring His human nature from heaven (as some have strangely and erroneously concluded from 1 Corinthians 15:47), but it was composed of the very substance of His mother. In clothing Himself with flesh and blood, Christ also clothed Himself with human feelings, so He did not differ from His brethren, sin only excepted.

While we always contend that Christ is God, let us never lose the conviction He is most certainly a man. He is not God humanized, nor a human deified; but, as to His Godhead, pure Godhead, equal and coeternal with the Father; as to His manhood, perfect manhood, made in all respects like the rest of mankind, sin alone excepted. His humanity is real, for He was born. He lay in the virgin's womb, and in due time was born. The gate by which we enter our first life he passed through also. He was not created, nor transformed, but His humanity was begotten and born. As He was born, so in the circumstances of His birth, he is completely human. He was as weak and feeble as any other babe. He is not even royal, but human. Those born in marble halls of old were wrapped in purple garments, and were thought by the common people to be a superior race. But this Babe was wrapped in swaddling clothes and had a manger for a cradle, so that the true humanity of His being would come out.

As He grows up, the very *growth* shows how completely human He is. He does not spring into full manhood at once, but He grows in wisdom and stature, and in favor with God and man. When he reaches man's estate, He gets the common stamp of manhood upon His brow. "In the *sweat* of thy brow shalt thou eat bread" is the common heritage of us all, and He receives no better. The carpenter's shop must witness to the toils of a Saviour, and when He becomes the preacher and the prophet, still we read such significant words as these—"Jesus, being weary sat thus on the well." We find Him needing to betake Himself to rest in *sleep.* He slumbers at the stern of the vessel when it is tossed in the midst of the tempest. Brethren, if *sorrow* be the mark of real manhood, and "man is born unto trouble as the sparks fly upward," certainly Jesus Christ has the truest evidence of being a man. If to hunger and to thirst be signs that He was no shadow, and His manhood no fiction, you have these. If to associate with His fellow-men, and eat and drink as they did, will be proof to your mind that He was none other than a man, you see Him sitting at a feast one day, at another time He graces a marriage supper, and on another occasion He is hungry and "hath not where to lay His head." (C. H. Spurgeon)

They who deny Christ's derivation of real humanity through His mother undermine the atonement. His very brotherhood with us (Hebrews 2:11), as our Kinsman-Redeemer, depended on the fact that He obtained His humanity from Mary. Without this He would neither possess the natural nor the legal union with His people, which must lie at the foundation of His representative character as the "last Adam." To be our *Goel* (Redeemer), His humanity could neither be brought from heaven nor immediately created by God, but must be derived, as ours was, from a human mother. But with this difference: His humanity never existed in Adam's covenant to entail guilt or taint.

The humanity of Christ was holy. Intrinsically so, because it was "of the Holy Ghost" (Matthew 1:20); absolutely so, because taken into union with God, the Holy One. This fact is expressly affirmed in Luke 1:35, "that holy thing," which is contrasted with "but we are all as an unclean thing" (Isaiah 64:6), and that because we are "shapen in iniquity" and conceived "in sin" (Psalm 51:5). Though Christ truly became partaker of our nature, yet He was "holy, harmless, undefiled, separate from sinners" (Hebrews 7:26). For this reason He could say, "For the prince of this world cometh, and hath nothing in me" (John 14:30). There was nothing in His pure humanity which could respond to sin or Satan.

It was truly remarkable when man was made in the image of God (Genesis 1:26). But bow in wonderment and worship at the amazing condescension of God being made in the image of man! How this manifests the greatness of His love and the riches of His grace! It was for His people and their salvation that the eternal Son assumed human nature and abased Himself even to death. He drew a veil over His glory that He might remove our reproach. Surely, pride must be forever renounced by the followers of such a Saviour.

Inasmuch as "the man Christ Jesus" (1 Timothy 2:5) lived in this world for thirty-three years, He has left us "an example, that [we] should follow his steps: who did no sin, neither was guile found in his mouth:

who, when he was reviled, reviled not again . . . but committed himself to him that judgeth righteously" (1 Peter 2:21–23). He "did no sin," nor should we (2 Corinthians 5:21). "Neither was guile found in his mouth," nor should it be in ours (Colossians 4:6). "When he was reviled, he reviled not again," nor must His followers. He was weary in body, but not in well-doing. He suffered hunger and thirst, yet never murmured. He "pleased not himself" (Romans 15:3), nor must we (2 Corinthians 5:15). He always did those things which pleased the Father (John 8:29). This too must ever be our aim (2 Corinthians 5:9).

Chapter 30

THE
PERSON
OF CHRIST

e enter with fear and trembling upon this high and holy subject. Christ's name is called "Wonderful" (Isaiah 9:6), and even the angels of God are commanded to worship Him (Hebrews 1:6). There is no salvation apart from a true knowledge of Him (John 17:3). "Whosoever denieth the Son [either His true Godhead, or His true and holy humanity] . . . hath not the Father" (1 John 2:23). They are thrice-blessed to whom the Spirit of Truth communicates a supernatural revelation of the Being of Christ (Matthew 16:17). It will lead them in the only path of wisdom and joy, for in Him "are hid all the treasures of wisdom and knowledge" (Colossians 2:3) until they are taken to be where He is and behold His supernal glory forever (John 17:24). An increasing apprehension of the truth concerning the person of Christ should be our constant aim.

"Without controversy great is the mystery of godliness: God was manifest in the flesh" (1 Timothy 3:16). In view of such a divine declaration as this, it is both useless and impious for any man to attempt an explanation of the wondrous and unique person of the Lord Jesus. He cannot be fully comprehended by any finite intelligence. "No man knoweth the Son, but the Father" (Matthew 11:27). Nevertheless, it is our privilege to grow "in the knowledge of our Lord and Saviour Jesus Christ" (2 Peter 3:18). So too it is the duty of His servants to hold up the person of the God-man as revealed in Holy Scriptures, as well as to warn against errors which cloud His glory.

The One born in Bethlehem's manger was "The mighty God" (Isaiah 9:6), "Emmanuel" (Matthew 1:23), "the great God and our Saviour" (Titus 2:13). He is also the true Man, with a spirit, a soul, and a body, for these are essential to human nature. None could be real man without all three. Nevertheless, the humanity of Christ ("that holy thing," Luke 1:35) is not a distinct person, separate from His Godhead, for it never had a separate existence before taken into union with His deity. He is the God-man, yet "one Lord" (Ephesians 4:5). As such He was born, lived here in this world, died, rose again, ascended to heaven, and will continue thus for all eternity. As such He is entirely unique, and the Object of lasting wonder to all holy beings.

The Person of Christ is a composite one. Two separate natures are united in one peerless Person; but they are not fused into each other, instead, they remain distinct and different. The human nature is not divine, nor has it been, intrinsically, deified, for it possesses none of the attributes of God. The humanity of Christ, absolutely and separately considered, is neither omnipotent, omniscient, nor omnipresent. On the other hand, His deity is not a creature and has none of the properties which pertain to such. Taking to Himself a human nature did not effect any change in His divine being. It was a divine person who wedded to Himself a holy humanity, and though His essential glory was partly veiled, yet it never ceased to be, nor did His divine attributes cease to function. As the God-man, Christ is the "one mediator" (1 Timothy 2:5). He alone was fitted to stand between God and men and effect a reconciliation between them.

It needs to be maintained that the two natures are united in the one person of Christ, but that each retains its separate properties, just as the soul and body of men do, though united. Thus, in His divine nature, Christ has nothing in common with us—nothing finite, derived, or dependent. But in His human nature, He was made in all things like to His brethren, sin excepted. In that nature He was born in time and did not exist from all eternity. He increased in knowledge and other endowments. In the one nature He had a comprehensive knowledge of all things; in the other, He knew nothing but by communication or derivation. In the one nature He had an infinite and sovereign will; in the other, He had a creature will. Though not opposed to the divine will, its conformity to it was of the same kind with that in imperfect creatures.

The necessity for the two natures in the one person of our Saviour is self-evident. It was fitting that the Mediator should be both God and man, that He might partake of the nature of both parties and be a middle person between them, filling up the distance and bringing them near to each other. Only thus was He able to communicate His benefits to us, and only thus could He discharge our obligations. As Hermann Witsius, the Dutch theologian (1690), pointed out: "None but God could restore us to true liberty. If any creature could redeem us we should be the peculiar property of that creature: but it is a manifest contradiction to be free and yet at the same time be the servant of any creature. So too none but God could give us eternal life: hence the two are joined together— 'The true God, and eternal life' (1 John 5:20)."

It was equally necessary that the Mediator be Man. He was to enter our Law-place, be subject to the Law, keep it, and merit by keeping it. "But when the fulness of the time was come, God sent forth his Son, made of a woman, made under the law" (Galatians 4:4). Note the order. He must first be "made of a woman" before He could be "made under the law." But more, He had to endure the curse of the Law, suffer its penalty. He was to be "made sin" for His people, and the wages of sin is death. But that was impossible to Him until He took upon Him a nature capable of mortality. "Forasmuch then as the children are partakers of flesh and blood, he also himself likewise took part of the same; that through death he might destroy him that had the power of death, that is, the devil" (Hebrews 2:14).

Thus, the person of the God-man is unique. His birth had no precedent and His existence no analogy. He cannot be explained by referring Him to a class, nor can He be illustrated by an example. The Scriptures, while fully revealing all the elements of His person, yet never present in one formula an exhaustive definition of that person, nor a connected statement of the elements which constitute it and their mutual relationships. The "mystery" is indeed great. How is it possible that the same Person should be at the same time infinite and finite, omnipotent and helpless? He altogether transcends our understanding. How can two complete spirits coalesce in one Person? How can two consciousnesses, two understandings, two memories, two wills, constitute one Person? No one can explain it. Nor are we called upon to do so. Both natures act in concert in one Person. All the attributes and acts of both natures are referred to one Person. The same Person who gave His life for the sheep possessed glory with the Father before the world was!

This amazing Personality does not center in His humanity, nor is it a compound one originated by the power of the Holy Spirit when He brought those two natures together in the womb of the virgin Mary. It was not by adding manhood to Godhead that His personality was formed. The Trinity is eternal and unchangeable. A new person is not substituted for the second member of the Trinity; neither is a fourth added. The person of Christ is just the eternal Word, who in time, by the power of the Holy Spirit, through the instrument of the virgin's womb, took a human nature (not at that time a man, but the seed of Abraham) into personal union with Himself. The Person is eternal and divine; His humanity was introduced into it. The center of His personality is always in the eternal and personal Word, or Son of God.

Though no analogy exists by which we may illustrate the mysterious person of Christ, there is a most remarkable type in Exodus 3:2–6. The "flame of fire" in the midst of the "bush" was an emblem of the presence of God indwelling the Man Christ Jesus. Observe that the One who appeared there to Moses is termed, first, "the angel of the LORD," which declares the relation of Christ to the Father, namely, "the angel (messenger) of the covenant." But secondly, this angel said unto Moses, "I am . . . the God of Abraham"; that is what He was absolutely in Himself. The fire emblem of Him who is a "consuming fire"—placed itself in a bush (a thing of the earth), where it burned, yet the bush was not consumed. A remarkable foreshadowing this was of the "fulness of the Godhead" dwelling in Christ (Colossians 2:9). That this is the meaning of the type is clear, when we read of "the good will of him that dwelt in the bush" (Deuteronomy 33:16).

The great mystery of the Trinity is that one Spirit should subsist eternally as three distinct Persons; the mystery of the person of Christ is that two separate spirits (divine and human) should constitute but one Person. The moment we deny the unity of His person we enter the bogs of error. Christ is the God-man. The humanity of Christ was not absorbed by His deity, but preserved its own characteristics. Scripture does not hesitate to say, "Jesus increased in wisdom and stature, and in favour with God and man" (Luke 2:52). Christ is both infinite and finite, self-sufficient and dependent at the same time, because His person embraces two different natures, the divine and the human.

In the incarnation the second Person of the Trinity established a personal union between Himself and a human spirit, soul, and body. His two natures remained and remain distinct, and their properties or active powers are inseparable from each nature respectively.

> The union between them is not mechanical, as that between oxygen and nitrogen in our air; neither is it chemical, as between oxygen and hydrogen when water is formed; neither is it organic, as that subsisting between our hearts and brains; but it is a union more intimate, more profound, and more mysterious than any of these. It is *personal*. If we cannot understand the nature of the simpler unions, why should we complain because we cannot understand the nature of the most profound of all unions? (A. A. Hodge, to whom we are also indebted for a number of other thoughts in this article.)

Is there a thing beneath the sun
That strives with Thee my heart to share?
O tear it thence, and reign alone,
The Lord of every motion there.
Then shall my heart from earth be free,
When it has found repose in Thee.

Chapter 31

THE
SUBSISTENCE
OF CHRIST

The ground we now tread upon is quite unknown even to the majority of God's people (so great has been the spiritual and theological deterioration of the last century)—though it was familiar to the better-taught saints of the Puritans' times and of those who followed. That the Son of God is coequal with the Father and the Spirit, and that nearly two thousand years ago the Word became flesh and was made in the likeness of men, is still held firmly (and will be) by all truly regenerated souls. That it is the union of the divine and human natures in His wondrous Person which fits Him for His mediatorial office is also apprehended more or less clearly. But that is about as far as the light of nearly all Christians can take them. That the God-man subsisted in heaven before the world was is a blessed truth which has been lost to the last few generations.

A thoughtful reader who ponders a verse such as John 6:62 must surely be puzzled: "What and if ye shall see the Son of man ascend up where he was before?" Mark it well that our Redeemer there spoke of Himself not as the Son before He became incarnate. But ignorant as we may be of this precious truth, Old Testament saints were instructed therein, as evident from Psalm 80, where Asaph prays, "Let thy hand be upon the man of thy right hand, upon the son of man whom thou madest strong for thyself" (v. 17). Yes, the Man Christ Jesus, taken into union with Himself by the second Person of the Trinity, subsisted before the Father from all eternity, and was the object of the Old Testament saints' faith.

When first presented, the last statement appears to be mysticism run wild, or downright heresy. It would be if we had said that the soul and body of the Son of Man had any existence before He was born at Bethlehem. But this is not what Scripture teaches. What the written Word affirms is that the Mediator (Christ in His two natures) had a real subsistence before God from all eternity. First, He was "foreordained before the foundation of the world" (1 Peter 1:20). He was chosen by God to be the Head of the whole election of grace (see Isaiah 42:1). But more; it was not only purposed by God that the Mediator (the Man Christ Jesus wedded to the eternal Word, John 1:1, 14) should have an historical existence when the "fulness of the time" (Galatians 4:4) had arrived, but He had an actual subsistence before Him long before that. But how could this be?

In seeking the answer, it will help us to contemplate something which, though not strictly analogous, on a lower plane serves to illustrate the principle. Hebrews 11:1 records that "faith is the substance of things hoped for." The Greek word for *substance* more properly signifies "a real subsistence." It is opposed to what is only an image of the imagination; it is the antithesis of fantasy. Faith gives a real subsistence in the mind and heart of things which are yet to be, so that they are enjoyed now and their power is experienced in the soul. Faith lays hold of the things God has promised so that they become actually present.

If faith possesses the power to add reality to what as yet has no historical actuality; if faith can enjoy in the present that whose existence is yet future, how much more was God able to give the Mediator a covenant subsistence endless ages before He was born. In consequence, Christ was the Son of Man in heaven, secretly before God, before He became the Son of Man openly in this world. As Christ declared of His Father in the language of prophecy, "In the shadow of his hand hath he hid me, and made me a polished shaft; in his quiver hath he hid me" (Isaiah 49:2). Note that the verses which follow refer to the everlasting covenant. The "quiver" of God is a fine expression to denote the secrecy and security in which the purpose of God was concealed.

Many passages speak of this wondrous subject. Perhaps the clearest, and the one with the most detail, is Proverbs 8. The term *wisdom* (v. 12) is one of the names of Christ (see 1 Corinthians 1:24). That *wisdom* has reference to a person is clear (v. 17), and to a divine person (v. 15). The whole passage (vv. 13–36) has Christ in view, but in what character has not been clearly discerned. While it is evident that what is said (vv. 15–16, 32–36) could only apply to a divine person, it should be equally plain that some of the terms (vv. 23–25) cannot be predicated of the Son of God. Contemplated only as coeternal and coequal with the Father, it could not be said that Christ was ever "brought forth."

From all the terms used in Proverbs 8:13–36 it should be apparent that some are impossible to understand of Christ's deity (separately considered), as others of them cannot be of His humanity only. But the difficulties disappear once we see that the whole passage contemplates the Mediator, the God-man in His two natures. The Man Christ Jesus, as united to the second Person of the Godhead, was "possessed" (v. 22) by the Triune God from all eternity. Let us note some things about this marvelous passage.

"The Lord possessed me in the beginning of his way, before his works of old" (v. 22). The speaker is the Mediator, who had a covenant subsistence before God ere the universe came into being. The Man Christ Jesus, taken into union with the eternal Son, was "the beginning" of the Triune God's "way." It is difficult to speak of eternal matters as first, second, and third, yet God set them forth in the Scriptures for us, and it is permissible to use such distinctions to aid our understanding. The first act or counsel of God had respect to the Man Christ Jesus. He was appointed to be not only the Head of His Church, but also "the firstborn of all creation" (Colossians 1:15 RV). The predestination of the Man Christ Jesus unto the grace of divine union and glory was the first of God's decrees: "in the head [Greek] of the book" it was written of Him (Hebrews 10:7; see also Isaiah 42:1; Revelation 13:8).

The Person of the God-man Mediator was the foundation of all the divine counsels (see Ephesians 1:9–10; 3:11). He was ordained to be the cornerstone on which all creation was to rest. As such, the Triune Jehovah "possessed" or "embraced" Him as a treasury in which all the divine counsels were laid up, as an efficient Agent for the execution of all His works. As such, He is both "the wisdom of God" and "the power of God" executively, being a perfect vehicle through which to express Himself. As such, He was "the beginning" of God's way. The "way" of God signifies the outworking of His eternal decrees, the accomplishing of His purposes by wise and holy dispensations (see Isaiah 55:8–9).

"I was set up from everlasting" (v. 23). This could not be spoken of the Son Himself, for as God He was not capable of being "set up." Yet how could He be set up as the God-man Mediator? By mediatorial settlement, by covenant-constitution, by divine subsistence before the mind of God. From the womb of eternity, in the "counsel of peace" (Zechariah 6:13), before all worlds, Jesus Christ was in His official character "set up." Before God planned to create any creature, He first set up Christ as the great Archetype and Original. There was an order in God's counsels as well as creation, and Christ has "the preeminence" in all things.

The Hebrew verb for "set up" is *anointed,* and should have been so translated. The reference is to the appointing and investing of Christ with the mediatorial office, which was done in the everlasting covenant. All the glory our Lord possesses as Mediator was then granted to Him, on the condition of His obedience and sufferings. Therefore, when He finished His work, He prayed, "Glorify thou me with thine own self with the glory which I had with thee before the world was" (John 17:5). The glory which is there expressly in view is that exalted place which had been given to Him as the Head of all creation. In the timeless transactions of the everlasting covenant, in the unique honor which had been accorded Him as the "beginning" of God's "way," the "firstborn of all creation," He had this glory. For the open manifestation of it He now prayed—answered at His ascension.

"When there were no depths, I was brought forth" (v. 24). "Brought forth" out of the womb of God's decrees; "brought forth" into covenant subsistence before the divine mind; "brought forth" as the Image of the invisible God; "brought forth" as the Man Christ Jesus, after whose likeness Adam was created. Though Adam was the first man by open manifestation on earth, Christ had the priority as He secretly subsisted in heaven. Adam was created in the image and after the likeness of Christ as He actually, but secretly, subsisted in the person of the Son of God, who, in the fulness of time, was born openly.

"Then I was by him, as one brought up with him" (v. 30). Gesenius says that the Hebrew verb here is connected with one which means "to prop,

stay, sustain"; and hence "such as one may safely lean on." It is rendered *nurse* in Ruth 4:16 and 2 Samuel 4:4. As men commit their children to a nurse to cherish and train, so God committed His counsels to Christ. The Hebrew word for "brought up" also signifies a "master workman" (RV). Christ took the fabric of the universe upon Himself, to contrive the framing of it with the most exquisite skill. It is akin to the Hebrew word *amen,* which has the same letters as the verb to which Gesenius refers, only with different vowel points. How blessedly it describes Him who could be relied upon to carry out the Father's purpose!

"And I was daily his delight, rejoicing always before him" (v. 30).

It is not absolutely the mutual eternal delight of the Father and the Son, arising from the perfection of the same Divine excellency in each person that is intended. But respect is plainly had unto the counsels of God concerning the salvation of mankind by Him who is His "Wisdom" and "Power" unto that end. The counsel of "peace" was between Jehovah and the Branch (Zechariah 6:13), or the Father and the Son as He was to become incarnate. For therein was He "foreordained before the foundation of the world" (1 Peter 1:20), namely, to be a Saviour and Deliverer, by whom all the counsels of God were to be accomplished, and this by His own will and concurrence with the Father. And such a foundation was laid of the salvation of the Church in those counsels of God, as transacted between the Father and the Son, that it is said (Titus 1:2), "eternal life" was "promised before the world began." (J. Owen)

Chapter 32

THE SERVITUDE OF CHRIST

God has many servants, not only on earth, but also in heaven. The angels are "all ministering spirits" (Hebrews 1:14) who "do his commandments, hearkening unto the voice of his word" (Psalm 103:20). But what we now contemplate is not any servant of God or from God, but something infinitely more blessed and amazing, the Divine Servant Himself. What a remarkable phenomenon, an anomaly in any other connection. Yes, what amounts to a contradiction in terms, for supremacy and subordination, Godhood and servanthood are opposites. Yet this is the surprising conjunction Holy Writ sets before us: that the Most High abased Himself; the Lord of glory assumed the form of a menial; the King of kings became a subject. Most of us at least were taught from childhood that the Son of God took unto Himself our nature and was born as a Babe at Bethlehem. Perhaps our familiarity with this tended to blunt our sense of wonderment at it. Let us ponder not so much the miracle or mystery of the Divine Incarnation, but the fact itself.

"Behold, my servant shall deal prudently, he shall be exalted and extolled, and be very high" (Isaiah 52:13). There are four things here. First, the note

of exclamation, "Behold"; second, the subject, the divine "servant"; third, the perfection of His work, "shall deal prudently"; fourth, the reward bestowed upon Him, "he shall be exalted and extolled." The opening, "behold," is not only a call for us to focus our gaze upon and adoringly consider the One before us, but also and primarily as an exclamation or note of wonderment. What an amazing spectacle to see the Maker of heaven and earth in the form of a Servant, the Giver of the Law Himself become subject to it. What an astonishing phenomenon that the Lord of Glory should take upon Him such an office. How this ought to stir our souls. "Behold!" Wonder at it, be filled with holy awe, and then consider what our response ought to be.

"Behold, my servant." None other than the Father Himself owns Christ in this office. This is most blessed, for it is in sharp contrast from the treatment He received at the hands of men. It was because the Messiah appeared in servant form that the Jews despised and rejected Him. "Is not this the carpenter, the son of Mary.... And they were offended at him" (Mark 6:3). Apparently the holy angels were nonplused at such an incredible sight, for they received, and needed, the divine order, "Let all the angels of God worship him" when He brought His first begotten into the world (Hebrews 1:6). "Let," as though they were uncertain, as well they might be now that their Maker had assumed creature form; "all the angels of God," none excepted, the highest as well as the lowest, archangel, cherubim, seraphim, principalities, and powers; "worship him," render homage and praise unto Him, for far from His self-abasement having tarnished His personal glory, it enhanced it.

How blessed to hear the Father testifying of His approbation of the One who had entered Bethlehem's manger, bidding the angels not to be staggered by so unparalleled a sight, but to continue worshiping the second Person in the Holy Trinity even though He now wore a menial garb. Nor has the Holy Spirit failed to record their obedience, for He has told us that while the shepherds were keeping watch over their flock by night, a celestial messenger announced the Saviour's birth, "And suddenly there was with the angel a multitude of the heavenly host praising God, and saying, Glory to God in the highest, and on earth peace, good will toward men" (Luke 2:13–14). How jealous the Father was of His incarnate Son's honor! It was evidenced again when He condescended to be baptized in the Jordan, for "the heavens were opened unto him," the Spirit of God descended like a dove and abode upon Him, and the

Father declared, "This is my beloved Son, in whom I am well pleased" (Matthew 3:16–17). "Behold, my servant," He says to us.

"Shall deal prudently." Here we need to be on our guard, lest we interpret carnally. In the judgment of the world, to "deal prudently" is to act tactfully. Nine times out of ten tact is nothing more than a compromise of principle. Measured by the standards of unregenerate "policy," Christ acted very imprudently. He could have spared Himself much suffering had He been "less extreme" and followed the religious tide of His day. He could have avoided much opposition had He been milder in His denunciations of the Pharisees or withheld those aspects of the truth which are most distasteful to the natural man. Had He been more tactful as this evil generation considers things, He had never overthrown the tables of the money changers in the temple and charged such unholy traffickers with making His Father's house "a den of thieves," for it was then He began to "make so much trouble for Himself." But from the spiritual viewpoint, from the angle of ever having the Father's glory in view, from the side of seeking the eternal good of His own, Christ ever dealt "prudently." None other than the Father testifies to the fact.

Instead of illustrating where Christ dealt "prudently," we have sought to dispose of a general misconception and warn against interpreting that expression in a fleshly manner. It is true the Christian may, in rashness or acting with a zeal that is not according to knowledge, bring upon himself much unnecessary trouble; yet if he is faithful to God and uncompromising in his separation from the world, he is certain to incur the hatred and opposition of the ungodly. He must expect religious professors to tell him he has only himself to blame, that his lack of tact has made things so unpleasant for him. Christ's dealing prudently means He acted wisely. He never erred, never acted foolishly, never did anything which needed to be corrected; but the wisdom from which He acted was not of this world, but was "from above," and therefore was "pure, then peaceable, gentle" (James 3:17). Oh, for more of such prudence—obtained by communion with Christ, drinking in of His Spirit.

"He shall be exalted and extolled, and be very high." This tells of the reward given Christ for His willingness to become a "servant" and for His faithfulness in discharging that office. It tells us first of the Father's own valuation of His Son's condescension and of the recompense He has made the One who became obedient unto death. "Wherefore God also hath highly exalted him, and given him a name which is above every

name: that at the name of Jesus every knee should bow, of things in heaven, and things in earth, and things under the earth; and that every tongue should confess that Jesus Christ is Lord, to the glory of God the Father" (Philippians 2:9–11). The perfect Servant has been exalted to the Throne, seated "on the right hand of the Majesty on high" (Hebrews 1:3), "angels and authorities and powers being made subject unto him" (1 Peter 3:22). It tells also of Christ's exaltation in the affections of His people. Nothing endears the Redeemer more to their hearts than the realization that it was for their sakes He "became poor" and abased Himself. "Worthy is the Lamb that was slain to receive power, and riches, and wisdom, and strength, and honour, and glory, and blessing" (Revelation 5:12) is their united testimony.

Chapter 33

THE DESPISEMENT OF CHRIST

"He is despised and rejected of men" (Isaiah 53:3) forms part one of the messianic predictions. God made known long beforehand the treatment His Son would receive when He became incarnate. The prophecy of Isaiah was in the hands of the Jews seven hundred years before Jesus was born at Bethlehem; yet, so exactly did it describe what befell Him that it might well have been written by one of the apostles. Here is one of the incontrovertible proofs of the divine inspiration of Scriptures, for only One who knew the end from the beginning could have written this history beforehand.

It might have been supposed that the coming to earth of the Lord of glory would meet with a warm welcome and reverent reception; and more so in view of His appearing in human form and His going about doing good. Since He came not to judge, but to save; since His mission was one of grace and mercy; since He ministered to the needy and healed the sick, will not men gladly receive Him? Many would naturally think so, but in so doing they overlook the fact that the Lord Jesus is "the Holy One." None but those who have the principle of holiness in their hearts can appreciate ineffable Purity. Such an assumption as just mentioned ignores the solemn fact of human depravity: the heart of fallen man is "desperately wicked" (Jeremiah 17:9). How can the Holy One appear attractive to those who are full of sin!

Nothing so clearly evidences the condition of the human heart, nor so solemnly demonstrates its corruption, as its attitude toward Christ. Much is recorded against man in the Old Testament (see Psalm 14:1–4); yet, dark as its picture is of fallen human nature, it fades into insignificance before what the New Testament sets before us. "The carnal mind is enmity against God" (Romans 8:7). Never was this so frightfully patent as when He was manifested in flesh. "If I had not come, and spoken unto them, they had not had sin: but now they have no cloke for their sin" (John 15:22). The appearing of Christ fully exposed man and brings to light as nothing else has the desperate wickedness of his heart. Let us consider three questions: Who was (and still is) "despised and rejected of men"? Why is He so grievously slighted? In what way is He scorned?

Who was so unwelcome here? First, the One who pressed upon men the absolute sovereignty of God. Few things are so distasteful to the proud human heart as the truth that God does as He pleases, without consulting with the creature; that He dispenses His favors entirely according to His imperial will. Fallen man has no claims upon Him, is destitute of any merit, and can do nothing whatever to win God's esteem. Fallen man is a spiritual pauper, entirely dependent upon divine charity. In bestowing His mercies, God is regulated by nothing but His own "good pleasure" (Luke 12:32; Ephesians 1:5, 9; Philippians 2:13; 2 Thessalonians 1:11). "Is it not lawful for me to do what I will with mine own?" (Matthew 20:15) is His unanswerable challenge; yet, as the context shows, man wickedly murmurs against this.

The Lord Jesus came to glorify His Father; therefore we find Him maintaining His crown-rights and emphasizing His sovereignty. In His first message, in the Capernaum synagogue, He pointed out there were many widows in Israel during the days of Elijah. But when there was great famine throughout the land, the prophet was not sent to any but one at Zarephath; and though there were many lepers in Israel in the time of Elisha, none were healed, except by distinguishing mercy shown to Naaman, the Syrian. The sequel was "All they in the synagogue, when they heard these things, were filled with wrath, and rose up, and thrust him out of the city, and led him unto the brow of the hill whereon their city was built, that they might cast him down headlong" (Luke 4:28–29). For pressing the truth of God's absolute sovereignty, Christ was "despised and rejected of men."

Who was so unwelcome here? Second, the One who upheld God's Law. In it is the divine authority expressed, and complete subjection to it is required from the creature; thus Christ pressed the demands of God's Law upon man. "Think not that I am come to destroy the law, or the prophets: I am not come to destroy, but to fulfil" (Matthew 5:17); "All things whatsoever ye would that men should do to you, do ye even so to them: for this is the law and the prophets" (7:12). But fallen men resent restraints and want to be a law unto themselves. Their language concerning God and His Christ is "Let us break their bands asunder, and cast away their cords from us" (Psalm 2:3). Because the Lord Jesus enforced the requirements of the Decalogue He was "despised and rejected of men." A solemn illustration of this occurs when He spoke to the Jews: "Did not Moses give you the law, and yet none of you keepeth the law? Why go ye about to kill me?" (John 7:19). What was their response? "The people answered and said, Thou hast a devil" (v. 20).

Who was so unwelcome here? Third, the One who denounced human tradition in the religious sphere. Despite the Fall, man is essentially a religious creature. The image of God in which he was originally created has not been completely destroyed. The world over, people from all nations and people groups pay homage to gods of their own devising; there are few things on which they are more tender than their sacerdotal superstitions. He who condemns, or even criticizes, the devotees of any form or order of worship will be greatly disliked. Christ drew upon Himself the hatred of Israel's leaders by His denunciation of their inventions. He charged them with "making the word of God of none effect through [their] tradition" (Mark 7:13). When He cleansed the temple, the chief priests and scribes were "sore displeased" (Matthew 21:15).

Who was so unwelcome here? Fourth, the One who repudiated an empty profession. Nothing so infuriated the Jews as Christ's exposure and denunciation of their vain pretensions. Since He was omniscient, it was impossible to impose upon Him; inflexibly righteous, He could not accept deceptions; absolutely holy, He must insist upon sincerity and reality. When they declared, "Abraham is our father," He answered, "If ye were Abraham's children, ye would do the works of Abraham." When they added, "We have one Father, even God," He replied, "If God were your Father, ye would love me. . . . Ye are of your father the devil, and the lusts of your father ye will do." This so riled them that they exclaimed, "Say we not well that thou art a Samaritan, and hast a devil?" (John 8:39–48).

On another occasion, the Jews asked Him, "How long dost thou make us to doubt? If thou be the Christ, tell us plainly" (John 10:24). He at once exposed their hypocrisy by saying, "I told you, and ye believed not. . . . But ye believe not, because ye are not of my sheep. . . . My sheep hear my voice, and I know them, and they follow me" (vv. 25–27). They were so angry they "took up stones again to stone him" (v. 31). Men will not tolerate One who pierces their religious disguise, exposes their shams, and repudiates their fair but empty profession. It is the same to-day.

Who was so unwelcome here? Fifth, the One who exposed and denounced sin. This explains why Christ was not wanted here. He was a constant thorn in their sides. His holiness condemned their unholiness. Men wish to go their own way, to please themselves, to gratify their lusts. They want to be comfortable in their wickedness; therefore, they resent that which searches the heart, pierces the conscience, rebukes their evil. Christ was absolutely uncompromising. He would not wink at wrongdoing but unsparingly denounced it, in whomever He found it. He boldly affirmed, "For judgment I am come into this world" (John 9:39), that is, to discover men's secret characters, to prove they are blind in spiritual things, to demonstrate they love darkness rather than light. His Person and preaching tested everything and everyone with whom He came into contact.

Why was (and is) Christ "despised and rejected of men"? First, because He required inward purity. Here is the great difference between all human religions and divine: the former concern themselves with external performances; the latter with the source of all conduct. "Man looketh on the outward appearance, but the LORD looketh on the heart" (1 Samuel 16:7). Christ's exposition and enforcement of this truth made Him unpopular with the leaders.

> Woe unto you, scribes and Pharisees, hypocrites! for ye make clean the outside of the cup and of the platter, but within they are full of extortion and excess. Thou blind Pharisee, cleanse first that which is within the cup

and platter, that the outside of them may be clean also. Woe unto you, scribes and Pharisees, hypocrites! for ye are like unto whited sepulchres, which indeed appear beautiful outward, but are within full of dead men's bones, and of all uncleanness. Even so ye also outwardly appear righteous unto men, but within ye are full of hypocrisy and iniquity. (Matthew 23:25–28)

Why was Christ "despised and rejected of men"? Second, because He demanded repentance. "Repent ye, and believe the gospel" (Mark 1:15) was His demanding call. That order is unchanging, for it is impossible to believe the Gospel till the heart be contrite. Repentance is taking sides with God against ourselves. It is the unsparing judgment of ourselves because of our high-handed rebellion. It is a ceasing to love and tolerate sin, and to excuse ourselves for committing it. It is a mourning before God because of our transgressions of His holy Law. Therefore, Christ taught, "Except ye repent, ye shall all likewise perish" (Luke 13:3), for He would not condone evil. He came to save His people *from* their sins, and not in them.

Why was Christ "despised and rejected of men"? Third, because He insisted on the denial of self. This is on two principal points, namely, indulging and exalting of self. All fleshly lusts are to be unsparingly mortified, and self-righteousness is allowed no place in the gospel scheme. This was unmistakably plain in our Lord's teaching: "If any man will come after me, let him deny himself, and take up his cross, and follow me" (Matthew 16:24). Yet nothing is more contrary to the desires of the natural man, and Christ's insistence upon these terms of discipleship causes Him to be despised and rejected of men.

How is Christ "despised and rejected of men"? In different ways, and in varying degrees: professedly and practically, in words and in works. It is most important to clearly recognize this, for Satan deceives a great many souls at this point. He deludes them into supposing that because they are not guilty of what pertains to the avowed infidel and blatant atheist, therefore they are innocent of the fearful sin of slighting and defying the Lord Jesus. My reader, the solemn fact remains that there are millions of people in Christendom who, though not atheists and infidels, yet despise and reject the Christ of God. "They profess that they know God; but in works they deny him, being abominable, and disobedient, and unto every good work reprobate" (Titus 1:16). That verse clearly enunciates the principle.

Christ's authority is "despised" by those who disregard His precepts and commandments. Christ's yoke is "rejected" by those who are determined to be lord over themselves. Christ's glory is "despised" by those who bear His name yet have no concern whether their walk honors Him or not. Christ's Gospel is "rejected" by those who on the one hand affirm that sinners may be saved without repenting of and turning away from their sins, and on the other hand by those who teach heaven may be won by our own good works.

There are some who intellectually reject Christ by repudiating His claims, denying that He is God the Son, assumed a holy and impeccable humanity, and died a vicarious death to save His people from their sins. Others virtually and practically reject Christ. There are those who profess to believe in the existence of God, own His power, and talk about His wondrous handiwork; yet they have not His fear upon them and are not in subjection to Him. So there are many who claim to trust in the finished work of Christ, yet their daily walk is no different from that of thousands of respectable worldlings. They profess to be Christians; yet are covetous, unscrupulous, untruthful, proud, self-willed, uncharitable; in a word, utterly unchristian.

Chapter 34

THE CRUCIFIXION OF CHRIST

"They crucified him. . . . And sitting down they watched him there" (Matthew 27:35–36). The reference is to Roman soldiers, as is clear from John 19:23 and confirmed by Matthew 27:54. They were authorized to carry out the death sentence passed by Pilate, and into their hands the governor had delivered the Saviour (vv. 26–27). With coarse scurrility they executed the task. Adding insult to injury, they exposed the Lord Jesus to the indignities of a mock coronation: robing Him in scarlet, crowning Him with thorns, hailing Him as King of the Jews. Giving full expression to their enmity, they spat upon Him, smote Him with a reed, and mocked Him. Restoring to Him His raiment, they conducted Him to Golgotha and affixed Him to the cross. Having gambled for His garments, they sat down to watch Him to frustrate any attempt at rescue His friends might make and to wait until life was extinct. Let us note three things:

First, *the circumstances.* The religious leaders of Israel had taken the initiative, for there "assembled together the chief priests, and the scribes, and the elders of the people, unto the palace of the high priest, who was called Caiaphas, and consulted that they might take Jesus by subtilty, and kill him" (Matthew 26:3–4). How many of the foulest crimes which have blackened the pages of history were perpetrated by ecclesiastical dignitaries. Yet the common people were in full accord with their leaders, for "the multitude" (Mark 15:8) requested Pilate to adhere to his custom of releasing a prisoner to them. When he gave them the choice between Christ and Barabbas, they preferred the latter; and when the governor asked what was their pleasure concerning the former, they cried, "Crucify him" (15:13). It was to "content the people" that Pilate released Barabbas (v. 15). When Pilate reasoned with them, "all the people . . . said, His blood be on us, and on our children" (Matthew 27:25). And Pilate, the administrator of the Roman law, which boasted of justice, acceded to their unjust demands.

Second, *the scene.* It was the outskirts of Jerusalem, a city more memorable than either Rome, London, or New York; the residence of David, the royal city, the seat of Israel's kings. The city witnessed the magnificence of Solomon's reign, and here the temple stood. Here the Lord Jesus had taught and wrought miracles, and into this city He had ridden a few days earlier, seated upon a donkey as the multitudes cried, "Hosanna to the son of David: Blessed is he that cometh in the name of the Lord; Hosanna in the highest" (Matthew 21:9)—so fickle is human nature. Israel had rejected their King, and therefore He was conducted beyond the bounds of the city, so that He "suffered without the gate" (Hebrews 13:12). The actual place of the crucifixion was Golgotha, signifying "the place of a skull." Nature had anticipated the awful deed, since the contour of the ground resembled a death's head. Luke gives the Gentile name "Calvary" (Luke 23:33), for the guilt of that death rested on both Jew and Gentile.

Third, *the time.* This was as significant and suggestive as the historical and topographical associations of the place itself. Christ was crucified on the fourteenth of Nisan, or about the beginning of April. It was the first of Israel's great national feasts, the most important season in the Jewish year. It was the Passover, a solemn celebration of that night when all the firstborn sons of the Hebrews were spared from the Angel of Death in the land of Egypt. At this season great multitudes thronged Jerusalem, for it was one of the three annual occasions when every male Israelite was commanded to appear before Jehovah in the temple (Deuteronomy 16:16). Thus, huge crowds had journeyed there from all parts of the land.

It was in no obscure corner nor in secret that the Great Sacrifice was offered up to God. And the fourteenth of Nisan was the day appointed for it, for the Lord Jesus was the antitypical Lamb. "Christ our passover is sacrificed for us" (1 Corinthians 5:7). On no other day could He be slain. At an earlier date they "sought to take him: but no man laid hands on him, because his hour was not yet come" (John 7:30).

"They crucified him. . . . And sitting down they watched him there." My divisions are simple: What they saw; What I see; What do you see?

WHAT THEY SAW

They beheld the most amazing event of all history, the most awe-inspiring spectacle men ever saw, the most tragic and yet the most glorious deed ever performed. They beheld God incarnate taken by wicked hands and slain—and at the same time the Redeemer voluntarily laying down His life for those who have forfeited every claim upon Him. To the soldiers it was an ordinary event, the execution of a criminal; and thus it is with most who hear the Gospel. It falls on their ears as a religious commonplace. To the Roman soldiers, at least for a while, Christ appeared only as a dying Jew; thus it is with the multitude today.

They beheld the incomparable perfections of the Crucified One. How immeasurably different the mien of the suffering Saviour from what they had witnessed from others in similar circumstances! No cursing of His lot, no reviling of His enemies, no maledictions upon themselves. The very reverse. His lips were engaged in prayer. "Father," He said, "forgive them; for they know not what they do" (Luke 23:34). How amazed they must have been as they heard the Blessed One on the tree making "intercession for the transgressors" (Isaiah 53:12). The two thieves crucified with Him mocked the Redeemer (Matthew 27:44); but at the eleventh hour one of them was "granted repentance unto life" (Acts 11:18). Turning to Jesus, he said, "Lord, remember me when thou comest into thy kingdom" (Luke 23:42). The Lord did not decline his appeal and say, "You have sinned beyond the reach of mercy"; but answered, "Verily I say unto thee, To day shalt thou be with me in paradise" (v. 43). They witnessed an unparalleled display of sovereign grace to one of the greatest of sinners.

They beheld the most mysterious phenomena. They sat down to "watch Him," but after a while they were no longer able to do so. At midday it suddenly became midnight. "From the sixth hour [after sunrise] there was darkness over all the land unto the ninth hour" (Matthew 27:45). It was as though the sun refused to shine on such a scene, as though nature itself mourned over such a sight. During those three hours a transaction took place between Christ and God which was infinitely too sacred for finite eyes to gaze upon, a mystery which no mortal mind can fully enter. As soon as the Saviour committed His spirit into the hands of the Father, "behold, the veil of the temple was rent in twain from the top to the bottom; and the earth did quake, and the rocks rent; and the graves were opened; and many bodies of the saints which slept arose" (vv. 51–52). This was no ordinary sufferer; it was the Creator of heaven and earth, and heaven and earth expressed their sympathy.

They beheld and heard what was blessed to their conviction and conversion. Pharaoh witnessed a most remarkable display of God's power in the plagues which He sent upon Egypt, but far from inclining him to repentance he continued to harden his heart. Thus it always is with the unregenerate while they are left to themselves; neither the most astonishing tokens of God's goodness nor the most awe-inspiring of judgments melt them. But God was pleased to soften the callous hearts of these Roman soldiers and illumine their heathen minds. "Now when the centurion, and they that were with him, watching Jesus, saw the earthquake, and those things that were done, they feared greatly, saying, Truly this was the Son of God" (Matthew 27:54). We regard this as another of the miracles at Calvary—a miracle of amazing grace. And we expect to meet in heaven the man who hammered the nails into the Saviour's hands and thrust the spear into His side—God's answer to Christ's prayer, "Father, forgive them." So there is hope for the vilest sinner if he will surrender to the Lordship of Christ and trust in His blood.

WHAT I SEE

I see an unveiling of the character of man. "All things that are discovered [marginal reading] are made manifest by the light: for whatsoever doth make manifest is light" (Ephesians 5:13). Christ is "the true Light" (John 1:9)—the essential, divine, all-revealing light; consequently, all men and all things stand exposed in His presence. The worst things predicated in Scripture of fallen human nature were exemplified in the days of Christ. God says that "the heart [of man] is . . . desperately wicked" (Jeremiah 17:9), and it was so demonstrated by the treatment of His beloved Son. Scarcely was He born into this world than men made a determined effort to slay Him. Though He constantly went about doing good, relieving the distressed, and ministering to the souls and bodies of the needy, He was so little appreciated that He had to say, "The foxes have holes, and the birds of the air have nests; but the Son of man hath not where to lay his head" (Matthew 8:20). On one occasion "they besought him that he would depart out of their coasts" (v. 34).

Not only was Christ unwelcome here, but also men hated Him "without a cause" (John 15:25). He gave them every reason to admire Him, but they had an inveterate aversion for Him. The Word declares, "The carnal mind is enmity against God" (Romans 8:7). Multitudes go through the form of paying homage to God, but of a "god" of their own imagination. They hate the living God, and, were it possible, would rid the universe of Him. This is clear from their treatment of Christ, for He was none other than "God . . . manifest in the flesh" (1 Timothy 3:16). They hated and hounded Him to death, and nothing short of death by crucifixion would appease them. At Calvary the real character of man was revealed, and the desperate wickedness of his heart laid bare.

I see an unveiling of sin. Sin! That "abominable thing," which the Lord hates (Jeremiah 44:4), is regarded so lightly by those who commit it. Sin! It caused our first parents to be banished from Eden and is responsible for all the woe in the world. Sin! It produces strife and bloodshed and has turned this "land of the living" into a mammoth cemetery. Sin! A hideous monster we so much dislike hearing about and which we are so ready to excuse. Sin! Satan employs all his subtle arts to render it attractive and sets it forth in the most appealing colors. One of the great designs of the Incarnation was to bring to light the hidden things of darkness. The presence here of the Holy One served as a brilliant light in a long-neglected room, revealing its squalor and filth. "If I had not come and spoken unto them, they had not had sin: but now they have no cloke for their sin" (John 15:22).

Christ here spoke *comparatively*. Evil as man had shown himself through history; the coming of Immanuel to earth brought sin to a head. All that had gone before was a trifling thing when compared to the monstrous wickedness done against Love incarnate. In the treatment the Son of God received at the hands of men we see sin in its true colors, stripped of all disguise, exposed in all its hideous reality, in its true nature as rebellion against God. At Calvary we behold the climax of sin, the fearful, horrible lengths to which it is capable of going. What germinated in Eden culminated in the Crucifixion. The first sin occasioned spiritual suicide; the second, fratricide (Cain murdered his brother); but here at Calvary it resulted in Deicide, the slaying of the Lord of glory. We also see the fearful wages of sin—death and separation from God. Since Christ hung there as the Sinbearer, He received the punishment due to them.

I see an unveiling of the character of God. The heavens declare His glory and the firmament shows His handiwork, but nowhere are His perfections more prominently displayed than at the cross. Here is His ineffable holiness. The holiness of God is the delight He has in all that is pure and lovely; therefore, His nature burns against whatever is evil. God hates sin wherever it is found, and He made no exception of Christ when He saw it imputed on His beloved Son. There God "laid on him the iniquity of us all" (Isaiah 53:6). He dealt with Him accordingly, pouring out His holy wrath upon Him. God is "of purer eyes than to behold evil, and canst not look on iniquity" (Habakkuk 1:13); therefore He turned His back on the Sinbearer. "My God, my God, why hast thou forsaken me?" the suffering Saviour cried, then answered His own query, "Thou art holy" (Psalm 22:1, 3).

I see God's inflexible justice. The pronouncement of His Law is this: "The soul that sinneth, it shall die" (Ezekiel 18:4, 20). No deviation from it can be made, for Jehovah has expressly declared He "will by no means clear the guilty" (Exodus 34:7). But will He not make an exception if the One who He testifies is the Lamb "without blemish and without spot" (1 Peter 1:19)? No! For though Christ was sinless both by nature and action, because the sins of His people had been laid upon Him God "spared not his own Son" (Romans 8:32). Because sin was transferred to Him, punishment must be visited upon Him. Therefore, God cried, "Awake, O sword, against my shepherd, and against the man that is my fellow, saith the Lord of hosts: smite the shepherd" (Zechariah 13:7). God would not abate one iota of His righteous demand or allow sentiment to sully the fair face of His government. He claims to be *par excellence* the Judge who is without "respect of persons" (2 Chronicles 19:7; Romans 2:11; Ephesians 6:9; 1 Peter 1:17). How fully that was demonstrated at Calvary by His refusal to exempt the person of His Beloved, the One in whom His soul delighted (Isaiah 42:1), when He occupied the place of the guilty.

I see God's amazing grace. "God commendeth his love toward us [His people], in that, while we were yet sinners, Christ died for us" (Romans 5:8). Had He so pleased, God could have consigned the whole of Adam's race to everlasting woe. That is what each of us richly deserves. And why should He not do so? By nature we are depraved and corrupt; by practice incorrigible rebels, with no love for Him nor concern for His glory. But out of His own goodness He determined to save a people from their sins, to redeem them by Christ "to the praise of the glory of his grace" (Ephesians 1:6). He determined to pluck them as brands from the burning so they might be the eternal monuments of His mercy. Because it was wholly outside their power to make atonement for their fearful crimes, He Himself provided an all-sufficient sacrifice for them. He is "the God of all grace" (1 Peter 5:10) and He has given innumerable tokens of this. But nowhere were the "riches of His grace" so lavishly and wondrously displayed as at Calvary.

See here God's *manifold wisdom.* The Word declares, "There shall in no wise enter into it any thing that defileth, neither whatsoever worketh abomination" (Revelation 21:27); then how is it possible that I can ever gain admittance into the heavenly Jerusalem? How can it be that one so completely devoid of righteousness could ever receive divine approbation? The Law says, "The soul that sinneth, it shall die." I have sinned and broken the Law; how then can I escape its penalty? Since I am a spiritual pauper, how can the necessary ransom be procured? These are problems that no human intelligence can solve. Nor is the knot to be cut by an appeal to the bare mercy of God, for His mercy is not an attribute which overrides His justice and integrity. But at the Cross the divine perfections shone out in glorious unity like the blending of the colors in the rainbow. There, "mercy and truth are met together; righteousness and peace have kissed each other" (Psalm 85:10). God's justice was satisfied by Christ, and therefore His mercy flows freely to all who repent and believe. The wisdom of God appears in creation and providence, but nowhere so grandly as at the cross.

I see myself. What? Yes, as I turn my gaze to the cross I behold myself, and so does everyone who looks with the eye of faith. Christ hung there as the Surety of His people, and there cannot be representation without identification. Christ identified with those whose sins He bears, believers identified with Him. In the sight of God they are one. Christ took my place, and faith appropriates that fact. In the Person of my Substitute I satisfied every requirement of God's Law. In the Person of Christ I paid the full price which divine justice demanded. In the Person of Christ I stand approved before God, for I am clothed with His meritorious perfections (Isaiah 61:10). The whole ransomed Church of God can say of Christ, "He was wounded for our transgressions, he was bruised for our iniquities" (53:5), "Who his own self bare our sins in his own body on the tree" (1 Peter 2:24). And faith individualizes it and declares, "I am crucified with Christ . . . who loved me, and gave himself for me" (Galatians 2:20). Hallelujah! What a Saviour.

WHAT DO YOU SEE?

You behold One whom you despise and reject, if you are unsaved. Perhaps you deny it, saying my attitude is merely negative. You err. If you are not the friend of Christ you are His enemy. There is no third class. "He that is not with me is against me" (Matthew 12:30) is His own verdict, and from that there is no appeal. You have despised His authority, flouted His laws, treated His claims with contempt. You reject His yoke and scepter and refuse to be ruled by Him; thus you unite with those who cast Him out and hounded Him to death.

You behold One who is presented as Saviour. Yes, despite your wicked treatment of Him hitherto, He is set before you in the Gospel as One willing and able to heal the wounds sin has made and to save your soul from eternal death. If you will throw down the weapons of your warfare against Him, surrender to His Lordship, and trust in His redeeming blood, He will accept you now. "Him that cometh to me I will in no wise cast out" (John 6:37).

You behold the One who is to be your Judge if you refuse to accept Him as Saviour. Come to Him now as a repentant sinner, as a spiritual pauper, casting yourself upon His grace, and He will pardon your iniquities and give you a royal welcome. "Come unto me, all ye that labour and are heavy laden, and I will give you rest" (Matthew 11:28) is His own invitation with promise. But continue to turn your back upon Him, and one day He will say to you, "Depart from me, ye cursed, into everlasting fire, prepared for the devil and his angels" (25:41).

Chapter 35

THE REDEMPTION OF CHRIST

Our righteous Redeemer—does such a title have a strange sound to the reader? Is that adjective unfamiliar in such a context? The great majority of us probably are far more accustomed to such expressions as "our loving Redeemer" and "our gracious Redeemer," or even "our mighty Redeemer." We employ the term here not because we are striving for originality. No, rather such an appellation is required by the teaching of Scripture. In fact, if we carefully observe where the Holy Spirit has placed His emphasis it is incumbent on us that we should conform our terminology thereto. See how many passages you can recall where either *loving* or *gracious* is used as an adjective in connection with Christ. If memory fails, consult a concordance, and you will be surprised that neither of them occurs a single time! Now try the word *righteous* and see how many passages refer to the Lord Jesus as such.

Christ is referred to as "my righteous servant" (Isaiah 53:11); as "a righteous Branch" (Jeremiah 23:5); and in the next verse as "THE LORD OUR RIGHTEOUSNESS"; as "the Sun of righteousness" (Malachi 4:2); as a "righteous man" (Luke 23:47); as "the righteous judge" (2 Timothy 4:8). He is seen as the antitypical Melchizedek, or "King of righteousness" ("Melchisedec," KJV; Hebrews 7:1–3); as our "advocate with the Father, Jesus Christ the righteous" (1 John 2:1). In addition, the same Greek word *dikaios* is rendered "just" in the following passages: Pilate's wife sent a warning to her husband, "Have thou nothing to do with that just [righteous] man" (Matthew 27:19); in the same chapter Pilate himself declared, "I am innocent of the blood of this just person" (v. 24). He is called "the Just" (Acts 3:14; James 5:6); and "the Just One" (Acts 7:52; 22:14); while in 1 Peter 3:18 are the well-known words, "Christ also hath once suffered for sins, the just for the unjust"—actually rendered "the righteous for the unrighteous" (RV). When Zechariah predicted His entry into Jerusalem, riding on a donkey, he said, "Behold, thy King cometh unto thee: he is just" (Zechariah 9:9; compare Matthew 21:5); in Revelation 19:11, where He is depicted on a white horse, it is said, "in righteousness he doth judge and make war."

In all of these passages, the Father's "fellow" and equal is viewed in His official character, as the God-man Mediator. Equally evident is that the verses intimate the Lord Jesus is righteous in His Person, in the administration of His office, in the discharge of the Great Commission given Him. Before His incarnation it was announced, "Righteousness shall be the girdle of his loins, and faithfulness the girdle of his reins" (Isaiah 11:5); and Christ affirmed by the spirit of prophecy, "I have preached righteousness in the great congregation" (Psalm 40:9). There was no fault or failure in His performing of the honored and momentous task committed to Him, as His own words to the Father prove: "I have glorified thee on the earth: I have finished the work which thou gavest me to do" (John 17:4). God's owning of Christ as "my righteous servant" signifies that He excellently executed the work entrusted to Him. As the Holy Spirit declares, He "was faithful to him that appointed him" (Hebrews 3:2). When the Father rewarded Him, He said, "Thou lovest righteousness, and hatest wickedness" (Psalm 45:7).

Further, Christ is the righteous Redeemer of His people because their righteousness is *in Him*. He wrought out a perfect righteousness for them. Upon their believing in Him, it is imputed or reckoned to their account; therefore He is designated "THE LORD OUR RIGHTEOUSNESS" (Jeremiah 23:6). Christ was righteous not as a private person, not for Himself alone, but for us sinners and our salvation. He acted as God's righteous Servant and as His people's righteous sponsor.

He lived and died that all the infinite merits of His obedience might be made over to them. In justifying His sinful people God neither disregarded nor dishonored His law; instead He "established" it (Romans 3:31). The Redeemer was "made under the law" (Galatians 4:4). Its strictness was not relaxed, nor was one iota of its requirements abated in connection with Him. Christ rendered to the Law a personal, perfect, and perpetual obedience; therefore He did "magnify the law, and make it honourable" (Isaiah 42:21). Consequently, God is not only gracious but "just" at the very moment He is "the justifier of him which believeth in Jesus" (Romans 3:26) because Jesus satisfied every requirement of righteousness on behalf of all who trust in Him.

In the righteous Redeemer we find the answer to the question, "How can those who have no righteousness of their own and who are utterly unable to procure any, become righteous before God?" How can man, who is a mass of corruption, draw nigh unto the ineffably Holy One and look up into His face in peace? He can do so by coming to God as unrighteous, acknowledging his inability to remove unrighteousness and offering nothing to palliate Him. Because we were unable to reach up to the holy requirements or righteousness of the Law, God brought His righteousness down to us: "I bring near my righteousness" (Isaiah 46:13). That righteousness was brought near to sinners when the Word became flesh and tabernacled among men; it is brought near to us in the Gospel, "for therein is the righteousness of God revealed from faith to faith" (Romans 1:17). This righteousness God imputes to all who believe and then deals with them according to its deserts.

"For he [God] hath made him [Christ] to be sin for us, who knew no sin; that we might be [not put into a capacity of acquiring a righteousness of our own, but] made the righteousness of God in him" (2 Corinthians 5:21). Here is the double imputation of our sins to Christ and of His righteousness to us. We are not said to be made righteous, but "righteousness" itself; and not righteousness only, but "the righteousness of God," the utmost that language can reach. In the same manner that Christ was made "sin," we are made "righteousness." Christ did not know actual sin, but in His mediatorial interposition on our behalf, He was dealt with as a guilty person. Likewise we are destitute of all legal righteousness; yet upon receiving Christ, we are viewed by the divine majesty as righteous creatures. Both were by imputation: an amazing exchange! So as to exclude the idea that any inherent righteousness is involved, it is said, "We [are] made the righteousness of God in him." As the sin imputed to Christ is inherent in us, so the righteousness by which we are justified is inherent in Him.

The divine plan of redemption fully satisfies the claims of the Law. There was nothing in all its sacred injunctions which Christ did not perform, nothing in its awful threatenings which He did not sustain. He fulfilled all its precepts by an unspotted purity of heart and a perfect integrity of life. He exhausted the whole curse when He hung on the cross, abandoned by God, for the sins of His people. His obedience conferred higher honor upon the Law than it could possibly have received from an uninterrupted compliance by Adam and his posterity. The perfections of God, which were dishonored by our rebellion, are glorified in our redemption. In redemption God appears inflexibly just in exacting vengeance and inconceivably rich in showing mercy. "The sword of justice and the sceptre of grace has each its due exercise, each its full expression" (James Hervey). The interests of holiness are also secured, for where redemption is received by faith it kindles in the heart an intense hatred of sin and the deepest love and gratitude to God.

Chapter 36

THE SAVIOURHOOD OF CHRIST

"My thoughts are not your thoughts, neither are your ways my ways, saith the LORD" (Isaiah 55:8). Solemnly these words manifest the terrible havoc sin has wrought in fallen mankind. They are out of touch with their Maker; nay more, they are alienated from the life of God through the ignorance that is in them, because of "the blindness of their heart" (Ephesians 4:18). As a consequence, the soul has lost its anchorage, everything has been thrown out of gear, and human depravity has turned all things upside down. Instead of subordinating the concerns of this life to the interests of the life to come, man devotes himself principally to the present and gives little or no thought to the eternal. Instead of putting the good of his soul ahead of the needs of the body, man is occupied chiefly about food and raiment. Instead of man's great aim being to please God, ministering to self has become his prime business.

Man's thoughts ought to be governed by God's Word, and his ways regulated by God's revealed will. But the converse is true. So the things which are of great price in the sight of God (1 Peter 3:4) are despised by the fallen creature, and "that which is highly esteemed among men is abomination in the sight of God" (Luke 16:15). Man has turned things topsy-turvy, sadly in evidence when he attempts to handle divine matters. The perversity which sin has caused appears in our *reversing* God's order. The Scripture speaks of man's "spirit and soul and body" (1 Thessalonians 5:23), but when the world refers to it, it says "body, soul, and spirit." Scripture declares that Christians are "strangers and pilgrims" in this scene; but nine times out of ten, even good men talk and write of "pilgrims and strangers."

This tendency to reverse God's order is part of fallen man's nature. Unless the Holy Spirit interposes and works a miracle of grace, its effects are fatal to the soul. Nowhere do we have a more tragic example of this than in the evangelistic message now being given, though scarcely anyone seems aware of it. That something is radically wrong with the world is widely recognized. That Christendom is in a sad state many are painfully conscious; that error abounds on every side, that practical godliness is at a low ebb, that worldliness has devitalized many churches, is apparent to increasing numbers. But few see *how* bad things are, few perceive that things are rotten to the very foundation; yet such is the case.

God's true way of salvation is little known today. The Gospel which is being preached, even in orthodox circles, is often an erroneous gospel. Even there man has *reversed* God's order. For many years it has been taught that nothing more is required for a sinner's salvation than to "accept Christ as his personal *Saviour*." Later, he ought to bow to Him as *Lord,* consecrate his life to Him, and serve Him fully. But even if he fails to do so, heaven is sure for him. He will lack peace and joy now, and probably miss some millennial crown; but having received Christ as his personal Saviour, he has been delivered from wrath to come. This is a reversal of God's order. It is the devil's lie, and only the day to come will show how many have been fatally deceived by it.

We are aware this is strong language, and it may come as a shock; but test it by this light: In nearly every passage where these two titles occur together, *Lord* appears before *Saviour* (Luke 1:46–47; 2 Peter 1:11; 2:20; 3:2, 18; Titus 1:4; contrast Luke 2:11; Philippians 3:20; 1 Timothy 1:1). Unless Jehovah had first become Mary's "Lord," most certainly He would not have been her "Saviour." No one who seriously ponders the matter has any difficulty perceiving this. How could a thrice-holy God save one who scorned His authority, despised His honor, and flouted His revealed will. It is infinite grace that God is ready to be reconciled to us when we throw the weapons of our rebellion against Him; but it would be an act of unrighteousness, putting a premium upon lawlessness, were He to pardon the sinner before he was first reconciled to His Maker.

The saints of God are bidden to make their "calling and election sure" (2 Peter 1:10), (and this, by adding to their faith the other graces enumerated in vv. 5–7). They are assured that if they do so they shall never fall, "for so an entrance shall be ministered [to them] abundantly into the everlasting kingdom of our [1] Lord and [2] Saviour Jesus Christ" (v. 11). But, again, particularly note *the order* in which Christ's titles are mentioned: it is not "our Saviour and Lord," but "Lord and Saviour." He becomes the *Saviour* of none until the heart and will unreservedly receive Him as *Lord*.

"For if after they have escaped the pollutions of the world through the knowledge of the Lord and Saviour Jesus Christ, they are again entangled therein, and overcome, the latter end is worse with them than the beginning" (2 Peter 2:20). Here the apostle refers to those who had a head knowledge of the Truth, and then apostatized. There had been a reformation outwardly in their lives, but no regeneration of the heart. For a while they were delivered from the pollution of the world, but with no supernatural work of grace having been wrought in their souls, the lustings of the flesh proved too strong. They were again overcome and returned to their former manner of life like the "dog [returning] to his own vomit" or the sow "to her wallowing in the mire" (v. 22). The apostasy is described as turning "from the holy commandment delivered unto them" (v. 21), which refers to the terms of discipleship made known in the Gospel. But what we are particularly concerned about is the Holy Spirit's order: these apostates had been favored with the "knowledge of [1] the Lord and [2] Saviour Jesus Christ."

God's people are exhorted to "grow in grace, and in the knowledge of our Lord and Saviour Jesus Christ" (2 Peter 3:18). Here again God's order is the opposite of man's. Nor is this merely a technical detail, concerning which a mistake is of little moment. No, the subject is basic, vital, and fundamental, and error at this point is fatal. Those who have not submitted to Christ as *Lord*, but who trust in Him as *Saviour* are deceived.

The same principle is illustrated in passages where other titles of Christ occur. Take the opening verse of the New Testament, Matthew

1:1, where He is presented as "Jesus Christ, [1] the son of David, [2] the son of Abraham." Waiving the dispensational signification of these titles, view them from the doctrinal and practical viewpoint, which should be our first consideration. "Son of David" brings in the throne, emphasizes His authority, and demands allegiance to His scepter. And "son of David" comes before "son of Abraham"! Again, we are told that God had exalted Jesus to his own right hand "to be [1] a Prince and [2] a Saviour" (Acts 5:31). The concept embodied in the title *Prince* is that of supreme dominion and authority, "The prince of the kings of the earth" (Revelation 1:5).

In the book of Acts we quickly discover that the message of the apostles was altogether different—not only in emphasis, but also in substance—from the preaching of our times. On the Day of Pentecost Peter declared, "Whosoever shall call on the name of the Lord shall be saved" (2:21), and reminded his hearers that God had made Jesus "both Lord and Christ" (v. 36), not Christ and Lord. To Cornelius and his household Peter presented Christ as "Lord of all" (10:36). When Barnabas came to Antioch, he "exhorted them all, that with purpose of heart they would cleave unto the Lord" (11:23); also Paul and Barnabas "commended them to the Lord, on whom they believed" (14:23). At the great synod in Jerusalem, Peter reminded his fellows that the Gentiles would "seek after [not only a Saviour, but] the Lord" (15:17). To the Philippian jailer and his household Paul and Silas preached "the word of the Lord" (16:32).

The apostles not only emphasized the Lordship of Christ, but also they made surrender to it essential to salvation. This is clear from many other passages: "And believers were the more added to [not Christ, but] the Lord" (Acts 5:14); "and all that dwelt at Lydda and Saron saw him, and turned to the Lord" (9:35); "and many believed in the Lord" (v. 42); "and much people was added unto the Lord" (11:24). "Then the deputy, when he saw what was done, believed, being astonished at the doctrine of the Lord" (13:12); "and Crispus, the chief ruler of the synagogue, believed on the Lord with all his house" (18:8).

Few today have a right conception of what a scriptural and saving conversion is. The call to it is set forth in Isaiah 55:7: "Let the wicked forsake his way, and the unrighteous man his thoughts: and let him return [having in Adam departed] unto the LORD, and he will have mercy upon him." The character of conversion is described in 1 Thessalonians

1:9, "Ye turned to God from idols to serve the living and true God." Conversion, then, is a turning from sin unto holiness, from self unto God, from Satan unto Christ. It is the voluntary surrender of ourselves to the Lord Jesus, not only by a consent of dependence upon His merits, but also by a willing readiness to obey Him, giving up the keys of our hearts and laying them at His feet. It is the soul declaring, "O LORD our God, other lords beside thee have had dominion over us [namely, the world, the flesh, and the devil]: but by thee only will we make mention of thy name" (Isaiah 26:13).

> Conversion consists in our being recovered from our present sinfulness to the moral image of God, or, which is the same thing, to a real conformity to the moral law. But a conformity to the moral law consists in a *disposition* to love God supremely, live to Him ultimately, and delight in Him superlatively, and to love our neighbor as ourselves; and *a practice agreeing thereto.* And therefore conversion consists in our being recovered from what we are by nature to such a disposition and practice. (James Bellamy, 1770)

Note the searching words in Acts 3:26, "Unto you first God, having raised up his Son Jesus, sent him to bless you, in turning away every one of you from his iniquities." This is Christ's way of blessing men—converting them. However the Gospel may instruct and enlighten men, so long as they remain the slaves of sin, it has conferred upon them no eternal advantage. "Know ye not, that to whom ye yield yourselves servants to obey, his servants ye are to whom ye obey; whether of sin unto death, or of obedience unto righteousness?" (Romans 6:16).

There is a very real difference between believing in the deity of Christ and surrendering to His lordship. Many are firmly persuaded that Jesus is the Son of God; they have no doubt He is the Maker of heaven and earth. But that is no proof of conversion. The demons owned Him as the "Son of God" (Matthew 8:29). What we press here is not the mind's assent to the Godhood of Christ, but the will's yielding to His authority, so that the life is regulated by His commandments. There must be a subjecting of ourselves to Him. The one is useless without the other. "He became the author of eternal salvation unto all them that obey him" (Hebrews 5:9).

Yet in the face of the clear teaching of Holy Writ, when unsaved people are concerned about their future destiny, and inquire, "What must we do to be saved?" the answer they are usually given is "Accept Christ as your personal Saviour." Little effort is made to press upon them (as Paul did the Philippian jailer) the Lordship of Christ. Many a blind leader of the blind glibly quotes, "But as many as received him, to them gave he power to become the sons of God" (John 1:12). Perhaps the leader objects, "But nothing is said there about receiving Christ as *Lord*." Directly, no; nor is anything said there about receiving Christ "as a personal *Saviour*"! It is a whole Christ which must be received, or none at all.

But if the objector will carefully ponder the context of John 1:12, he will quickly discover that it is as *Lord* Christ is presented, and as such must be received by us. In the previous verse it says, "He came unto his own, and his own received him not" (v. 11). In what character does that view Him? Clearly, as the Owner and Master of Israel; and it was as such they "received him not." Consider what He does for those who do receive Him: "To them gave he power [the right or prerogative] to become the sons of God" (v. 12). Who but the Lord of lords is vested with authority to give others the title to be sons of God!

In an unregenerate state, no sinner is subject to Christ as *Lord,* though he may be fully convinced of His deity and employ "Lord Jesus" when referring to Him. When we say that no unregenerate person "is subject to Christ as Lord," we mean that His will is not the rule of life; to please, obey, honor, and glorify Christ is not the dominant aim, disposition, and striving of the heart. Far from this being the case, his real sentiment is "Who is the LORD, that I should obey his voice?" (Exodus 5:2). The whole trend of his life is saying, "I will not have this man to reign over me" (see Luke 19:14). Despite all religious pretensions, the real attitude of the unregenerate toward God is "Depart from us; for we desire not the knowledge of thy ways. What is the Almighty, that we should serve [be in subjection to] him?" (Job 21:14–15). Their conduct intimates, "Our lips are our own: who is lord over us?" (Psalm 12:4). Instead of surrendering to God in Christ, every sinner turns "to his own way" (Isaiah 53:6), living only to please self.

When the Holy Spirit convicts of sin, He causes that person to see what sin really is. He makes the convicted one understand that sin is rebellion against God, a refusal to submit to the Lord. The Spirit causes him to realize that he has been an insurrectionist against Him who is exalted above all. He is now convicted not only of this sin, or that idol, but also is brought to realize his whole life has been a fighting against God; that he has knowingly, willfully, and constantly ignored and defied Him, deliberately choosing to go his own way. The work of the Spirit in God's elect is not so much to convince each of them they are lost sinners (the conscience of the natural man knows that, without any supernatural operation of the Spirit!); it is to reveal the exceeding "sinfulness of sin" (see Romans 7:13), by making us see and feel that all sin is a species of spiritual anarchy, a defiance of the Lordship of God.

When a man has really been convicted by the supernatural operation of the Holy Spirit, the first effect on him is complete and abject despair. His case appears to be utterly hopeless. He now sees he has sinned so grievously that it appears impossible for a righteous God to do anything but damn him for eternity. He sees what a fool he has been in heeding the voice of temptation, fighting against the Most High, and in losing his own soul. He recalls how often God has spoken to him in the past—as a child, as a youth, as an adult, upon a bed of sickness, in the death of a loved one, in adversities—and how he refused to listen and deliberately turned a deaf ear. He now feels he has sinned away his day of grace.

But the ground must be plowed and harrowed before it is receptive to seed. So the heart must be prepared by these harrowing experiences, the stubborn will broken, before it is ready for the healing of the Gospel. But how very few ever are savingly convicted by the Spirit! The Spirit continues His work in the soul, plowing still deeper, revealing the hideousness of sin, producing a horror of and hatred for it. The sinner next receives the beginning of hope, which results in an earnest inquiry, "What must I do to be saved?" Then the Spirit, who has come to earth to glorify Christ, presses upon that awakened soul the claims of His Lordship (see, for example, Luke 14:26–33) and makes us realize that Christ demands our hearts, lives, and all. Then He grants grace to the quickened soul to renounce all other lords, to turn away from all idols, and to receive Christ as Prophet, Priest, and King.

Nothing but the sovereign and supernatural work of the Spirit can bring this to pass. A preacher may induce a man to believe what Scripture says about his lost condition, persuade him to bow to the divine verdict, and then accept Christ as his personal Saviour. No man wants to go to hell, and if he is assured intellectually that Christ stands ready as a fire escape, on the sole condition that he jump into His arms ("rest on

His finished work"), thousands will do so. But a hundred preachers are unable to make an unregenerate person realize the dreadful nature of sin, or show him that he has been a lifelong rebel against God, or change his heart so that he now hates himself and longs to please God and serve Christ. Only the Spirit can bring man to the place where he is willing to forsake every idol, cut off a hindering right hand, or pluck out an offending right eye (see Matthew 5:27–30).

Probably some will say, "But the exhortations addressed to saints in the epistles show that it is Christians, and not the unsaved, who are to surrender to Christ's Lordship," citing Romans 12:1. Such a mistake only serves to demonstrate the gross spiritual darkness which has enveloped even orthodox Christendom. The exhortations of the Epistles simply signify that Christians are to continue as they began: "As ye have therefore received Christ Jesus the Lord, so walk ye in him" (Colossians 2:6). All the exhortations may be summed up in two words: "*Come* to Christ," "*Abide* in Him"; and what is abiding but coming to Christ constantly (1 Peter 2:4)? The saints (Romans 12:1) have already been bidden to "yield" themselves "unto God" (6:13). While we are on earth we will always need such admonitions. The backslidden church at Ephesus was told, "Repent, and do the first works" (Revelation 2:5).

And now a pointed question: Is Christ your Lord? Does He in fact occupy the throne of your heart? Does He actually rule your life? If not, then most certainly He is not your Saviour. Unless your heart has been renewed, unless grace has changed you from a lawless rebel to a loving subject, then you are yet in your sins, on the broad road to destruction.

Chapter 37

THE LORDSHIP OF CHRIST

ut sanctify in your hearts Christ as Lord" (1 Peter 3:15 RV). In view of the context it is striking to note that it was Peter whom the Spirit of God first moved to write these words. As he did so, his heart, no doubt, was filled with sorrow and deep contrition. He says, "If ye suffer for righteousness' sake, happy are ye: and be not afraid of their terror, neither be troubled" (v. 14). On a never-to-be forgotten occasion, he had been afraid of the "terror" of the wicked. In Pilate's palace the fear of man brought him a snare. But in our text he announces the divine remedy for deliverance from the fear of man.

"But sanctify in your hearts Christ as Lord." In the light of its setting, this means, first of all, to let the awe of the lordship of Christ possess your hearts. Dwell constantly on the fact that Christ is Lord. Because He is Lord, all power in heaven and earth is His; therefore, He is Master of every situation, sufficient for every emergency, able to supply every need. When a Christian trembles in the presence of his enemies, it is because he doubts or has lost sight of the faithfulness and power of Christ.

"But sanctify in your hearts Christ as Lord." The motive for obeying

this precept should not be our own peace and comfort, but His honor and glory. To guard against the fear of man, the saint is to cultivate the fear of the Lord, that Christ may be magnified. The Lord Jesus is glorified when His persecuted people preserve a calm demeanor and immovable fortitude in the face of all opposition. But this is possible only as our hearts are occupied with Him, and particularly with His lordship.

"But sanctify in your hearts Christ as Lord." These words have a wider application. How little professing Christians dwell on the lordship of Christ! How sadly inadequate are the real Christian's views of that One who has a name which is above every name! "That I may know [obtain a better knowledge of] him" (Philippians 3:10) should be the daily longing of our hearts and the earnest prayer of our lips. Not only do we need to grow in "grace" but also in "the knowledge of our Lord and Saviour Jesus Christ" (2 Peter 3:18).

How little we really know the Christ of God. "No man knoweth [perfectly] the Son, but the Father" (Matthew 11:27); yet much has been revealed concerning Him in the Scriptures. How little we study those Scriptures with the definite object of seeking a better, deeper, fuller knowledge of the Lord Jesus! How circumscribed is the scope of our studies! Many form their conceptions of Christ from the first four books of the New Testament and rarely read beyond those books.

The Gospels speak of Christ's life during the days of His humiliation. They view Him in the form of a Servant, who came not to be ministered unto, but to minister. True, Matthew's gospel sets forth the kingship of Him who was here as Jehovah's Servant; yet it is as the rejected King. True also, John's gospel portrays the divine glories of the incarnate Son; yet as the One who was unknown in the world which He had made and as rejected by His own to whom He came (John 1:10–11). It is not until we pass beyond the Gospels that we find the lordship of Jesus of Nazareth really made manifest.

On the Day of Pentecost, Peter said, "Let all the house of Israel know assuredly, that God hath made that same Jesus, whom ye have crucified, both Lord and Christ" (Acts 2:36). The humbled One is now victorious. He who was born in lowliness has been exalted "far above all principality, and power, and might, and dominion, and every name that is named, not only in this world, but also in that which is to come" (Ephesians 1:21). He who suffered His face to be covered with the vile spit of men has been given a name more excellent than the angels (see Hebrews

1:4). He whom man crowned with thorns has been "crowned with glory and honour" (2:9). He who hung, in apparent helplessness, upon a cross has taken His seat "on the right hand of the Majesty on high" (1:3).

The Epistles, in contrast to the Gospels, were all written from the viewpoint of an ascended Christ. They treat of a glorified Saviour. How much we lose by their neglect! Why is it that when Christ comes to our minds our thoughts turn back to the "days of his flesh" (Hebrews 5:7)? Why are our hearts so little occupied with the heavenly Christ? Why do we meditate so little upon His exaltation, His seat and session at God's right hand? Is it not because we read the Epistles so infrequently?

Many Christians find the Epistles so much more difficult than the Gospels. Of course they do, because they are so unfamiliar. Enter a strange city, and its layout, streets, and suburbs are unknown. It is hard to find your way about. So it is with the Epistles. The Christian must live in them to become acquainted with their contents.

It is in the Epistles alone that the distinctive character of Christianity is set forth; not in the Gospels; the Acts is transitionary; and most of the Revelation belongs to the future. The Epistles alone treat of the present dispensation. But present-day preaching rarely notices them. Christians, in their private reading of the Word, seldom turn to them. But in the Epistles only is Christianity expounded, and Christianity has to do with a risen, glorified, and enthroned Christ. Thus, if we are to "sanctify in [our] hearts Christ Jesus as Lord," we must spend much time in the Epistles.

Chapter 38

THE FRIENDSHIP OF CHRIST

*H*ow many have ever heard a sermon or read an article on this subject? How many of God's people think of Christ in this blessed relationship? Christ is the best Friend the Christian has, and it is both his privilege and duty to regard Him as such. Our scriptural support is in the following passages: "There is a friend that sticketh closer than a brother" (Proverbs 18:24), which can refer to none other than the Lord Jesus; "this is my beloved, and this is my friend, O daughters of Jerusalem" (Song of Songs 5:16). That is the language of His Spouse, the testimony of the Church, avowing this most intimate relationship. Add to these the witness of the New Testament when Christ was termed "a friend of publicans and sinners" (Luke 7:34).

Many and varied are the relationships in which Christ stands to a believer, and he is the loser if He is ignored in any of them. Christ is God, Lord, Head, Saviour of the Church. Officially He is our Prophet, Priest, and King personally. He is our Kinsman-Redeemer, our Intercessor, our Friend. That last title expresses the near union between the Lord Jesus and believers. They are as if but one soul actuated them; indeed, one and the same spirit does, for "he that is joined unto the Lord is one spirit" (1 Corinthians 6:17). "Christ stands in a nearer relation than a brother to the Church: He is her Husband, her Bosom friend" (John Gill). "We are members of his body, of his flesh, and of his bones" (Ephesians 5:30). But even those relationships fall short of fully expressing the nearness, spiritual oneness, and indissolubleness of the union between Christ and His people. There should be the freest approaches to Him and the most intimate fellowship with Him. To deny Christ that, is to ignore the fact that He is our best Friend.

"There is a friend that sticketh closer than a brother." That endearing title not only expresses the near relation between Him and His redeemed but also the affection which He bears them. Nothing has, does, or can dampen or quench its outflow. "Having loved his own which were in the world, he loved them unto the end" (John 13:1). That blessed title tells of the sympathy He bears His people in all their sufferings, temptations, and infirmities. "In all their affliction he was afflicted . . . : in his love and in his pity he redeemed them; and he bare them, and carried them all the days of old" (Isaiah 63:9). What demonstrations of His friendship! That title also tells of His deep concern for our interests. He has our highest welfare at heart; accordingly He has promised, "I will not turn away from them, to do them good" (Jeremiah 32:40). Consider more definitely the excellencies of our best Friend.

Christ is an ancient Friend. Old friends we prize highly. The Lord Jesus was our Friend when we were His enemies! We fell in Adam, but He did not cease to love us; rather, He became the last Adam to redeem us and "lay down his life for his friends" (John 15:13). He sent His servants to preach the Gospel unto us, but we despised it. Even when we were wandering in the ways of folly, He determined to save us, and He watched over us. In the midst of our sinning and sporting with death, He arrested us by His grace, and by His love overcame our enmity and won our hearts.

Christ is a constant Friend; One that "loveth at all times" (Proverbs 17:17). He continues to be our Friend through all the vicissitudes of life—He is no fair-weather friend who would fail us when we need him most. He is our Friend in the day of adversity equally as much as in the day of prosperity. Was He not so to Peter? He is "a very present help in trouble" (Psalm 46:1) and evidences it by His sustaining grace. Nor do our transgressions turn away His compassion from us; even then He acts as a Friend. "If any man sin, we have an advocate with the Father, Jesus Christ the righteous" (1 John 2:1).

Christ is a faithful Friend. His grace is not shown at the expense of righteousness, nor do His mercies ignore the requirements of holiness. Christ always has in view both the glory of God and the highest good of His people. "Faithful are the wounds of a friend" (Proverbs 27:6). A real friend performs his duty by pointing out my faults. In this respect, too, Christ does "shew himself friendly" (18:24). Often He says to each of us, "I have a few things against thee" (Revelation 2:14)—and rebukes us by His Word, convicts our conscience by His Spirit, and chastens us by His providence "that we might be partakers of his holiness" (Hebrews 12:10).

Christ is a powerful Friend. He is willing and able to help us. Some earthly friends may have the desire to help us in the hour of need, but lack the wherewithal; not so our heavenly Friend. He has both the heart to assist and also the power. He is the Possessor of "unsearchable riches" (Ephesians 3:8), and all that He has is at our disposal. "The glory which thou gavest me I have given them" (John 17:22). We have a Friend at court, for Christ uses His influence with the Father on our behalf. "He ever liveth to make intercession for [us]" (Hebrews 7:25). No situation can possibly arise which is beyond the resources of Christ.

Christ is an everlasting Friend. He does not desert us in the hour of crisis. "Though I walk through the valley of the shadow of death, I will fear no evil: for thou art with me" (Psalm 23:4). Nor does death sever us from this Friend who "sticketh closer than a brother," for we are with Him that very day in paradise. Death will have separated us from those on earth, but "absent from the body" we shall be "present with the Lord" (2 Corinthians 5:8). And in the future Christ will manifest Himself as our Friend, saying "Enter thou into the joy of thy lord" (Matthew 25:21, 23).

Since Christ is such a Friend to the Christian, what follows? Friendship should be answered with friendship! Negatively, there should be no coldness, aloofness, trepidation, hesitancy on our part; but positively, a free availing ourselves of such a privilege. We should delight ourselves in Him. Since He is a faithful Friend we may safely tell Him the secrets of our hearts, for He will never betray our confidence. But His friendship also imposes definite obligations—to please Him and promote His cause and daily seek His counsel.

Chapter 39

THE HELPFULNESS OF CHRIST

One of the apostle's purposes in writing the epistle to the Hebrews is to strengthen the faith of those who were sorely tried and wavering—and by parity of reason all who are weak in grace. "For in that he himself hath suffered being tempted, he is able to succour them that are tempted" (Hebrews 2:18). The method he followed in prosecuting that end was to set forth the transcendent excellency of Christ, with His goodwill to the sons of men. He exhibits at length the perfections of His person, His offices, and His work. He declares that He is the Son of God, who has been made the "heir of all things"; that He is "the brightness" of the Father's glory and the "express image" of His person (1:2–3). Full demonstration was made of His immeasurable superiority to angels (vv. 4–14), yet so infinite was His condescension and so great His love to those given Him by the Father that He took a place lower than that occupied by celestial creatures (2:7–8); yet, "in all things . . . to be made like unto his brethren" (v. 17). In His *offices* He is revealed as the supreme Prophet, the final spokesman of Deity (1:1–2), as a glorious King (v. 8), and as "a merciful and faithful high priest" (2:17). In His *work*

He is revealed as making "reconciliation [literally, "propitiation"] for the sins of the people" (v. 17), as ever living "to make intercession for them" (7:25), and as "bringing many sons unto glory" (2:10).

So amazing was the grace of this august Being that He not only partook of the nature of those He came here to save, but also He entered fully into their circumstances, became subject to their infirmities, was tempted in all respects as they are, inward corruption excepted (Hebrews 2:18). He shed His precious blood and died a shameful death in their stead and on their behalf; and all of this to manifest the reality and abundance of His mercy unto sinners, fire their hearts, and draw out the affections of believers to Him. The apostle points out one of the blessed consequences of the Son's having become incarnate and entered into fellowship with His suffering people. First, the Lord of glory came down into the realm of temptation. Scripture is always to be understood in its widest possible latitude; therefore "tempt" is signifying put to the proof, subjected to trials and troubles, solicited to evil. Christ was tempted by God, by men, by the devil. Second, He "suffered" while being tempted. Those temptations were not mere make-believe, but real and painful. It could not be otherwise, for not only did He partake of all human sensibilities, but also His holiness felt acutely every form of evil. Third, the remembrance of His sufferings makes Him the more mindful of ours.

"For in that he himself hath suffered being tempted, he is able to succour them that are tempted" (Hebrews 2:18). Let us consider first the timeliness and preciousness of those words to those to whom they were originally addressed. The Hebrew saints were Jews who had been converted in the days of Christ and under the preaching of the apostles, and they were in peculiarly trying circumstances. Their unconverted countrymen regarded them as apostates from Moses, and therefore from Jehovah Himself. They would have no fellowship with them, but instead regarded them with the utmost contempt and treated them most cruelly. This resulted in great distress and privation, so that they "endured a great fight of afflictions" and were "made a gazingstock both by reproaches and afflictions," even to "the spoiling of [their] goods" (10:32–34) because of their continued loyalty to Christ. Hence they were strongly tempted to abandon the Christian profession, resume their former place under Judaism, and thereby escape further trouble. Now it was to believers in such a situation that our text was addressed. The apostle reminds them that Christ Himself was severely tempted, that He was subjected to worse trials than ours; yet He endured the same and emerged a victorious Overcomer. Then he assured them that the Saviour was able to sustain, comfort, and strengthen them.

There are Christians today who are in circumstances similar to those of the oppressed Hebrews. The world hates them and does so in proportion to their fidelity and conformity to Christ. Some are treated harshly by ungodly relatives. Some suffer at the hands of graceless professors. Others experience divine chastisement or perplexing providences, or are passing through the waters of bereavement or a painful sickness. At such times Satan is particularly active, launching his fiercest attacks, tempting them in various ways. Here is relief—real, present, all-sufficient relief. Turn your heart and eye to the Saviour and consider how well qualified He is to succor you. He is clothed with our humanity, and therefore capable of being "touched with the feeling of our infirmities" (4:15). The experience through which He passed fit Him to pity us. He knows all about your case, fully understands your trials, and gauges the strength of your temptation. He is not an indifferent spectator, but full of compassion. He wept by the grave of Lazarus—and He is the same today as yesterday (13:8). He is faithful in responding to the appeals of His people.

"He is able to succour," no matter what form the temptation or trial takes. *Succor* is a comprehensive word: it means "to befriend," "to assist those in need," "to strengthen the weak." But the Greek term is even more striking and beautifully expressive: it signifies to hasten in response to a cry of distress, literally to "run in to the call" of another. Chrysostom interpreted it, "He gives out His hand unto them with all readiness." A blessed illustration is seen in the case of Christ stretching forth His hand to catch hold of Peter as he began to sink in the sea (Matthew 14:25–31). That was the Saviour succoring one of His own. The same tender benevolence was yet more fully exemplified where we behold Him as the good Samaritan tending the wounded traveler (Luke 10:30–37). "He is *able*." The Greek word implies both fitness and a willingness to do a thing. Christ is alike competent and ready to undertake for His people. There is no unwillingness in Him. The straitness is always in us.

"He is able also to save them to the uttermost that come unto God by him" (Hebrews 7:25) signifies readiness as well as ability. During His sojourn on this earth, was He not ever ready to heal diseased bodies? And do you think that He is now unwilling to minister to distressed souls? Perish the thought. He was always at the disposal of the maimed,

the blind, the palsied, yes, of the repellent leper too. He was ever prepared, uncomplainingly, to relieve suffering, though it cost Him something—"There went virtue out of him" (Luke 6:19)—and though
much unbelief was expressed by those He befriended. As it was then a
part of His mission to heal the sick, so it is now a part of His ministry to
bind up the brokenhearted. What a Saviour is ours! The almighty God,
the all-tender Man. One who is infinitely above us in His original nature and present glory, yet One who became flesh and blood, lived on
the same plane as we do, experienced the same troubles, and suffered as
we, though far more acutely. Then how well qualified He is to supply
your every need! Cast all your care upon Him, knowing that He cares
for you (1 Peter 5:7).

Whatever your circumstances, the succoring Saviour is all-sufficient
and enters sympathetically into your condition. He knew what it was to
be weary (John 4:6) and exhausted (Mark 4:36–38). He knew what it
was to suffer hunger and thirst. Are you homeless? He had not a place to
lay His head. Are you in straitened circumstances? He was cradled in a
manger. Are you grief-stricken? He was the Man of sorrows. Are you
misunderstood by fellow believers? So was He by His own disciples.
Whatever your lot, He can enter fully into it. He experienced all the
miseries of mankind and has not forgotten them. Are you assailed by Satan? So was He. Do blasphemous thoughts at times torment your mind?
The devil tempted Him idolatrously to worship him. Are you in such
desperation as to think of making an end of yourself? Satan challenged
Him to cast Himself down from the pinnacle of the temple. He "was in
all points tempted like as we are, sin excepted" (see Hebrews 4:15).

Angels may pity, but they can have no fellow feeling. But Christ's
compassion ("to suffer with") moves Him to succor. In some instances
He does so *before* the temptation comes, and in a variety of ways. He
prepares for it by forewarning of the same; as with Israel being afflicted
in Egypt (Genesis 15:13), and Paul (Acts 9:16)—in our case by causing
His providences to presage the temptation; by fitting us for them, as
Christ was anointed with the Spirit before the devil tempted Him; or by
melting the heart with a sense of His goodness, which moves us to say,
"How then can I do this great wickedness?" (Genesis 39:9).

He succors *under* temptation; in some cases by the powerful application of a precept or promise, which as a cable holds the heart fast amid
the storm; by a providential interposition which prevents our executing

the evil intention; or by removing the temptation itself; by giving us to prove the sufficiency of His grace (2 Corinthians 1:2). He succors *after* temptation, by giving us a spirit of contrition (Luke 22:61–62), moving us to confess our sins. As angels ministered to Him after His conflict with Satan, so He ministers to us. Then no matter how dire your situation or acute your suffering, apply to Christ for relief and deliverance and count upon His help. It is when the child is most ill that the mother comes and sits beside it (Isaiah 66:13).

Chapter 40

THE
CALL
OF CHRIST

"Come unto me, all ye that labour and are heavy laden, and I will give you rest. Take my yoke upon you, and learn of me; for I am meek and lowly in heart: and ye shall find rest unto your souls. For my yoke is easy, and my burden is light" (Matthew 11:28–30).

Familiar as the sound of those words are to professing Christians, there is a pressing need for their careful examination. Few portions of God's Word have received such superficial treatment. That these verses call for prayerful meditation some will admit, but few realize that such a "simple passage" demands protracted study. Many take it for granted they already understand its meaning; hence they make no diligent inquiry into the significance of its terms. The mere fact a verse is so frequently quoted is no proof that we really see its import; yet, such familiarity has precluded careful examination and renders it far more likely we do not rightly grasp its truth.

There is a vast difference between being acquainted with the *sound* of a verse of Holy Writ and entering into the *sense* of it. Our age is marked by industrial loafing and mental slackness. Work is detested; and how quickly a task may be disposed of, rather than how well it may be done, is the order of the day. The same dilatory spirit marks the products of both the pulpit and the printed page; hence the superficial treatment this passage commonly receives. No regard is paid to its context or no laborious attempt made to ascertain its coherence (the relation of one clause to another); no painstaking examination and exposition of its terms.

If ever a passage of Scripture were mutilated and its meaning perverted, it is this one. Only a fragment of it usually is quoted, with the part most unpalatable to the flesh omitted. A particular call is twisted into a promiscuous invitation by deliberately ignoring the qualifying terms there used by the Saviour. Even when the opening clause is quoted, no attempt is made to show what is involved in "come to Christ," so the hearer is left to assume he already understands its meaning. The special offices in which the Son of God is portrayed, namely as Lord and Master, as Prince and Prophet, are ignored and another substituted. The conditional promise made by Christ is falsified by making it an unconditional one, as though His "rest" could be obtained *without* our taking His "yoke" upon us, and *without* our "learning" of Him.

Such charges may be resented bitterly by a large number of churchgoers who do not wish to hear anyone criticized. But if they are prepared to remain "at ease in Zion," if they are content whether they be deceived or not, if they have such confidence in men that they are willing to receive the most valuable things of all secondhand, if they refuse to examine their foundations and search their hearts, then we must "let them alone" (Matthew 15:14). But there are still some who prize their souls so highly they consider no effort too great to ascertain whether or not they possess a saving knowledge of God's truth; whether or not they truly understand the terms of God's salvation; whether or not they are building on an unshakable foundation.

Take a closer look at the passage. It opens with "Come unto me . . . and I will give you rest" and closes with "and ye shall find rest unto your souls." It is not (as some have supposed) two different rests which are spoken of, but the same in both cases; namely, spiritual rest, saving rest. Nor are two different aspects of this rest portrayed, but rather one rest viewed from two distinct viewpoints. In the former, divine sovereignty is in view: "I will give"; in the latter, human responsibility is enforced: "Ye shall find." In the opening clause Christ affirms that He is the Giver of rest; in what follows He specifies the terms upon which He dispenses rest; or to express it another way, the conditions which we must meet if we are to obtain that rest. The rest is freely given, yet only to those who comply with the revealed requirements of its Bestower.

"Come unto Me." Who issues this call? Christ, you reply. True, but Christ in what particular character? Did Christ speak as King, commanding His subjects; as Creator, addressing His creatures; as Physician, inviting the sick; or as Lord, instructing His servants? But do you draw a distinction in your mind between the Person of Christ and the office of Christ? Do you not distinguish sharply between His office as Prophet, as Priest, and as King? Have you found such distinctions both necessary and helpful? Then why do people complain when we call attention to the varied relations which our Lord sustains and the importance of noting which of these relations He is acting in at any time? Attention to such details often makes all the difference between a right and wrong understanding of a passage.

To answer our query in what particular character Christ issued this call, it is necessary to look at the verses preceding. Attention to context is one of the very first concerns for those who would carefully ponder any particular passage. Matthew 11 opens with John the Baptist having been cast into prison from which he sent messengers to Christ to acquaint Him with his perplexity (vv. 2–3). Our Lord publicly vindicated His forerunner and magnified his unique office (vv. 4–15). Having praised the Baptist and his ministry, Christ went on to reprove those who had been privileged to enjoy both it and that of His own, because they did not profit from it, but had despised and rejected both. So depraved were the people of that day, they accused John of being demon-possessed and charged Christ with being a glutton and a winebibber (vv. 16–19).

One of the most solemn passages in Holy Writ (vv. 20–24) records some of the most fearful words which ever fell from the lips of the Son of God. He upbraided the cities where most of His mighty works were done because "they repented not" (v. 20). Note that Christ refused to gloss over the perversity of the people; instead, He charged them with their sins. And let antinomians observe that, so far from the Christ of God ignoring human responsibility or excusing men's spiritual powerlessness, He held them strictly accountable and blamed them for their impenitency.

Wilful impenitency is the great damning sin of multitudes that enjoy the Gospel, and which (more than any other) sinners will be upbraided with to eternity. The great doctrine that both John the Baptist, Christ Himself, and the apostles preached, was repentance: the great thing designed to both in the "piping" and in the "mourning" was to prevail with people to change their minds and ways, to leave their sins and turn to God; but this they would not be brought to. He does not say, because they *believed* not, for some kind of faith many of them had, that Christ was a "Teacher come from God"; but because they *"repented not"*—their faith did not prevail to the transforming of their hearts and the reforming of their lives. Christ reproved them for their other sins that He might lead them to repentance, but when they repented not, He upbraided them with that as their refusal to be healed. He upbraided them with it, that they might upbraid themselves, and might at length see the folly of it, as that which alone makes the sad case a desperate one and the wound incurable. (Matthew Henry)

The particular sin for which Christ upbraided them was that of impenitence. The special aggravation of their sin was that they had witnessed most of Christ's miraculous works, for in those cities the Lord had for some time resided and performed many of His miracles of healing. Some places enjoy the means of grace more plentifully than others. Just as certain parts of the earth receive a much heavier rainfall than others, certain countries and towns have been favored with purer Gospel preaching and more outpourings of the Spirit than others. God is sovereign in the distribution of His gifts, both natural and spiritual, and "unto whomsoever much is given, of him shall be much required" (Luke 12:48). The greater our opportunities, the greater our obligations; and the stronger the inducements we have to repent, the more heinous is impenitence and the heavier reckoning will be. Christ notes His "mighty works" among us, and will yet hold us to an account of them.

"Woe unto thee, Chorazin! woe unto thee, Bethsaida!" (Matthew 11:21). Christ came into the world to dispense blessing. But if His Person is despised, His authority rejected, and His mercies slighted, then He has terrible woes in reserve. But how many church attenders hear anything at all about this? Often the pulpiteer has deliberately taken the line of least resistance and sought only to please the pew, withholding what was unpalatable or unpopular. Souls are deceived if a sentimental Christ is substituted for the scriptural Christ, if His "Beatitudes" (Matthew 5) are emphasized and His "woes" (Matthew 23) are ignored.

In still further aggravation of their sin of impenitence, our Lord affirmed that the citizens of Chorazin and Bethsaida were worse at heart than the Gentiles they despised. He asserted that if Tyre and Sidon had enjoyed such privileges as they, they would have "repented long ago in sackcloth and ashes." Some of the blessings Christendom despises would be welcome in many parts of heathendom.

> We are not competent to solve every difficulty, or fully to understand the whole of this subject; it suffices that Christ knew the hearts of the impenitent Jews to be more hardened in rebellion and enmity, and less susceptible of suitable impressions from His doctrine and miracles, than those of the inhabitants of Tyre and Sidon would have been; and therefore their final condemnation would be proportionately more intolerable. (Thomas Scott)

On the one hand, this passage does not stand alone (see Ezekiel 3:6–7); on the other, the repentance spoken of by Christ is not necessarily one which leads to eternal salvation.

Still more solemn are the awful words of Christ in Matthew 11:23–24, where He announced the doom of highly favored Capernaum. Because of the unspeakable privileges enjoyed by its inhabitants, they had been lifted heavenwards. But because their hearts were so earthbound they scorned such blessings; therefore they would be "brought down to hell." The greater the advantages enjoyed, the more fearful the doom of those who abuse them; the higher the elevation, the more fatal a fall from it. Honorable Capernaum is then compared with dishonorable Sodom, which, because of its enormities, God had destroyed with fire and brimstone. It was in Capernaum the Lord Jesus had resided chiefly upon entry into His public ministry and where so many of His miracles of healing were accomplished. Yet so obdurate were its inhabitants, so wed to their sins, they refused to apply to Him for the healing of their souls. Had such mighty works been done by Him in Sodom, its people would have been affected and their city remain as a lasting monument of divine mercy.

"But I say unto you, That it shall be more tolerable for the land of Sodom in the day of judgment, than for thee" (v. 24). Yes, my reader, though you may hear nothing about it from the pulpit, there is a "day of judgment" awaiting the world. It is "the day of wrath and revelation of the righteous judgment of God; who will render to every man according to his deeds"; it is the day "when God shall judge the secrets of men by Jesus Christ according to my gospel" (Romans 2:5–6, 16); "for God shall bring every work into judgment, with every secret thing, whether it be good, or whether it be evil" (Ecclesiastes 12:14); "the Lord knoweth how to deliver the godly out of temptations, and to reserve the unjust unto the day of judgment to be punished" (2 Peter 2:9). The punishment then meted out will be in proportion to the opportunities given and rejected; the privileges vouchsafed and scorned; the light granted and quenched. Most intolerable will be the doom of those who have abused the greatest advancements heavenwards.

"At that time Jesus answered and said, I thank thee, O Father, Lord of heaven and earth, because thou hast hid these things from the wise and prudent, and hast revealed them unto babes" (Matthew 11:25). The connection between this and the preceding verses is most instructive. There the Lord Jesus intimates that the majority of His mighty works had produced no good effect upon those who saw them, that their beholders remained impenitent. So little influence had His gracious presence exerted upon Capernaum, where He spent much of His time, that its fate would be worse than Sodom's. Christ looks away from earth to heaven, and finds consolation in the sovereignty of God and the absolute security of His covenant. From upbraiding the impenitence of men, Christ turned to render thanks to the Father. On the word *answered,* Matthew Henry said, "It is called an answer though no other words are found recorded but His own, because it is so comfortable a reply to the melancholy considerations preceding it, and is aptly set in the balance against them."

A word of warning is needed at this point, for we are such creatures of extremes. In earlier paragraphs we referred to those who substituted a sentimental Christ for the true Christ; yet the reader must not infer from this that we believe in a stoical Christ, hard, cold, devoid of feeling. Not so. The Christ of Scripture is perfect Man as well as God the Son, possessed of human sensibilities; yes, capable of much deeper feeling than any of us, whose faculties are blunted by sin. The Lord Jesus was not unaffected by grief when He pronounced the doom of those cities, nor did He view them with fatalistic indifference as He found comfort in the sovereignty of God. Scripture must be compared with Scripture: He who wept over Jerusalem (Luke 19:41) would not be unmoved as He foresaw the intolerable fate awaiting Capernaum. The fact that He was "the man of sorrows" (Isaiah 53:3) precludes any such concept.

A similar warning is needed by hyper-Calvinists with fatalistic stoicism:

> It seems plain then, that those who are indifferent about the event of the Gospel, who satisfy themselves with this thought, that the elect shall be saved, and feel no concern for unawakened sinners, make a wrong inference from a true doctrine, and know not what spirit they are of. Jesus wept for those who perished in their sins. Paul had great grief and sorrow of heart for the Jews, though he gave them this character, "that they pleased not God, and were contrary to all men." It well becomes us, while we admire distinguishing grace to ourselves, to mourn over others: and inasmuch as secret things belong to the Lord, and we know not but some, of whom we have at present but little hopes, may at last be brought to the knowledge of the Truth, we should be patient and forebearing after the pattern of our heavenly Father, and endeavor by every proper and prudent means to stir them up to repentance, remembering that they cannot be more distant from God than by nature we were ourselves. (John Newton)

As perfect Man and as "minister of the circumcision" (Romans 15:8) the Lord Jesus felt acutely any lack of response to His arduous efforts. This is clear from His lament, "I have laboured in vain, I have spent my strength for nought" (Isaiah 49:4). But observe how He comforted Himself. "Yet surely my judgment is with the LORD, and my work [or "reward"] with my God" (v. 4). Thus, both in the language of prophecy and here in Matthew 11:25–26, the Lord Jesus sought relief from the discouragements of the Gospel by retreating into the divine sovereignty. "We may take great encouragement in looking upward to God, when round about us we see nothing but what is discouraging. It is sad to see how regardless most men are of their own happiness, but it is comfortable to think that the wise and faithful God will, however, effectually secure the interests of His own glory" (Matthew Henry).

Christ alluded here in verse 25 to the sovereignty of God in three details. First, by owning His Father as "Lord of heaven and earth," that is, as sole Proprietor thereof. It is well to remember, especially when it appears Satan is master of this lower sphere, that God not only "doeth according to his will in the army of heaven," but also "among the inhabitants of the earth," so that "none can stay his hand" (Daniel 4:35).

Second, by affirming, "Thou hast hid these things from the wise and prudent." The things pertaining to salvation are concealed from the self-sufficient and self-complacent, leaving them in nature's darkness. Third, by declaring, "And hast revealed them unto babes." By the effectual operation of the Holy Spirit a divine discovery is made by those who are helpless in their own esteem. "Even so, Father: for so it seemed good in thy sight" (Matthew 11:26) expressed the Saviour's perfect acquiescence.

"All things are delivered unto me of my Father: and no man knoweth the Son, but the Father; neither knoweth any man the Father, save the Son, and he to whomsoever the Son will reveal him" (Matthew 11:27). This verse supplies the immediate connecting link between the sovereignty of divine grace mentioned (vv. 25–26) and the communication of that grace through Christ (vv. 28–30). The settlements of divine grace were made and secured in the Everlasting Covenant; communication of it is by and through Christ as the Mediator of that covenant. First, here is the grand commission the Mediator received from the Father: all things necessary to the administration of the covenant were delivered unto Christ (compare Matthew 28:18; John 5:22; 17:2). Second, here is the inconceivable dignity of the Son: lest a false inference be drawn from the preceding clause, the essential and absolute deity of Christ is affirmed. Inferior in office, Christ's nature and dignity is the same as the Father's. As Mediator, Christ receives all from the Father, but as God the Son He is, in every way, equal to the Father in His incomprehensible Person. Third, here the work of the Mediator is summed up in one grand item: that of revealing the Father to those given to Him.

Thus the context of Matthew 11 reveals Christ in the following characters: as the Upbraider of the impenitent; as the Pronouncer of solemn "woe" upon those who were unaffected by His mighty works; as the Announcer of the day of judgment, declaring that the punishment awaiting those who scorned gospel mercies should be more intolerable than that meted out to Sodom; as the Affirmer of the high sovereignty of God who conceals and reveals the things pertaining to salvation; as the Mediator of the covenant; as the Son coequal with the Father; and as the One by whom the Father is revealed.

"Come unto me, all ye that labour and are heavy laden, and I will give you rest" (Matthew 11:28). Having examined the context of these words, so that we might the better see their connection and the particular characters in which Christ is portrayed, consider the persons addressed, the ones who were invited to the Rest-giver. This point brings some differences among commentators. Some give a narrower scope to this call of Christ, and some a wider. Note however, that all of the leading earlier expositors restricted this particular call to a special class:

> He now kindly invites to Himself those whom He acknowledges to be fit for becoming His disciples. Though He is ready to reveal the Father to all, yet the great part are careless about coming to Him, because they are not affected by a conviction of their necessities. Hypocrites give themselves no concern about Christ because they are intoxicated with their own righteousness, and neither hunger nor thirst after His grace. Those who are devoted to the world set no value on a heavenly life. It would be vain therefore for Christ to invite either of these classes, and therefore He turns to the wretched and afflicted. He speaks of them as "laboring" or being under a "burden," and does not mean generally those who are oppressed with griefs and vexations, but those who are overwhelmed by their sins, who are filled with alarm at the wrath of God and are ready to sink under so weighty a burden. (John Calvin)

> The character of the persons invited: all that labor and are heavy laden. This is a word in season to him that is weary (Isaiah 50:4). Those that complain of the burden of the ceremonial law, which was an intolerable yoke, and was made much more so by the tradition of the elders (Luke 11:46); let them come to Christ and they shall be made easy. . . . But it is rather to be understood of the burden of sin, both the guilt and the power of it. All those, and those only, are invited to rest in Christ that are sensible of sin as a burden and groan under it, that are not only convicted of the evil of sin—their own sin—but are contrite in soul for it; that are really sick of sin, weary of the service of the world and the flesh, that see their state sad and dangerous by reason of sin, and are in pain and fear about it: as Ephraim (Jeremiah 31:18–20), the prodigal (Luke 15:17), the publican (Luke 18:13), Peter's hearers (Acts 2:37), Paul (Acts 9), the jailer (Acts 16:29–30). This is a necessary preparative for pardon and peace. (Matthew Henry)

> Who are the persons here invited? They are those who "labor" (the Greek expresses toil with weariness) and are "heavy laden." This must here be limited to spiritual concerns, otherwise it will take in all mankind, even the most hardened and obstinate opposers of Christ and the Gospel. Referring to the self-righteous religionists, this writer went on to say, "You

avoid gross sins, you have perhaps a form of godliness. The worst you think that can be said of you is that you employ all your thoughts and every means that will not bang you under the lash of the law, to heap up money, to join house to house and field to field; or you spend your days in a complete indolence, walking in the way of your own hearts, and looking no further: and here you will say you find pleasure, and insist on it, that you are neither weary nor heavy laden . . . then it is plain that you are not the persons whom Christ here invites to partake of His rest." (John Newton)

The persons invited are not "all" the inhabitants of mankind, but with a restriction: "all ye that labor and are heavy laden," meaning not those who labor in the service of sin and Satan, are laden with iniquity and insensible of it those are not weary of sin nor burdened with it, nor do they want or desire any rest for their souls; but such who groan, being burdened with the guilt of sin on their consciences and are pressed down with the unsupportable yoke of the Law and the load of their trespasses, and have been laboring till they are weary, in order to obtain peace of conscience and rest for their souls by the observance of these things, but in vain. These are encouraged to come to Him, lay down their burdens at His feet and look to Him, and lay hold by faith on His person, blood and righteousness. (John Gill)

In more recent times many preachers have dealt with the text (Matthew 11:28) as though the Lord Jesus was issuing an indefinite invitation, regarding His terms as sufficiently general and wide in their scope to include sinners of every type. They supposed that the words "ye that labour and are heavy laden" refer to the misery and bondage which the Fall brought upon the human race, as its unhappy subjects vainly seek satisfaction in the things of time and sense, and endeavor to find happiness in the pleasures of sin. "The universal wretchedness of man is depicted on both its sides—the active and the passive forms of it" (Fausset and Brown). They are laboring for contentment by gratifying their lusts, only to add to their miseries by becoming more and more the burdened slaves of sin.

It is true the unregenerate "labour in the very fire" and they "weary themselves for very vanity" (Habakkuk 2:13); it is true they "labour in vain" (Jeremiah 51:58), and "what profit hath he that hath laboured for the wind?" (Ecclesiastes 5:16). It is true they "spend money for that which is not bread," and "labour for that which satisfieth not" (Isaiah 55:2), for "the eye is not satisfied with seeing, nor the ear filled with hearing" (Ecclesiastes 1:8). It is equally true that the unregenerate are heavy laden, "a people laden with iniquity" (Isaiah 1:4), yet they are totally insensible to their awful state. "The labour of the foolish wearieth every one of them, because he knoweth not how to go to the city" (Ecclesiastes 10:15). Moreover, "The wicked are like the troubled sea, when it cannot rest, whose waters cast up mire and dirt. There is no peace, saith my God, to the wicked" (Isaiah 57:20–21). They have neither peace of conscience nor rest of heart. But it is quite another matter to affirm these are the characters Christ invited to come unto Him for rest.

We prefer the view taken by the older writers. Over a century ago a latitudinarian spirit began to creep in, and even the most orthodox were often, unconsciously, affected by it. Those in the pews were more inclined to chafe against what they regarded as the "rigidity" and "narrowness" of their fathers; and those in the pulpit had to tone down those aspects of truth which were most repellent to the carnal mind, if they were to retain their popularity. Side by side with modern inventions, an increased means for travel, and the dissemination of news, came what was termed "a broader outlook" and "a more charitable spirit." Posing as an angel of light, Satan succeeded in Arminianizing many places of truth; and even where this was not accomplished, high Calvinism was whittled down to moderate Calvinism.

These are solemn facts which no student of ecclesiastical history can deny. Christendom has not fallen into its present condition all of a sudden; rather its present state is the outcome of a long and steady deterioration. The deadly poison of error was introduced here a little, there a little, with the quantity increased as less opposition came against it. As the acquiring of "converts" absorbed more and more of the attention and strength of the Church, the standard of doctrine lowered, sentiment displaced convictions, and fleshly methods were introduced. In a comparatively short time many of those sent out to "the foreign field" were rank Arminians, preaching "another gospel." This reacted upon the homeland, and soon the interpretations of Scripture given out from pulpits moved into line with the "new spirit" which had captivated Christendom.

While we do not affirm that everything modern is evil or that everything ancient was excellent, there is no doubt that the greater part of the boasted "progress" in Christendom of the nineteenth and twentieth centuries was a progress downward and not upward—away from

God and not toward Him, into the darkness and not the light. Therefore we need to examine with double caution any religious views which deviate from the common teachings of the godly Reformers and Puritans. We need not be worshipers of antiquity as such, but we need to regard with suspicion those "broader" interpretations of God's Word which have become popular in recent times.

We should point out some of the reasons why we do not believe that Christ was making a broadcast invitation that was issued promiscuously to the light-headed, gay-hearted, pleasure-crazy masses which had no appetite for the Gospel and no concern for eternal interests. This call was not addressed to the godless, careless, giddy, and worldly multitudes, but rather to those who were burdened with a sense of sin and longed for relief of conscience.

First, the Lord Jesus received no commission from heaven to bestow rest of soul upon all, but only upon the elect of God. "For I came down from heaven, not to do mine own will, but the will of him that sent me. And this is the Father's will which hath sent me, that of all which he hath given me I should lose nothing, but should raise it up again at the last day" (John 6:38–39). That, necessarily, regulated all His ministry.

Second, the Lord Jesus always practiced what He preached. To His disciples He said, "Give not that which is holy unto the dogs, neither cast ye your pearls before swine, lest they trample them under their feet, and turn again and rend you" (Matthew 7:6). Can we, then, conceive of our holy Lord inviting the unconcerned to come unto Him for that which their hearts abhorred? Has He set His ministers such an example? Surely, the word He would have them press upon the pleasure-intoxicated members of our generation is "Rejoice, O young man, in thy youth; and let thy heart cheer thee in the days of thy youth, and walk in the ways of thine heart, and in the sight of thine eyes: but know thou, that for all these things God will bring thee into judgment" (Ecclesiastes 11:9).

Third, the immediate context is entirely out of harmony with the wider interpretation. Christ pronounced most solemn "woes" on those who despised and rejected Him (Matthew 11:20–24), drawing consolation from the sovereignty of God and thanking Him because He had hidden from the wise and prudent the things which belonged unto their eternal peace but had revealed them unto babes (vv. 25–26). It is these "babes" He invites to Himself; and we find Him presented as the One commissioned by the Father and as the Revealer of Him (v. 27).

It must not be concluded that we do not believe in an unfettered Gospel, or that we are opposed to the general offer of Christ to all who hear it. Not so. His marching orders are far too plain for any misunderstanding; our Master has bidden us to "preach the Gospel to every creature," so far as Divine providence admits; and the substance of the Gospel message is that Christ died for sinners and stands ready to welcome every sinner willing to receive Him on His terms. The Lord Jesus announced the design of His incarnation in sufficiently general terms as to warrant any man truly desiring salvation to believe in Him. "I am not come to call the righteous, but sinners to repentance" (Matthew 9:13). Many are called even though but few are chosen (20:16). The way we spell out our election is by coming to Christ as lost sinners, trusting in His blood for pardon and acceptance with God.

In his excellent sermon on these words before us, John Newton pointed out that, when David was driven into the wilderness by the rage of Saul, "every one that was in distress, and every one that was in debt, and every one that was discontented, gathered themselves unto him; and he became a captain over them" (1 Samuel 22:2). But David was despised by those who, like Nabal (25:10), lived at their ease. They did not believe he should be a king over Israel; therefore, they preferred the favor of Saul, whom God had rejected. Thus it was with the Lord Jesus. Though a divine person, invested with all authority, grace, and blessings —and declaring that He would be the King of all who obeyed His voice—yet the majority saw no beauty that they should desire Him, felt no need of Him, and so rejected Him. Only a few who were consciously burdened believed His Word and came to Him for rest.

What did our Lord signify when He bade all the weary and heavy laden "come unto me"? First, it is evident that something more than a physical act or coming to hear Him preach was intended. These words were first addressed to those already in His presence. Many who attended His ministry and witnessed His miracles never came to Him in the sense intended. The same holds true today. Something more than a bare approach through the ordinances—listening to preaching, submitting to baptism, partaking of the Lord's Supper—is involved in coming to Christ. Coming to Christ in the sense He invited is a going out of the soul after Him, a desire for Him, a seeking after Him, a personal embracing and trusting Him.

Coming to Christ suggests first, and negatively, a *leaving* of something, for the divine promise is "He that covereth his sins shall not prosper: but whoso confesseth and forsaketh them shall have mercy" (Proverbs 28:13). Coming to Christ, then, denotes turning our backs upon the world and turning our hearts unto Him as our only Hope. It means to abandon every idol and surrender ourselves to His Lordship; it is repudiating our own righteousness and dependency, and the heart going out to Him in loving submission and trustful confidence. It is an entire going out of self with all its resolutions to cast ourselves upon His mercy; it is the will yielding itself to His authority, to be ruled by Him and to follow where He leads. In short, it is the whole soul of a self-condemned sinner turning unto a whole Christ, exercising all our faculties, responding to His claims upon us, and prepared to unreservedly trust, unfeignedly love, and devotedly serve Him.

Thus, coming to Christ is the turning of the whole soul to Him. Perhaps this calls for amplification. There are three principal faculties in the soul: the understanding, the affections, and the will. Since each of these were operative and affected by our original departure from God, so they are and must be active in our return to Christ. Of Eve it is recorded, "When the woman saw that the tree was good for food, and that it was pleasant to the eyes, and a tree to be desired to make one wise, she took of the fruit thereof" (Genesis 3:6). First, she "saw that the tree was good for food," she perceived the fact mentally, a conclusion drawn from her understanding. Second, "and that it was pleasant to the eyes." That was the response of her affections to it. Third, "and a tree to be desired to make one wise." Here was the moving of her will. "She took of the fruit thereof, and did eat," was the completed action.

So it is in the sinner's coming to Christ. First, there is apprehension by the understanding. The mind is enlightened and brought to see a deep need of Christ and His suitability to meet those needs. The intelligence sees He is "good for food," the Bread of life for the nourishment of our souls. Second, there is the moving of the affections. Before, we saw no beauty in Christ that we should desire Him, but now He is "pleasant to the eyes" of our souls. It is the heart turning from the love of sin to the love of holiness, from self to the Saviour. Third, in coming to Christ there is an exercise of the will, for He said to those who would not receive Him, "Ye will not come to me, that ye might have life" (John 5:40). This exercise of the will is a yielding of ourselves to His authority.

None will come to Christ while they remain in ignorance of Him.

The understanding must accept His suitability for sinners before the mind can turn intelligently to Him as He is revealed in the Gospel. Neither can the heart come to Christ while it hates Him or is wedded to the things of time and space. The affections must be drawn out to Him. "If any man love not the Lord Jesus Christ, let him be Anathema" (1 Corinthians 16:22). Equally evident is it that no man will come to Christ while his will is opposed to Him: it is the enlightening of his understanding and the firing of his affections which subdues his enmity and makes the sinner willing in the day of God's power (Psalm 110:3). Observe that these exercises of the three faculties of the soul correspond in character to the threefold office of Christ: the understanding enlightened by Him as Prophet; the affections moved by His work as Priest; and the will bowing to His authority as King.

In the days on earth the Lord Jesus stooped to minister to the needs of men's bodies, and not a few came unto Him and were healed. In that we may see a foreshadowing of Him as the Great Physician of souls and what is required of sinners if they are to receive spiritual healing at His hand. Those who sought out Christ to obtain bodily relief were persuaded of His mighty power, His gracious willingness, and of their own dire need. But note that then, as now, this persuasion in the Lord's sufficiency and His readiness to nourish varied in different cases. The centurion spoke with full assurance, "Speak the word only, and my servant shall be healed" (Matthew 8:8). The leper expressed himself more dubiously, "Lord, if thou wilt, thou canst make me clean" (v. 2). Another used fainter language, "If thou canst do any thing, have compassion on us, and help us" (Mark 9:22); yet even there the Redeemer did not break the bruised reed nor quench the smoking flax, but graciously wrought a miracle on his behalf.

But observe that in each of these cases there was a personal, actual application to Christ; and it was this very application which manifested their faith, even though it was as small as a grain of mustard seed. They were not content with having heard of His fame, but improved it. They sought Him out for themselves, acquainted Him with their case, and implored His compassion. So it must be with those troubled about soul concerns. Saving faith is not passive, but operative. Moreover, the faith of those who sought Christ for physical relief refused to be deterred by difficulties. In vain the multitudes charged the blind man to be quiet (Mark 10:48). Knowing that Christ was able to give sight, he cried so much the more. Even when Christ appeared to manifest a great reserve, the woman refused to leave till her request was granted (Matthew 15:22–28).

Chapter 41

THE
REST
OF CHRIST

"Come unto me, all ye that labour and are heavy laden, and I will give you rest" (Matthew 11:28). In a message on these words John Newton pointed out:

The dispensation of the Gospel may be compared to the cities of refuge in Israel. It was a privilege and honor to the nation in general that they had such sanctuaries of Divine appointment, but the real value of them was known and felt by only a few. Those alone who found themselves in that case for which they were provided could rightly prize them. Thus it is with the Gospel of Christ: it is the highest privilege and honor of which a professing nation can boast, but it can be truly understood and esteemed by none except weary and heavy laden souls, who have felt their misery by nature, are tired of the drudgery of sin, and have seen the broken Law pursuing them like the avenger of blood of old. This is the only consideration which keeps them from sinking into abject despair, in that God has graciously provided a remedy by the Gospel, and that Christ bids them "Come unto Me, and I will give you rest."

If awakened, convicted, and distressed souls would but appropriate the full comfort of that blessed invitation and obey its terms, their complaints would end; but remaining ignorance, the workings of unbelief, and the opposition of Satan combine to keep them back. Some will say, "I am not qualified to come to Christ: my heart is so hard, my conscience so insensible, that I do not feel the burden of my sins as I ought, nor my need of Christ's rest as I should." Others will say, "I fear that I do not come aright. I see from the Scriptures and hear from the pulpit that repentance is required from me and that faith is an absolute essential if I am to be saved; but I am concerned to know whether my repentance is sincere and deep enough and if my faith is anything better than a historical one—the assent of the mind to the facts in the Gospel."

We may discover from those who sought healing from Him what is meant by the invitation Christ makes to those who have sought the approval of God and met His requirements in the Law. First, they were persuaded of His power and willingness and of their own deep need of His help. So it is in the matter of salvation. The sinner must be convinced that Christ is "mighty to save" (Isaiah 63:1), that He is ready to receive all who are sick of sin and want to be healed. Second, they made an application to Him. They were not content to hear of His fame but wanted proof of His wonder-working power. So, too, the sinner must not only credit the message of the Gospel, but also he must seek Him and trust Him.

Those who sought Christ as a Physician of souls continued with Him and became His followers. They received Him as their Lord and Master, renounced what was inconsistent with His will (Luke 9:23, 60), professed an obedience to His precepts, and accepted a share in His reproach. Some had a more definite call to Him, such as Matthew, who was sitting at the receipt of custom, indifferent to the claims of Christ until He said, "Follow me" (Matthew 9:9). That word was accompanied with power and won his heart, separating him from worldly pursuits in an instant. Others were drawn to Him more secretly by His Spirit, such as Nathaniel (John 1:45–49), and the weeping penitent (Luke 7:38). The ruler came to the Lord with no other intention than to obtain the life of his son (John 4:53), but he secured much more than he expected, and he believed, with all his house.

These things are recorded for our encouragement. The Lord Jesus is not on earth in visible form, but He promised His spiritual presence to abide with His Word, His ministers, and His people to the end. Weary sinners do not have to take a hard journey to find the Saviour, for He is always near (Acts 17:27) wherever His Gospel is preached.

> But the righteousness which is of faith speaketh on this wise, Say not in thine heart, Who shall ascend into heaven? (that is, to bring Christ down from above:) or, Who shall descend into the deep? (that is, to bring up Christ again from the dead.) But what saith it? The word is nigh thee, even in thy mouth, and in thy heart: that is, the word of faith, which we preach. (Romans 10:6–8)

If you cannot come to Christ *with* a tender heart and burdened conscience, then come to Him for them.

> Is it a sense of your load which makes you say you are not able? Then consider that this is not a work, but a rest. Would a man plead, I am so heavy laden that I cannot consent to part with my burden; so weary that I am not able either to stand still or to lie down, but must force myself farther? The greatness of your burden, so far from being an objection, is the very reason why you should instantly come to Christ, for He alone is able to release you. But perhaps you think you do not come aright. I ask, how would you come? If you come as a helpless unworthy sinner, without righteousness, without any hope but what arises from the worth, work, and Word of Christ, this is to come aright. There is no other way of being accepted. Would you refresh and strengthen yourself, wash away your own sins, free yourself from your burden, and then come to Him to do these things for you? May the Lord help you to see the folly and unreasonableness of your unbelief. (John Newton)

There is no promise in Scripture that God will reward the careless, halfhearted, indolent seeker; but He has declared, "Ye shall seek me, and find me, when ye shall search for me with all your heart" (Jeremiah 29:13). He has a fixed time for everyone whom He receives. He knew how long the poor man had waited at the pool (John 5:6), and when His hour came He healed him. So endeavor to be found in the way: where His Word is preached; and diligently search His Word in the privacy of your room. Be much in prayer. Converse with His people, and He may join you unexpectedly, as He did the two disciples walking to Emmaus.

"I will give you rest." What a claim! No mere man, no matter how godly and spiritual, could promise this. Abraham, Moses, or David could not bid the weary and heavy laden to come unto him with the assurance that he would give them rest. To impart rest of soul to another is beyond the power of the most exalted creature. Even the holy angels are incapable of bestowing rest upon others, for they are dependent on the grace of God for their own rest. Thus this promise of Christ manifested His uniqueness. Neither Confucius, Buddha, nor Muhammad ever made such a claim. It was no mere Man who uttered these words, "Come unto me, all ye that are weary and heavy laden, and I will give you rest." He was the Son of God. He made man, and therefore He could restore him. He was the Prince of peace, thus capable of giving rest.

As Christ is the only One who can bestow rest of soul, so there is no true rest apart from Him. The creature cannot impart it. The world cannot communicate it. We cannot manufacture it. One of the most pathetic things in the world is to see the unregenerate vainly seek happiness and contentment in the material things. At last they discover these are all broken cisterns which hold no water. Observe them turning to priests or preachers, penance or fastings, reading and praying, only to find, as the Prodigal Son did when he "began to be in want," that "no man gave unto him" (Luke 15:14, 16); or see the poor woman who had "suffered many things of many physicians, and had spent all that she had, and was nothing bettered, but rather grew worse" (Mark 5:26). All the unregenerate, illiterate or learned, find "the way of peace have they not known" (Romans 3:17).

It is much to be thankful for when we realize experientially that none but Christ can do helpless sinners any good. This is a hard lesson for man, and we are slow to learn it. The fact is not involved in itself, but the devilish pride of our hearts makes us self-sufficient until divine grace humbles us. It is part of the gracious work of the Holy Spirit to bring us off our creature dependence, to knock the props from under us, to make us see that Jesus Christ is our only hope. "Neither is there salvation in any other: for there is none other name under heaven given among men, whereby we must be saved" (Acts 4:12). Strikingly this was illustrated by the dove sent forth by Noah. "But the dove found no rest for the sole of her foot, and she returned unto him into the ark, for the waters were on the face of the whole earth: then he put forth his hand, and took her, and pulled her in unto him into the ark" (Genesis 8:9). Significantly, the very name *Noah* meant "rest" (5:29, margin); and it was only as the dove was "caused to come unto him" that she obtained rest. So it is with the sinner.

What is the nature of this rest Christ gives to all who come to Him?

> The Greek word expresses something more than rest, or a mere relaxation from toil; it denotes refreshment likewise. A person weary with long bearing a heavy burden will need not only to have it removed, but likewise he wants food and refreshment to restore his spirits and to repair his wasted strength. Such is the rest of the Gospel. It not only puts a period to our fruitless labor, but it affords a sweet reviving cordial. There is not only peace, but joy in believing. (John Newton)

Thus it is a spiritual rest, a satisfying rest, "rest for the soul" as the Saviour declares in this passage. It is such a rest the world can neither give nor take away.

In particularizing upon the nature of this rest we may distinguish between its present and future forms. Concerning the former, *first,* it is a deliverance from that vain and wearisome quest which absorbs the sinner before the Spirit opens his eyes to see his folly and moves him to seek true riches. Piteous it is to behold those who are made for eternity wasting their energies in wandering from object to object, searching for what will not satisfy, only to be mortified by repeated disappointments. It is so with all until they come to Christ, for He has written about all the pleasures of this world, "Whosoever drinketh of this water shall thirst again" (John 4:13). For example, Solomon, who had everything the heart could desire and gratified his lusts to the full, found that, "behold, all is vanity and vexation of spirit" (Ecclesiastes 1:14). From this vexation of spirit Christ delivers His people, for He declares, "Whosoever drinketh of the water that I shall give him shall never thirst" (John 4:14).

Second, it is the easing and tranquilizing of a burdened conscience. Only one who has been convicted by the Holy Spirit appreciates what this means. When one has to cry out, "The arrows of the Almighty are within me, the poison whereof drinketh up my spirit: the terrors of God do set themselves in array against me" (Job 6:4); when the curse of God's broken Law thunders in our ears; when we have an inward sense of divine wrath and the terrors of a future judgment fall upon the soul, then there is indescribable anguish of mind. When a true work is wrought in the heart by the Spirit we exclaim, "Thine arrows stick fast in me, and thy hand presseth me sore. There is no soundness in my flesh because of thine anger; neither is there any rest in my bones because of my sin"

(Psalm 38:2–3). When we first see the wondrous love of God for us and how vilely we have repaid Him, then we are cut to the quick; when by faith we come to Christ all this is altered. As we see Him dying in our stead and that there is now no condemnation for us, the intolerable load falls from our conscience—and a peace which passeth all understanding is ours.

Third, it is a rest from the dominion and power of sin. Here, again, only those who are the subjects of His grace can enter into what is meant. The unawakened are unconcerned about the glory of God and indifferent as to whether their conduct pleases Him. They have no concept of the sinfulness of sin and no realization of how completely sin dominates them. Only when the Spirit of God illumines their minds and convicts their consciences do they see the awfulness of their state; and only then, as they try to reform their ways, are they conscious of the might of their inward foe and of their inability to cope with him. In vain deliverance is sought in resolutions and endeavors in our own strength. Even after we are quickened and begin to understand the Gospel, for a season (often a lengthy one) it is rather a fight than a rest. But as we grow more out of ourselves and are taught to live in Christ and draw our strength from Him by faith, we obtain a rest in this respect also.

Fourth, there is a rest from our own works. As the believer realizes more clearly the sufficiency of the finished work of Christ, he is delivered experientially from the Law and sees that he no longer owes it service. His obedience is no longer legal but evangelical, no longer out of fear, but out of gratitude. His service to the Lord is not in a servile, but in a gracious spirit. What was formerly a burden is now a delight. He no longer seeks to earn God's favor, but acts in the realization that the smile of God is upon him. Far from rendering him careless, this will spur him on to strive to glorify the One who gave His own Son as a sacrifice. Thus, bondage gives place to liberty; slavery, to sonship; toil, to rest. And the soul reposes on the unchangeable Word of Christ and follows Him steadily through light and darkness.

There is also a future rest beyond any that can be experienced here, although our best conceptions of the glory awaiting the people of God are inadequate. *First,* in heaven there will be a perfect resting from all sin, for nothing shall enter there which could defile or disturb our peace. What it will mean to be delivered from indwelling corruptions no tongue can tell. The closer a believer walks with the Lord, and the more intimate his communion with Him is, the more bitterly he hates that within him which ever fights against his desire for holiness. Therefore the apostle cried, "O wretched man that I am! who shall deliver me from the body of this death?" (Romans 7:24). But we will not carry this burden beyond the grave.

Second, we shall be delivered from beholding the sins of others. No more will our hearts be pained by the evils which flood the earth. Like Lot in Sodom, we are grieved with the conversation of the godless. "Who that has any love to the Lord Jesus, any spark of true holiness, any sense of the worth of souls in his heart, can see what passes amongst us without trembling? How openly, daringly, almost universally, are the commandments of God broken, His Gospel despised, His patience abused, and His power defied" (John Newton). If that were the state of affairs two hundred years ago, what would this writer say were he on earth today to witness not only the wickedness of a profane world, but also the hypocrisy of Christendom? As the believer sees how the Lord is dishonored in the house of those who pose as His friends, how often he thinks, "Oh that I had wings like a dove! for then would I fly away, and be at rest" (Psalm 55:6).

Third, there will be perpetual rest from all outward afflictions; for in heaven none will harass the people of God. No more will the saint live in the midst of an ungodly generation, which may not actively persecute him, yet will only reluctantly tolerate his presence. Though afflictions are needful, and when sanctified to us are also profitable, nevertheless they are grievous to bear. But a day is coming when these tribulations will no longer be necessary, for the fine gold will have been purged from the dross. The storms of life will be behind, and an unbroken calm will be the believer's lot forever. Where there will be no more sin, there will be no more sorrow. "God shall wipe away all tears from their eyes; and there shall be no more death, neither sorrow, nor crying, neither shall there be any more pain: for the former things are passed away" (Revelation 21:4).

Fourth, it will be a rest from Satan's temptations. How often he disturbs the present rest of believers! How often they have cause to say with the apostle, "Satan hindered [me]" (1 Thessalonians 2:18). Satan seeks in various ways to hinder believers from attending the public means of grace; to hinder them when they try to meditate on the Word or pray. The devil cannot bear to see one of Christ's people happy, so he tries constantly to disturb their joy. One reason God permits this is that they may be conformed to their Head. When He was here on earth the devil continually hounded Him. Even when believers come to the hour of departure from this world, their great enemy seeks to rob them of assurance, but he can pursue them no further. "Absent from the body," they are "present with the Lord," forever out of the reach of their adversary (2 Corinthians 5:8).

Finally, they rest from unsatisfied desires. When one has really been born of the Spirit, he wants to be done with sin forever. He longs for perfect conformity to the image of Christ and for unbroken fellowship with Him. But such longings are not realized in this life. Instead, the old nature within the believer ever opposes the new, bringing him into captivity to the law of sin (Romans 7:23). But death affords final relief from indwelling corruptions, and he is made "a pillar in the temple of [his] God, and he shall go no more out" (Revelation 3:12). On the morning of the resurrection the believer's body shall be "fashioned like unto his [Christ's] glorious body" (Philippians 3:21), and his soul's every longing shall then be fully realized. The change from grace to glory will be as radical as the change from nature to grace.

Chapter 42

THE
YOKE
OF CHRIST

*C*ome unto me, all ye that labour and are heavy laden, and I will give you rest." This is not a broadcast invitation, addressed indefinitely to the careless, giddy masses; rather, it is a gracious call to those who seriously seek peace of heart, yet are still bowed down with a load of guilt. It is addressed to those who long for rest of soul, but who know not how it is to be obtained, nor where it is to be found. To such Christ says, "Come unto me, and I will give you rest." But He does not leave it there. He goes on to explain. Our Lord makes the bare affirmation that He is the giver of rest (Matthew 11:28). In what follows He specifies the terms on which He dispenses it, conditions which we must meet if we are to obtain it. The rest is freely "given," but only to those who comply with the revealed requirements of its Bestower.

"Take my yoke upon you, and learn of me; for I am meek and lowly in heart: and ye shall find rest unto your souls" (Matthew 11:29). In those words Christ voiced the conditions which men must meet if they are to obtain rest of soul. We are required to take His yoke upon us. The yoke is a figure of subjection. The force of this figure may be understood if we con-

trast oxen running wild in the field with oxen harnessed to a plow, where their owner directs their energies. Hence we read, "It is good for a man that he bear the yoke in his youth" (Lamentations 3:27). That means unless youths are disciplined, brought under subjection, and taught to obey their superiors, they are likely to develop into sons of Belial, intractable rebels against God and man. When the Lord took Ephraim in hand and chastised him, he bemoaned that he was like "a bullock unaccustomed to the yoke" (Jeremiah 31:18).

The natural man is born "like a wild ass's colt" (Job 11:12), completely unmanageable and self-willed, determined to have his own way at all costs. Having lost his anchor by the Fall, man is like a ship entirely at the mercy of winds and waves. His heart is unmoored, and he runs wild to his own destruction. Thus he has a need for the yoke of Christ if he is to obtain rest for his soul. In its larger sense, the yoke of Christ signifies complete dependence, unequaled obedience, unreserved submission to Him. The believer owes this to Christ both as his rightful Lord and his gracious Redeemer. Christ has a double claim upon him. He is the creature of His hands, and Christ gave him being, with all his capacities and faculties. Christ has redeemed him and acquired an additional claim on him. The saints are His purchased property. Therefore, the Holy Spirit says, "Know ye not that . . . ye are not your own? For ye are bought with a price: therefore glorify God in your body, and in your spirit, which are God's" (1 Corinthians 6:19–20).

"Take my yoke upon you." By which Christ meant: Surrender yourself to My Lordship, submit to My rule, let My will be yours. As Matthew Henry pointed out:

> We are here invited to Christ as Prophet, Priest and King, to be saved, and *in order to this,* to be ruled and taught by Him. As the oxen are yoked in order to submit to their owner's will and to work under his control, so those who would receive rest of soul from Christ are here called upon to yield to Him as their King. He died for His people that they should not henceforth live unto themselves, "but *unto him* which died for them, and rose again" (2 Corinthians 5:15). Our holy Lord requires absolute submission and obedience in all things, both in the inward life and the outward, even to "bringing into captivity every thought to the obedience of Christ" (2 Corinthians 10:5). Alas that this is so little insisted upon in a day when the

high claims of the Saviour are whittled down in an attempt to render His Gospel more acceptable to the unregenerate.

It was different in the past, when those in the pulpit kept back nothing profitable for their hearers. God honored such faithful preaching by granting the anointing of His Spirit, so that the Word was applied in power. Take this sample:

> No heart can truly open to Christ that is not made willing, upon due deliberation, to receive Him with His cross of sufferings and His yoke of obedience: "If any man will come after me, let him deny himself, and take up his cross, and follow me. . . . Take my yoke upon you, and learn of me" (Matthew 16:24; 11:29). Any exception against either of these is an effectual barrier to union with Christ. He looks upon that soul as not worthy of Him that puts in such an exception: "He that taketh not his cross, and followeth after me, is not worthy of me" (Matthew 10:38). If thou judgeth not Christ to be worthy of all sufferings, all losses, all reproaches, He judges thee unworthy to bear the name of His disciple. So, for the duties of obedience—called His "yoke"—he that will not receive Christ's yoke can neither receive His pardon nor any benefit by His blood. (John Flavel, 1689)

"Take my yoke upon you." Note carefully that the yoke is not laid upon us by another, but one which we place upon ourselves. It is a definite act on the part of one who seeks rest from Christ, and without which His rest cannot be obtained. It is a specific act of mind, an act of conscious surrender to His authority, to be ruled only by Him. Saul took this yoke upon him when, convicted of his rebellion and conquered by a sense of the Saviour's compassion, he said, "Lord, what wilt thou have me to do?" (Acts 9:6). To take Christ's yoke upon us signifies setting aside of our wills and completely submitting to His sovereignty, acknowledging His Lordship in a practical way. Christ demands something more than lip service from His followers, even a loving obedience to all His commands, "Not every one that saith unto me, Lord, Lord, shall enter into the kingdom of heaven; but he that doeth the will of my Father which is in heaven. . . . Whosoever heareth these sayings of mine, and doeth them, I will liken him unto a wise man, which built his house upon a rock" (Matthew 7:21, 24).

"Take my yoke upon you." Our coming to Christ necessarily implies turning of our backs upon all that is opposed to Him. "Let the wicked

forsake his way, and the unrighteous man his thoughts: and let him return unto the LORD, and he will have mercy upon him" (Isaiah 55:7). So taking His yoke presupposes our throwing off the yoke we had worn before: the yoke of sin and Satan, of self-will and self-pleasing. "O LORD our God, other lords beside thee have had dominion over us" confessed Israel of old (26:13). Then they added, "But by thee only will we make mention of thy name." Thus, taking Christ's yoke upon us denotes a change of master, a conscious, cheerful change on our part. "Neither yield ye your members as instruments of unrighteousness unto sin. . . . Know ye not, that to whom ye yield yourselves servants to obey, his servants ye are to whom ye obey; whether of sin unto death, or of obedience unto righteousness?" (Romans 6:13, 16).

"Take my yoke upon you." It may sound much like a paradox—to bid those who labor and are heavy laden, who come to Christ for "rest," to take a "yoke" upon them. Yet, in reality, it is far from the case. Instead of the yoke of Christ bringing its wearer into bondage, it introduces a real liberty, the only genuine liberty there is. The Lord Jesus said to those who believed in Him, "If ye continue in my word, then are ye my disciples indeed; and ye shall know the truth, and the truth shall make you free" (John 8:31–32). There must first be a continuing in His Word, a constant walking in it. As we do this, He makes good His promise: "And ye shall know the truth": know it in an experiential way, know its power and its blessedness. The consequence is: "The truth shall make you free"—free from prejudice, from ignorance, from folly, from self-will, from the grievous bondage of Satan and the power of sin. Then the obedient disciple discovers that divine commandments are "the perfect law of liberty" (James 1:25). David said, "I will walk at liberty: for I seek thy precepts" (Psalm 119:45).

By the yoke, two oxen were united together in the plow. The yoke, then, is a figure of practical union. This is clear from "Be ye not unequally yoked together with unbelievers: for what fellowship hath righteousness with unrighteousness? and what communion hath light with darkness?" (2 Corinthians 6:14). The Lord's people are forbidden to enter into any intimate relationships with unbelievers; prohibited from marrying, forming business partnerships, or having any religious union with them. This yoke speaks of a union which results in a close communion. Christ invites those who come to Him for rest to enter into a practical union with Him so that they may enjoy fellowship together. So it was with Enoch, who "walked with God" (Genesis 5:24). But "Can two walk together, except they be agreed?" (Amos 3:3). They cannot. They must be joined together in aim and unity of purpose: to glorify God.

"Take my yoke upon you." He does not ask us to wear something He has not worn. O the wonder of this!

> Let this mind be in you, which was also in Christ Jesus: who, being in the form of God, thought it not robbery to be equal with God: but made himself of no reputation, and took upon him the form of a servant, and was made in the likeness of men: and being found in fashion as a man, he humbled himself, and became obedient unto death, even the death of the cross. (Philippians 2:5–8)

The One who was equal with God "made himself of no reputation." He, the Lord of glory, took upon Him "the form of a servant." The very Son of God was "made of a woman, made under the law" (Galatians 4:4). "Even Christ pleased not himself" (Romans 15:3); "I came down from heaven, not to do mine own will, but the will of him that sent me" (John 6:38). This was the yoke to which He gladly submitted, complete subjection to the Father's will, loving obedience to His commands. And here He says, "Take my yoke upon you." Do as I did, making God's will yours. John Newton pointed out this is threefold.

First, *the yoke of His profession,* putting on of the Christian uniform and owning the banner of our Commander. This is no irksome duty; rather, is it a delight. Those who have "tasted that the Lord is gracious" (1 Peter 2:3) are far from being ashamed of Him and of His Gospel. They want to tell all who will hear what God has done for their souls. This was true of Andrew and Philip (John 1:40–46) and of the woman of Samaria (4:28–29). As someone has said, "Many young converts in the first warmth of their affection have more need of a bridle than of a spur in this concern." No Christian should ever be afraid to show his colors; nevertheless, he should not flaunt them before those who detest them. We will not go far wrong if we heed, "Be ready always to give an answer to every man that asketh you a reason of the hope that is in you with meekness and fear" (1 Peter 3:15). It is only when, like Peter, we follow Christ "afar off," that we are in danger of denying our discipleship.

Second, *the yoke of His precepts.*

These the gracious soul approves and delights in: but still we are renewed but in part. And when the commands of Christ stand in direct opposition to the will of man, or call upon us to sacrifice a right hand or a right eye; though the Lord will surely make those who depend upon Him victorious at the last, yet it will cost them a struggle; so that, when they are sensible how much they owe to His power working in them, and enabling them to overcome, they will, at the same time have a lively conviction of their own weakness. Abraham believed in God, and delighted to obey, yet when he was commanded to sacrifice his only son, this was no easy trial of his sincerity and obedience; and all who are partakers of his faith are exposed to meet, sooner or later, with some call of duty little less contrary to the dictates of flesh and blood. (John Newton)

Third, *the yoke of His dispensations,* His dealings with us in Providence. If we enjoy the favor of the Lord, it is certain that we will be out of favor with those who hate Him. He has plainly warned, "If ye were of the world, the world would love his own: but because ye are not of the world, but I have chosen you out of the world, therefore the world hateth you" (John 15:19). It is useless to suppose that, by acting prudently and circumspectly, we can avoid this. "All that will live godly in Christ Jesus shall suffer persecution" (2 Timothy 3:12). It is only by unfaithfulness, by hiding our light under a bushel, by compromising the Truth, by attempting to serve two masters, that we can escape "the reproach of Christ" (Hebrews 11:26). He was hated by the world and has called us to fellowship with His sufferings. This is part of the yoke He requires His disciples to bear. Moreover, "Whom the Lord loveth he chasteneth" (12:6). It is hard to bear the opposition of the world, but it is harder still to endure the rod of the Lord. The flesh is still in us and resists vigorously when our wills are crossed; nevertheless, we are gradually taught to say with Christ, "The cup which my Father hath given me, shall I not drink it?" (John 18:11).

"And learn of me: for I am meek and lowly in heart." Once, again, we call attention to the deep importance of observing our Lord's order here. Just as there can be no taking of His yoke upon us until we "come" to Him, so there is no learning of Him (in the sense meant) until we have taken His yoke upon us—until we have surrendered our wills to His and submitted to His authority. This is far more than an intellectual learning of Christ; it is an experiential, effectual, transforming learning. By painstaking effort any man may acquire a theological

knowledge of the person and doctrine of Christ. He may even obtain a clear concept of His meekness and lowliness; but that is vastly different from learning of Him in so far as to be "changed into the same image from glory to glory" (2 Corinthians 3:18). To "learn" of Him we must be completely subject to Him and in close communion with Him.

What is it that we most need to be taught of Him? How to do what will make us objects of admiration in the religious world? Or how to obtain such wisdom that we will be able to solve all mysteries? How to accomplish such great things that we will be given the preeminence among our brethren? No, indeed, nothing resembling these, for "that which is highly esteemed among men is abomination in the sight of God" (Luke 16:15). What, then, Lord? This: "Learn of me: for I am meek and lowly in heart." These are the graces we most need to cultivate, the fruits which the Husbandman most highly values. Of the former grace, it is said, "Even the ornament of a meek and quiet spirit, which is in the sight of God of great price" (1 Peter 3:4); of the latter, the Lord declared, "I dwell in the high and holy place, with him also that is of a contrite and humble spirit" (Isaiah 57:15). Do we really believe these Scriptures?

"For I am meek." What is meekness? We may best discover the answer by observing the word in other verses. For example, "Now the man Moses was very meek, above all the men which were upon the face of the earth" (Numbers 12:3). This refers to the gentleness of Moses' spirit under unjust opposition. Instead of returning evil, he prayed for the healing of Miriam. So far from being weakness (as the world supposes), meekness is the strength of the man who can rule his own spirit under provocation, subduing his resentment of wrong, and refusing to retaliate. The "meek and quiet spirit" also has to do with the subjection of a wife to her husband (1 Peter 3:1–6); her "chaste conversation" ("behavior"), which is to be "coupled with fear" (v. 2); even as Sarah "obeyed Abraham, calling him lord" (v. 6). It is inseparably associated with gentleness: "The meekness and gentleness of Christ" (2 Corinthians 10:1); "gentle, shewing all meekness unto all men" (Titus 3:2). The "spirit of meekness" is in sharp contrast from the apostle using "a rod" (1 Corinthians 4:21).

Thus we may say that meekness is the opposite of self-will. It is pliability, yieldedness, offering no resistance, as clay in the Potter's hands; when the Maker of heaven and earth exclaimed, "I am a worm, and no man" (Psalm 22:6), He referred not only to the unparalleled depths of shame into which He descended for our sakes, but also to His lowliness and submission to the Father's will. A worm has no power of resistance, not even when it is stepped on. So there was nothing in the perfect Servant which opposed the will of God. Behold in Him the majesty of meekness, when He stood like a lamb before her shearers, committing Himself to the righteous Judge. Contrast Satan, who is represented as "a great red dragon" (Revelation 12:3), while the Lamb stands as the symbol of the meekest and gentlest.

The meekness of Christ appeared in His readiness to become the covenant head of His people and to assume our nature; in being subjects to His parents during the days of His childhood; in submitting to the ordinance of baptism; in His entire subjection to the Father's will. He made no retaliation; He counted not His life dear unto Himself, but freely laid it down for others. We most need to learn of Him, not how to become great or self-important, but how to deny self, to become tractable and gentle, to be servants—not only His servants, but also the servants of our brethren.

"For I am meek and lowly in heart." As meekness is the opposite of self-will, so lowliness is the reverse of self-esteem and self-righteousness. Lowliness is self-abasement; yes, self-effacement. It is more than a refusing to stand up for our own rights. Though He was so great a Person, this grace was preeminently displayed by Christ. "The Son of man came not to be ministered unto, but to minister" (Matthew 20:28); "I am among you as he that serveth" (Luke 22:27). Behold Him as He performed the menial duties of washing the feet of His disciples. He was the only One born into this world who could choose the home and the circumstances of His birth. What a rebuke to our foolish pride His choice was! My reader, we must indeed learn of Him if this choice flower of paradise is to bloom in the garden of our souls.

Chapter 43

THE QUINTESSENCE OF CHRIST

*T*he Lord Jesus uttered a gracious invitation which is accompanied by a precious promise—"Come unto me, all ye that labour and are heavy laden, and I will give you rest. Take my yoke upon you, and learn of me: for I am meek and lowly in heart: and ye shall find rest unto your souls" (Matthew 11:28–29)—and then He proceeded to make known the conditions of that promise. To those whose consciences are weighted down by a burden of guilt and who are anxious for relief, He says, "Come unto me and rest." But His rest can only be obtained as we meet His requirements: that we take His "yoke" upon us, and that we "learn" of Him. Taking Christ's yoke upon us consists of surrendering our wills to Him, submitting to His authority, consenting to be ruled by Him (see chap. 42). Now consider what it means to "learn" of Him.

Christ is the antitypical Prophet, to whom all of the Old Testament prophets pointed. He alone was personally qualified to fully make known the will of God. "God, who at sundry times and in divers manners spake in time past unto the fathers by the prophets, hath in these last days spoken unto us by his Son" (Hebrews 1:1–2). Christ is the grand

Teacher of His Church; all others are subordinate to and appointed by Him. "He gave some, apostles; and some, prophets; and some, evangelists; and some, pastors and teachers; for the perfecting of the saints, for the work of the ministry, for the edifying of the body of Christ" (Ephesians 4:11–12). Christ is the chief Shepherd and Feeder of His flock (1 Peter 5:4); His undershepherds learn of and receive from Him. Christ is the personal Word in whom and through whom the divine perfections are illustriously displayed. "No man hath seen God at any time; the only begotten Son, which is in the bosom of the Father, he hath declared him" (John 1:18). So we must come to Christ to be instructed in heavenly doctrine and built up in our holy faith.

"*Learn of me.*" Christ is not only the final Spokesman of God, the One by whom the divine will is fully uttered, but He is also the grand Exemplar set before His people. Christ did more than proclaim the Truth; He became the embodiment of it. He did more than utter the will of God; He was the personal exemplification of it. The divine requirements were perfectly set forth in the character and conduct of the Lord Jesus. And therein He differed radically from all who went before Him and all who come after Him. The lives of the prophets (Old Testament) and the apostles (New Testament) shed scattered rays of light, but they were merely reflections of *the* Light. Christ is "the Sun of righteousness" (Malachi 4:2), and therefore is fully qualified to say, "Learn of me." There was no error in His teaching, nor the slightest blemish in His character, or flaw in His conduct. The life He lived presents to us a perfect standard of holiness, a perfect pattern for us to follow.

When His enemies asked, "Who art thou?" He answered, "Even the same that I said unto you from the beginning" (John 8:25). The force of that remarkable answer (expressed in the Greek) is brought out yet more plainly in Bagster's *Interlinear* and the margin of the *American Revised Version,* "Altogether that which I also spoke unto thee." In reply to their interrogation, the Son of God affirmed that He was essentially and absolutely what He declared Himself to be: I have spoken of "light"; I *am* that light. I have spoken of "truth"; I *am* that truth—the incarnation, personification, and exemplification thereof. None but He could really say, "I am Myself what I am speaking to you about." The child of God may speak the truth and walk in *the* truth, but he is not the truth. Christ is! A Christian may let his light shine, but he is not *the* light. Christ was—and therein we see His exalted uniqueness. "We may know him that is true" (1 John 5:20); not "him who *taught* the truth," but "him that is true."

Because the Lord Jesus could make this claim: "I am altogether that which I spoke unto thee": I am the living embodiment, the personal exemplification of all which I teach; because He is the perfect Pattern for us to follow, He can say, "Learn of me." He has "[left] us an example, that [we] should follow his steps" (1 Peter 2:21). Since we bear His name (Christians) we should imitate His holiness. "Be ye followers of me, even as I also am of Christ" (1 Corinthians 11:1). The best of men are but men at the best. They have their errors and defects, which they freely acknowledge; therefore, where they differ from Christ, it is our duty to differ from them. No man, however wise or holy, is a perfect rule for other men. The standard of perfection is in Christ alone; He is the rule of every Christian's walk. "Not as though I had already attained, either were already perfect: but I follow after, if that I may apprehend that for which also I am apprehended of Christ Jesus" (Philippians 3:12). Though we fall far short of teaching such a standard in this life, nothing short of it should be our aim.

"He that saith he abideth in him ought himself also so to walk, even as he walked" (1 John 2:6). Many reasons might be given in proof of *ought*. It is vain for any man to profess he is a Christian unless he evidences that it is both his desire and endeavor to follow the example Christ left His people. As the Puritans said, "Let him either put on the life of Christ, or put off the name of Christ; let him show the hand of a Christian in works of holiness and obedience, or else the tongue and language of a Christian must gain no belief or credit." God has predestinated His people "to be conformed to the image of his Son" (Romans 8:29). The work was begun here and perfected after death, but that work is not consummated in heaven unless it is commenced on earth. "We may as well hope to be saved without Christ, as to be saved without conformity to Christ" (John Flavel).

This practical conformity between God's Son and His sons is indispensable to their relation in grace, this relationship between body and Head. Believers are members of a living organism of which Christ is the Head; of *members:* "By one Spirit are we all baptized into one body, whether we be Jews or Gentiles, whether we be bond or free; and have been all made to drink into one Spirit" (1 Corinthians 12:13); of *Christ:* "And [God] gave him to be the head over all things to the church, which is his body, the fulness of him that filleth all in all" (Ephesians 1:22–23). The two together (*members* and *Head*) form Christ-mystical. Now as Christ, the Head, is pure and holy, so also must be the members. An animal with a human head would be a monstrosity. For the sensual and godless to claim oneness to Christ is to misrepresent Him before the world, as though His mystical Body were like the image of Nebuchadnezzar, with the head of fine gold and the feet of iron and clay (Daniel 2:32–45).

This resemblance to Christ appears necessary from the communion which all believers have with Him in the same Spirit of grace and holiness. Christ is the "firstborn among many brethren" (Romans 8:29), and God anointed Him "with the oil of gladness above [his] fellows" (Psalm 45:7). That oil of gladness is an emblem of the Holy Spirit, and God gives the same to each of the "fellows," or partners. Where the same Spirit and principle is, there the same fruits and works must be produced, according to the proportions of the Spirit of grace bestowed. This is the very reason the Holy Spirit is given to believers. "But we all, with open face beholding as in a glass the glory of the Lord, are changed into the same image from glory to glory, even as by the Spirit of the Lord" (2 Corinthians 3:18).

Also, the very honor of Christ demands conformity of Christians to His example. In what other way can they close the mouths of those who reject their Master and vindicate His blessed name from the reproaches of the world? How can Wisdom be justified of her children except in this way? The wicked will not read the inspired record of His life in the Scriptures; therefore, there is all the more need to have His excellencies set before them in the lives of His people. The world sees what we practice, as well as hears what we profess. Unless there is consistency between our profession and practice, we cannot glorify Christ before a world which has cast Him out.

Then there must be an inward conformity to Christ before there can be any resemblance on the outside. There must be an experiential oneness before there can be a practical likeness. How can we possibly be conformed to Him in external acts of obedience unless we are conformed to Him in those springs from which such actions proceed? We must "live in the Spirit" before we can "walk in the Spirit" (Galatians 5:25). "Let this mind be in you, which was also in Christ Jesus" (Philippians 2:5), for the mind should regulate all our other faculties. Therefore we are told, "For to be carnally minded is death: but to be spiritually minded is life and peace" (Romans 8:6). What was "the mind which was in Christ Jesus"? It was that of self-abnegation and devotedness to the Father. That we must begin with inward conformity to Christ is evident from our text; after saying "learn of me," He at once added, "for I am meek and lowly in heart."

We need to attend closely to our Lord's order in this passage, insisting we cannot possibly "learn" of Him (in the sense meant here) until we have taken His "yoke" upon us: until we *surrender* ourselves to Him. It is not merely to an intellectual learning of Him which Christ calls us, but to an experiential, effectual, and transforming learning; and in order to obtain that, we must be completely subject to Him. John Newton suggested that there is yet another relation between these two things: Not only is our taking of Christ's yoke upon us an indispensable requirement for our learning of Him, but also our learning of Him is His duly appointed means to enable us to wear His yoke.

"Learn of me." Be not afraid to come to Me for help and instruction, "for I am meek and lowly in heart." Here is encouragement. You need not hesitate to come to such a One, the Maker of heaven and earth, the King of kings and Lord of lords. He is the One before whom all the angels of heaven prostrate themselves in homage, yet the One who is the Friend of sinners. He is able to solve our every problem and supply strength for the weakest; because He is Man, possessed of human sensibilities, therefore is He capable of being "touched with the feeling of our infirmities" (Hebrews 4:15).

"Learn of me." I know why these things appear so hard. It is owing to the pride and impatience of your hearts. To remedy this, take Me for your example; I require nothing of you but what I have performed before you, and on your account: in that path I mark out for you, you may perceive My own footsteps all the way. This is a powerful argument, a sweet recommendation, the yoke of Christ, to those who love Him, that He bore it Himself. He is not like the Pharisees, whom He censured (Matthew 23:4) on this very account: who bound heavy burdens, and grievous to be borne, and laid them on men's shoulders, but they themselves would not move them with one of their fingers.

1. Are you terrified with the difficulties attending *your profession* [of belief in Christ]: disheartened by hard usage, or too ready to show

resentment against those who oppose you? Learn of Jesus, admire and imitate His constancy:"Consider him who endured the contradiction of sinners against himself" (Hebrews 12:3). Make a comparison (so the word imports) between yourself and Him, between the contradiction which He endured and that which you are called to struggle with; then surely you will be ashamed to complain. Admire and imitate His meekness: when He was reviled, He reviled not again; when He suffered, He threatened not; He wept for His enemies, and prayed for His murderers. Let the same mind be in you which was also in Christ Jesus.

2. Do you find it hard to walk steadfastly in His *precepts,* especially in some particular instances, when the maxims of worldly prudence and the pleadings of flesh and blood, are strongly against you? Learn of Jesus. He pleased not Himself (Romans 15:3): He considered not what was safe and easy, but what was the will of His heavenly Father. Entreat Him to strengthen you with strength in your soul, that as you bear the name of His disciples, you may resemble Him in every part of your conduct, and shine as lights in a dark and selfish world, to the glory of His grace.

3. Are you tempted to repine at the dispensations of Divine *providence?* Take Jesus for your pattern. Did He say, when the unspeakable sufferings He was to endure for sinners were just coming upon Him, "The cup which my Father hath given me, shall I not drink it?" (John 18:11); and shall we presume to have a will of our own? especially when we further reflect, that as His sufferings were wholly on our account, so all our sufferings are by His appointment, and all designed by Him to promote our best, that is our spiritual and eternal welfare? (John Newton).

"Learn of me." Christ, then, taught His disciples not only by precept, but also by example; not only by word of mouth, but also by His own perfect life of obedience to the Father's will. When He uttered these words (Matthew 11:29), He was wearing the "yoke" and personally exemplifying meekness and lowliness. What a perfect Teacher, showing us in His own selflessness what these graces really are. He did not associate with the noble and mighty, but made fishermen His ambassadors and sought out the most despised, so that He was dubbed "a friend of publicans and sinners" (v. 19).

"And learn of me: for I am meek and lowly in heart." Those heavenly graces, the roots from which all other spiritual excellencies spring, can

only be learned from Christ. The colleges and seminaries cannot impart them, preachers and churches cannot bestow them, no self-culture can attain unto them. They can only be learned experientially at the feet of Christ, only as we take His yoke upon us. They can only be learned as we commune with Him and follow the example He left us. They can only be learned as we pray that we may be more fully conformed to His image and trustfully seek the enablement of His Spirit to "mortify the deeds of the body" (Romans 8:13).

What causes have we to mourn that there is so little meekness and lowliness in us! How we need to confess unto God our lamentable deficiency. Yet, merely mourning does not improve matters. We must go to the root of our folly and judge it. Why have I failed to learn these heavenly graces? Has it not to be said of me, as of Israel, "Ephraim is a bullock unaccustomed to the yoke"? (see Jeremiah 31:18). Not until my proud spirit is broken and my will completely surrendered to Christ can I truly "learn of Him."

And taking Christ's yoke upon us and learning of Him is a daily thing. Christianity is far more than a creed or ethical code—it is a being conformed practically to the image of God's Son. So many make the great mistake in supposing that coming to Christ and taking His yoke is a single act, which may be done once and for all. Not so! It is to be a continuous and daily act: "To whom coming [again and again], as unto a living stone" (1 Peter 2:4). We need to continue as we began. The mature Christian who has been fifty years in the way needs Christ as urgently now as he did the first moment he was convicted of his lost condition. He needs to daily take His yoke and learn of Him.

Chapter 44

THE LEADERSHIP OF CHRIST

"or my yoke is easy, and my burden is light" (Matthew 11:30).
As pointed out (see chap. 42), the yoke, employed figuratively, is the symbol of service. Such an instrument united oxen together in pulling the plow or wagon, so they worked for their master. Our text refers to the service of Christ, in contrast to the service of sin and Satan. The devil promises his subjects a grand time if they follow his promptings; but sooner or later, they discover that "the way of transgressors is hard" (Proverbs 13:15). Sin deceives. Its deluded victims imagine they enjoy liberty while indulging the lusts of the flesh; but when failing health suggests they had better change their ways, they discover they are bound by habits they cannot break. Sin is a more cruel taskmaster than were the Egyptians to the Hebrews. And the service of Satan imposes far heavier burdens than Pharaoh ever placed upon his slaves. But "My yoke is easy, and my burden is light."

This declaration of the Saviour may also be the sequel to His opening words in this passage. There He invited those who labored and were heavy laden, which may be understood in a twofold sense: those who were sick of sin and bowed down by a sense of its guilt, and those who labored to meet the requirements of divine holiness and are cast down by their inability to do so. Those who seek to fulfill the letter of God's Law, far from finding it "easy," discover it is very hard; while those who endeavor to work out a righteousness of their own to gain God's esteem, find it a heavy task and not a "light burden."

"For my yoke is easy, and my burden is light." Exactly what is the relation between this verse and the ones preceding? To which of the previous clauses is it more immediately connected? We cannot discover that any commentator has made any specific attempt to answer this question. We deem it wise to link these closing words of the Redeemer with each of the earlier utterances. Thus, "Come unto me, all ye that labour and are heavy laden, and I will give you rest. . . . for my yoke is easy, and my burden is light." There is encouragement for us to come and proof that He will give us rest. "Take my yoke upon you": you need not fear to do so, "for my yoke is easy, and my burden is light." "And learn of me," for not only am I "meek and lowly in heart: and ye shall find rest unto your souls," but "for my yoke is easy."

"For my yoke is easy." The Greek word is variously rendered, "good," "kind," "gracious." There is nothing to chafe or hurt; rather, it is pleasant to wear. The question has been raised if Christ spoke absolutely or relatively. That is, did He describe what the yoke was in itself, or how that yoke appeared to His people? We believe both senses are included. Assuredly Christ's yoke or service is a light or gracious one in itself, for all His commandments are framed by infinite wisdom and love and are designed for the good of those who receive them. So far from being a harsh tyrant who imposes hard duties for the mere sake of exerting His authority, Christ is a gracious Master who ever has in mind the welfare and highest interests of His subjects. His commandments "are not grievous" in themselves, but beneficent. It is the "father of lies" who declares Christ's yoke to be difficult and heavy.

But not only is the yoke of Christ "easy" in itself, but also it should be so in the sense and apprehension of His people. It will be so, if they do as He bids. The unregenerate find the yoke of Christ irksome and heavy, for it grates against the carnal nature. The service of Christ is drudgery to those in love with the world and who find their delight in fleshly lusts; but to one whose heart has been captivated by Christ, to be under His yoke is pleasant. If we come to Christ daily to be renewed by

His grace, to yield ourselves afresh to His rule; if we sit at His feet to be taught of Him the loveliness of meekness and lowliness; if we enjoy spiritual communion with Him and partake of His rest, then whatsoever *He* commands is delightful to us, and we prove for ourselves that wisdom's ways "are ways of pleasantness, and all her paths are peace" (Proverbs 3:17).

Here the Christian may discover the most conclusive evidence that a good work of grace has begun in his heart. How many poor souls are deeply distressed over this point. They ask themselves continually, *Have I been genuinely converted, or am I yet in a state of nature?* They keep themselves in needless suspense because they fail to apply the scriptural methods of confirmation. Instead of measuring themselves by the rules in the Word, they await some extraordinary sensation in their heart. But many have been deceived at this point, for Satan can produce happy sensations in the heart and deep impressions on the mind. How much better is the testimony of an enlightened conscience. Judging things by the Word of God, it perceives that the yoke of Christ is easy and light.

But this principle works both ways. If we find by experience that Christ's yoke is easy and His burden is light, then what must be said of a vast number of professing Christians who, by their own conduct, often avow that the Lord's service is burdensome? Though members of evangelical churches, may we conclude that they are of the class who have a name that they live, and yet are dead (Revelation 3:1)? Certainly we cannot allow that Christ made a false predication of His yoke. Then only one alternative is left. We are obliged to regard as strangers to godliness those who find a life of communion with the Lord and devotedness to His service dull or irksome.

Do not misunderstand this point. We are not affirming the Christian life is nothing but a bed of roses, or that when a person comes to Christ and takes His yoke that his troubles end. Not so. Instead, in a real sense his troubles only then begin. It is written, "Yea, and all that will live godly in Christ Jesus shall suffer persecution" (2 Timothy 3:12). Wearing the yoke of Christ unites us to Him, and union with Him brings us into "fellowship with His sufferings." The members of Christ's body share the experience of their Head. The world hated and persecuted Him, and it hates those who bear His image. But the more closely we walk with Christ, the more we will suffer the hostility of Satan, for his rage is stirred up when he finds he has lost another of his captives.

Not only does the one who truly comes to Christ and takes upon him His yoke evoke the hatred of Satan and of the world, but also he is now the subject of inward conflicts. The corrupt nature which was his at birth is neither removed nor refined when he becomes a Christian. It remains within him, unchanged. But now he is more conscious of its presence and its vileness. Moreover, that evil nature opposes every movement of the holy nature he received at the new birth. "The flesh lusteth against the Spirit, and the Spirit against the flesh: and these are contrary the one to the other" (Galatians 5:17). This discovery of the plague of his own heart and that within there is opposition to holy aspirations, is a source of deep anguish to the child of God. He often cries, "O wretched man that I am! who shall deliver me from the body of this death?" (Romans 7:24).

We cannot affirm that the Christian's life is one of unclouded sunshine; yet we must not convey the impression the believer's lot is far from being envious, and that he is worse off than the unbeliever. Far from it. If the Christian uses diligently the means of God's appointing, he will possess a peace which passeth all understanding, and experience joys the worldling knows nothing about. The world may frown and the devil rage against him, but an approving conscience, the smile of God, the communion with fellow believers, and the assurance of eternity with his Beloved are ample compensation.

What is there in the yoke of Christ which makes such amends for the enmity it evokes and the suffering it entails, so that the believer will attest that it is an easy one? In seeking to answer this question we shall avail ourselves of the help of John Newton's sermons, in outline. *First,* those who wear the yoke of Christ *act from a principle which makes all things easy.* This is love. Any yoke will chafe when resisted, but even one of cast iron would be pleasant if it were lined with felt and padded with wool. And this is what renders the yoke of Christ easy to His people. It is *lined with love,* His to them, and theirs to Him. Whenever the shoulder becomes sore, look to the lining! Keep the lining right and the yoke will be no more a burden to us than wings are to a bird, or a wedding ring to a bride.

Scripture records that when Jacob served a hard master seven years for Rachel, they seemed but a few days to him "for the love he had to her" (Genesis 29:20). What a difference it makes when we perform a difficult task, whether for a stranger or a dear friend, an exacting employer or a close relative. Affection makes the hardest joy easy. But there is no love like that which a redeemed sinner bears to Him who died in his stead. We are willing to suffer much to gain the affection of one we highly esteem, even though we are not sure of success; but when we know the affection is reciprocal, it gives added strength for the endeavor. The believer does not love with uncertainty. He knows that Christ loved him before he had any love for the Saviour; yes, loved him even when his own heart was filled with enmity against Him. This love supplies two sweet and effectual motives in service:

A desire to please. This is the question love is ever asking. What can I do to gratify, to make happy the object of my affection? Love is ever ready to do whatever it can and regrets that it cannot do more. Neither time, difficulties, nor expense concern the one whose heart is warmly engaged. But the world is not in the secret. They neither know nor appreciate the principles which motivate the people of God. Not only are they at a loss to understand why the Christian is no longer willing to join with them in the pleasures of sin, but also they fail to see what satisfaction he finds in reading the Scriptures, in secret prayer, or public worship. They suppose that some mental derangement is responsible, and advise him to leave such gloomy exercises to those on the verge of the grave. But the believer can answer, "The love of Christ constraineth me" (see 2 Corinthians 5:14).

A pleasant assurance of acceptance. What a difference it makes when we are able to determine whether or not what we do will be favorably received. If we have reason to fear that the one for whom we work does not appreciate our efforts, we find little delight in the task and are tempted to spare ourselves. But if we have good reason to believe that our labors will meet with a smile of approval, how much easier is the labor and how much more readily will we do it with our might. It is this encouragement which stimulates Christ's disciples. They know that He will not overlook the smallest service in His name or the slightest suffering endured for His sake; for even a cup of cold water given on His account is acknowledged as though proffered immediately to Him (Mark 9:41).

Second, service is still easier and lighter if it is *agreeable to our inclinations.* Esau would probably have done anything to please his father to obtain the blessing. But no commandment could have been more agreeable to him than to be sent for venison, because he was a hunter (Genesis 25:27). The Christian has received from God a new nature; he has been made a "[partaker] of the divine nature" (2 Peter 1:4). Just as the magnetic needle ever points to the North Star, so this spiritual principle ever turns to its Author. Consequently, God's Word is its food, communion with Him its desire, His Law its delight. True, he still groans under inward corruption, but these are part of sin's burden and no part of Christ's yoke. He groans because he cannot serve Him better. But just so far as he exercises his faith he rejoices in every part of Christ's yoke. Professing His name is a holy privilege, His precepts are a profitable meditation, and suffering for Christ's sake is counted a high honor.

Third, the burden of Christ is light because *sustaining grace* is granted to its wearer. Service to a loved one would be impracticable if you were infirm and incapacitated. Nor could you take a long journey to minister to a friend, no matter how dear, if you were crippled. But the yoke of Christ is easy in this respect too—He supplies sufficient strength to the bearer. What is hard to flesh and blood is easy to faith and grace. It is true, apart from Christ the believer "can do nothing" (John 15:5); but it is equally true he "can do all things" through Christ strengthening him (Philippians 4:13). It is true that "even the youths shall faint and be weary, and the young men shall utterly fall"; yet we are divinely assured that "they that wait upon the LORD shall renew their strength; they shall mount up with wings as eagles; they shall run, and not be weary; and they shall walk, and not faint" (Isaiah 40:30–31). What more can we ask? It is entirely our own fault if we are not "strong in the Lord, and in the power of his might" (Ephesians 6:10).

Whatever the Lord may call upon us to do, if we depend on Him in the use of appointed means, He will most certainly equip us for it. He is no Pharaoh, requiring us to make bricks and providing no straw for the same. So far from it, He promises, "As thy days, so shall thy strength be" (Deuteronomy 33:25). Moses may complain, "I am slow of speech, and of a slow tongue," but the Lord assures him, "I will be with thy mouth, and teach thee what thou shalt say" (Exodus 4:10, 12). Paul acknowledged, "Not that we are sufficient of ourselves to think any thing as of ourselves"; yet he at once added, "But our sufficiency is of God" (2 Corinthians 3:5). So too whatever sufferings the Lord calls upon His people to endure for His sake, He will assuredly grant sustaining grace. "All power . . . in heaven and in earth" belongs unto Christ (Matthew 28:18), and therefore is He able to make our enemies flee before us and deliver us from the mouth of the lion. Even though He permits His servants to be beaten and cast into prison, yet songs of praises are put into their mouths (Acts 16:25).

Finally, the easiness of Christ's yoke appears in *the rich compensations that accompany it.* Under sin's yoke we spent our strength for what did not satisfy, but when wearing Christ's yoke we find rest for our souls. If we live a life of pleasing self and seeking our own honor, then we reap misery and woe; but when self is denied and Christ is glorified, peace and joy are ours. No man serves Christ for nothing; in keeping His commandments there is "great reward" (Psalm 19:11)—not of debt, but of grace, after. The Christian may have much to cast him down, but he has far more to cheer him up and send him on his way rejoicing. He has free access to the throne of grace, precious promises to rest upon, and the consolation of the Holy Spirit to comfort his soul. He has a Friend who sticketh closer than a brother, a loving Father who supplies his every need, and the blessed assurance that when the appointed hour arrives he shall go to another world, where there is no sin or sorrow, but "fulness of joy" and "pleasures for evermore" (Psalm 16:11).

Chapter 45
THE
EXAMPLE
OF CHRIST

*T*wo serious mistakes have been made by men in taking or not taking Christ for their example. It is difficult to determine which is the more evil and fatal of the two. First, those who held up the perfect life of the Lord Jesus before the unconverted maintained that they must imitate it in order to find acceptance with God. In other words, they made emulating Christ "the way of salvation" to lost sinners. This is a fundamental error, which cannot be resisted too strenuously. It repudiates the total depravity and spiritual helplessness of fallen man. It denies the necessity for the new birth. It nullifies the atonement by emphasizing Christ's flawless life at the expense of His sacrificial death. It substitutes works for faith, creature efforts for divine grace, man's faulty doings for the Redeemer's finished work. If the Acts and the Epistles are searched, it will be revealed that the apostles never preached imitating Christ as the way to obtain forgiveness of sins and secure peace with God.

But in recent generations the pendulum has swung to the opposite extreme. If, a century ago, the example which Christ has left His people was made too much of, our moderns make far too little of it; if they gave it a place in preaching to the unsaved which Scripture does not warrant, we have failed to press it upon Christians to the extent Scripture requires. If those a century ago are to be blamed for misusing the example of Christ in connection with justification, we are guilty of failing to use it in connection with sanctification. While it is true that the moral perfections which Christ displayed during His earthly sojourn are still extolled in many places, how rarely one hears (or reads) of those who insist that emulating Christ is absolutely essential for the believer's preservation and ultimate salvation. Would not the great majority of orthodox preachers be positively afraid to make any such assertion, lest they be charged with legality?

The Lord Jesus Christ is not only a perfect and glorious Pattern of all graces, holiness, virtue, and obedience, to be preferred above all others, but also *He alone* is such. In the lives of the best of the saints, Scripture records what it is our duty to avoid, as well as what we ought to follow. Sometimes one is puzzled to know whether it is safe to conform to them or not. But God has graciously supplied us with a sure rule which solves that problem. If we heed it we will never be at a loss to see our duty. Holy men and women of Scripture are to be imitated by us only as far as they were themselves conformed unto Christ (1 Corinthians 11:1). The best of their graces, the highest of their attainments, the most perfect of their duties were spoiled by blemishes; but in Christ there is no imperfection whatever, for He had no sin and did no sin.

Christ is not only the perfect, but also the pattern Man; and therefore is His example suitable for all believers. This remarkable fact presents a feature which has not received the attention it deserves. There is nothing so distinctive in personality as racial and national characteristics. The greatest of men bear unmistakable marks of their heredity and environment. Racial peculiarities are imperishable; to the last fiber of his being, Luther was a German, Knox a Scot; and with all his largeness of heart, Paul was a Jew. In sharp contrast, Jesus Christ rose above heredity and environment. Nothing local, transient, national, or sectarian dwarfed His wondrous personality. Christ is the only truly catholic man. He belongs to all ages and is related to all men, because He is "the Son of man." This underlies the universal suitability of Christ's example to believers of all nations, who one and all may find in Him the perfect realization of their ideal.

This is indeed a miracle and exhibits a transcendent perfection in the Man Christ Jesus which is rarely pondered. How remarkable that the converted Englishman may find in Christ's character and conduct a pattern as well-suited to him as to a saved Chinese; that His example is as appropriate for the regenerated Zulu as for a born-again German. The needs of Lord Bacon and Sir Isaac Newton were as truly met in Christ as were those of the half-witted youth who said, "I'm a poor sifter and nothing at all, but Jesus Christ is my all in all." How remarkable that the example of Christ is as appropriate for believers of the twentieth century as it was for those of the first; that it is as suitable for a Christian child as for his grandparent!

He is appointed of God for this very purpose. One end why God sent His Son to become flesh and tabernacle in the world was that He might set before us an example in our nature, in One who was like unto us in all things, sin excepted. Thereby He exhibited to us that renewal to His image in us, of that return to Him from sin and apostasy, and of that holy obedience He requires of us. Such an example was needful so that we might never be at a loss about the will of God in His commandments, having a glorious representation of it before our eyes. That could be given us no other way than in our own nature. The nature of angels was not suited as an example of obedience, especially in the exercise of such graces as we specially stand in need of in this world. What example could angels set us in patience in afflictions or quietness in sufferings, when their nature is incapable of such things? Nor could we have had a perfect example in our nature except in one who was holy and "separate from sinners."

Many Scriptures present Christ as the believer's Exemplar: "Take my yoke upon you and learn of me; for I am meek and lowly in heart" (Matthew 11:29)—learn by the course of My life as well as by My words; "when he putteth forth his own sheep, he goeth before them, and the sheep follow him" (John 10:4)—He requires no more of us than He rendered Himself; "I have given you an example, that ye should do as I have done to you" (13:15); "now the God of patience and consolation grant you to be likeminded one toward another according to Christ Jesus" (Romans 15:5); "let this mind be in you, which was also in Christ Jesus" (Philippians 2:5). "Let us run with patience the race that is set before us, looking unto Jesus the author and finisher of our faith" (Hebrews 12:1–2); "but if, when ye do well, and suffer for it, ye take it patiently, this is acceptable unto God. For even hereunto were ye called: because Christ also suffered for us, leaving us an example, that ye should follow his steps" (1 Peter 2:20–21); "he that saith he abideth in him ought himself so to walk, even as he walked" (1 John 2:6).

Example is better than precept. Why? Because a precept is more or less an abstraction, whereas an example sets before us a concrete representation and therefore has more aptitude to incite the mind to imitation. The conduct of those with whom we are in close association exerts a considerable influence upon us, either for good or evil. The fact is clearly recognized in the Scriptures. For example, we are enjoined, "Make no friendship with an angry man; and with a furious man thou shalt not go: lest thou learn his ways, and get a snare to thy soul" (Proverbs 22:24–25). It was for this reason that God commanded the Israelites to utterly destroy all the inhabitants of Canaan, so that they might not learn their evil ways and be contaminated by them (Deuteronomy 7:2–4). Contrariwise, the example of the pious exerts an influence for good; that is why they are called "the salt of the earth" (Matthew 5:13).

In keeping with this principle, God has appointed the consideration of Christ's character and conduct as a special means to increase the piety in His people. As their hearts contemplate His holy obedience, it has a peculiar efficacy to their growing in grace beyond all other examples. It is in beholding the Lord Jesus by faith that salvation comes to us. "Look unto me, and be ye saved, all the ends of the earth" (Isaiah 45:22). Christ is presented before the sinner in the Gospel, with the promise that whosoever believingly looks to Him shall not perish, but have everlasting life (John 3:14–15). This is a special ordinance of God, and it is made effectual by the Spirit to all who believe. In like manner, Christ is presented to the saints as the grand Pattern of obedience and Example of holiness, with the promise that as they contemplate Him as such we shall be changed into His image (2 Corinthians 3:18). Our response to that appointment of God is rewarded by a growing in piety.

But to get down to details: What is involved in the saints' imitating of Christ? First, it presupposes that they be already regenerate. The hearts of His followers must be sanctified before their lives can be conformed to Him. The spirit and principle of obedience must be imparted to the soul before there can be an external imitation of Christ's practice. This order is plainly enunciated in, "I will give them one heart, and I will put a new spirit within you; and I will take the stony heart out of their flesh, and will give them an heart of flesh: that they may walk in my statutes, and keep mine ordinances, and do them: and they shall be my people, and I will be their God" (Ezekiel 11:19–20). One who is yet in the gall of bitterness and the bond of iniquity has no heart for spiritual things; therefore the tree must be made good before it can produce good fruit. We must first *live* in the Spirit and then *walk* in the Spirit (Galatians 5:25). One might as well urge the Ethiopian to change his skin or the leopard his spots, as call upon the unconverted to follow the example Christ has left His people.

Second, imitating Christ definitely denotes that no Christian may govern himself or act according to his own will. Those who are a rule to themselves act in fearful defiance of the Most High. "O LORD, I know that the way of man is not in himself: it is not in man that walketh to direct his steps" (Jeremiah 10:23). A man may as well feign to be his own creator as his own guide. No man has wisdom enough to direct himself. When born again we are conscious of this fact. Our proud hearts are humbled and our rebellious wills broken, and we feel the need of being led by Another. The cry of a converted heart is, "Lord, what wouldst thou have me to do?" His answer to us today: Follow the example which I have left you; learn of Me; walk as I walked.

Third, if this imitating of Christ clearly implies that no man may pretend to be his own master, it is equally evident that no matter how wise or how holy he is, no Christian has the right or is qualified to rule others. Christ alone is appointed and fitted to be the Lord of His people. It is true that we read in the Word, "That ye be not slothful, but followers of them who through faith and patience inherit the promises" (Hebrews 6:12); and "obey them that have the rule over you, and submit yourselves: for they watch for your souls, as they that must give account" (13:17). Yet that must be taken in subordination to the example of Christ. The best of men are but men at the best; they have their errors and faults, and where they differ from Christ it is our duty to differ from them. It is very important that we be quite clear upon this point, for much mischief has resulted from allowing some to deprive others of a vital part of their rightful liberty.

It is not that Scripture teaches an ecclesiastical democracy; that is as far from the truth as the Romish hierarchy at the opposite extreme. God has placed rulers in the Church, and its members are commanded to obey them; but their rule is administrative and not legislative—to enforce the laws of Christ, and not invent rules of their own. Paul affirmed, "Not for that we have dominion over your faith, but are helpers of your joy: for by faith ye stand" (2 Corinthians 1:24); and Peter declared of the elders or bishops, "Neither as being lords over God's heritage, but being ensamples to the flock" (1 Peter 5:3). Filled with so great a measure of the Spirit of wisdom and holiness as Paul was, yet he goes no higher than this: "Be ye followers of me, even as I also am of Christ" (1 Corinthians 11:1).

Fourth, the imitation of Christ plainly intimates that true Christianity is very strict and exacting, and in no wise countenances licentiousness or the indulgence of fleshly lusts. This needs emphasis in such a day as ours, when so much laxity prevails. People suppose they may be followers of Christ and yet ignore the path which He traveled; that they may decline the unpleasant task of denying self and yet make sure of heaven. What a delusion! The vital necessity of the careful imitation of Christ disallows all loose walking and rejects the claim of any to being real Christians if they do not heed His example. Neither worldliness nor self–indulgence can find any protection beneath the wings of the Gospel. The unvarying rule, binding on all who claim to be His, is "Let every one that nameth the name of Christ depart from iniquity" (2 Timothy 2:19). Let him either follow the example of Christ, or cease claiming to belong to Him; let him tread the highway of holiness, or all his fair words are worthless.

Fifth, the imitation of Christ necessarily implies the blemishes of the best of men. If the life of Christ is our pattern, then the holiest among His followers are obliged to admit they come far short of this standard of duty, and not in a few details, but in every respect. The character and conduct of the Lord Jesus were without spot or blemish; therefore, they are so high above our poor attainments that we are filled with shame when we measure ourselves by them. Self-satisfied religionists may take delight in comparing themselves with others, as the Pharisee did with the publican. Deluded souls who suppose that all Christian holiness consists of is measuring up to some humanly invented standard of perfection (or entering into some peculiar experience), may pride themselves that they have "received the second blessing" or "have the fulness or baptism of the Spirit"; yet all who honestly measure themselves by the perfections of Christ will find abundant cause to be humbled.

This, too, is a point of tremendous practical importance. If I place my handkerchief against a dark background, it will appear spotlessly clean; but, if I lay it upon newly fallen snow, the imperfection of its whiteness is quickly apparent. If I compare my own life with that preached by certain "victorious life" advocates, I may conclude that my life is quite acceptable. But if I diligently apply to myself the plumb line of Christ's example, then I must at once acknowledge, like Peter of old, that I am but following Him "afar off." Surely none was more proficient in holiness and punctilious in obedience than Paul; yet, when he compared himself to Christ, he declared, "Not as though I had already attained, either were already perfect: but I follow after, if that I may apprehend" (Philippians 3:12).

Sixth, the imitation of Christ as our pattern clearly implies His transcendent holiness; that His holiness is high above that of all creatures. Therefore it is the greatest of the Christian's ambitions to be conformed to His image (Philippians 3:10). Christ has a double perfection: a perfection of being and a perfection of working. His life on earth supplies a perfect rule for us because there was no blot or error therein. He was "holy, harmless, undefiled, separate from sinners"; and such a High Priest became *us* (Hebrews 7:26). Thus the conformity of professing Christians to Christ's example is both the test and measure of all their graces. The nearer anyone approaches to this Pattern, the closer he comes to perfection.

Finally, the Christian's imitation of Christ, under the penalty of forfeiting his claim to any saving interest in Christ, necessarily denotes that sanctification and obedience are the evidences of our justification and acceptance with God. Scriptural assurance is unattainable without sincere and strict obedience. "The work of righteousness [not of loose living] shall be peace" (Isaiah 32:17). "We have it not for our holiness, but we always have it in the way of holiness. Let men talk what they will of the immediate sealings and comforts of the Spirit, without any regard to holiness, or respect to obedience: sure I am, whatever delusion they meet with in that way, true peace and consolation is only to be found and expected here" (John Flavel, to whom we are indebted for much in the seven points).

"Christ also suffered for us, leaving us an example, that ye should follow his steps" (1 Peter 2:21). We have seen that not only is the perfect life of Christ a suitable pattern of holiness and obedience for His people to imitate, but also that God has expressly appointed it for that purpose. This is so that we may have a sure rule to walk by, the Law of God translated into concrete terms and its requirements set before us by a personal representation; and also for the purpose of humbling our proud hearts, by revealing to us how far short we come of measuring up to God's standard of righteousness. Furthermore, God has appointed that the example of Christ should be followed by His people so that His Son might be honored by them; to distinguish His followers from the world; and so that they should evidence the reality of their profession. Imitating Christ, then, is not optional, but obligatory.

But here a very real difficulty confronts those who sincerely seek grace to heed this divine appointment. In what particular respects are we to regard Christ as our Exemplar? All things recorded of Him in Holy Writ are for our instruction, but not all for our imitation. There were some things Christ did as God; for example, He wrought miracles. "My Father worketh hitherto, and I work. . . . For as the Father raiseth up the dead, and quickeneth them; even so the Son quickeneth whom he will" (John 5:17, 21); "but that ye may know that the Son of man hath power on earth to forgive sins, (then saith he to the sick of and palsy,) Arise, take up thy bed, and go unto thine house" (Matthew 9:6)—even the apostles never performed such deeds in their own name or by their own power. Again, as Mediator, He performed works of merit, thus making expiation for the sins of His people and "[bringing] in everlasting righteousness" for them (Daniel 9:24) and obtaining their justification and reconciliation. So now His intercession secures their preservation. No mere man can do anything meritorious, for at best we are all "unprofitable servants" (Luke 17:10).

Even as Man, Christ performed extraordinary acts which are not for our emulation: fasting for forty days and nights (Matthew 4:2), walking on the water (14:25–26; John 6:19), spending a whole night in prayer (Luke 6:12)—we do not read in Scripture of anyone else doing so—are cases in point. So He performed certain temporary works which pertained to the time in which He lived, which are not for our imitation—such as His being circumcised and His keeping the Passover.

Wherein, then, is Christ to be imitated by us? First, in all those moral duties which pertain to all men at all times, which are neither extraordinary nor temporary, comprehended in the loving of God with all our hearts and our neighbors as ourselves (Mark 12:30–31; Luke 10:27;

compare Deuteronomy 6:4–5). Second, in such duties as belong to a like calling: as the child obeying its parents (Luke 2:51); the citizen paying his taxes (Matthew 17:27); the minister of the Gospel diligently (Luke 8:1) and faithfully (Hebrews 3:2) discharging his office. Third, in all such works as have like reason and occasion for doing them (Matthew 12:12; John 8:29).

The believer's conformity to Christ corresponds to the states through which He passed. Christ Jesus first entered a state of humiliation before God rewarded Him by bringing Him into a state of exaltation; therefore God has ordered that the members shall resemble their Head. They are called upon to endure sufferings before they enter into the promised glory. The disciples of the Lord Jesus have to experience a measure of opposition, persecution, hatred, and affliction; and they do so for their hope of a better life to come. In that, they do but follow "the captain of their salvation," who was made "perfect through sufferings" (Hebrews 2:10). Has not God declared, "If we be dead with him [Christ], we shall also live with him: if we suffer, we shall also reign with him" (2 Timothy 2:11–12). That order is inescapable: "Always bearing about in the body the dying of the Lord Jesus, that the life also of Jesus might be made manifest in our body" (2 Corinthians 4:10).

In like manner, the Christian is to be conformed to the special acts of Christ's mediation, which are His death and resurrection. These are of paramount consideration, for they are not only a pattern proposed to our meditation, but also a great influence upon our dying to sin and living unto holiness. This is evidenced from the fact that those effects of grace in us are ascribed to those acts of Christ's mediation which carry most correspondence with them. Thus our mortification is ascribed to Christ's crucifixion (Galatians 2:20); our vivification to His rising unto life (Philippians 3:10); and our heavenly mindedness to His ascension (v. 20); so that all of those chief acts of Christ are verified in His people. We die to sin as Christ died for it.

But in descending to more specific details, it is in Christ's graces we are to be conformed to Him. All the graces and virtues of the Spirit were represented in their grandest glory and brightest luster in His life here on earth. First, the *purity and holiness of His life* is proposed as a glorious pattern for the saints to imitate. "Every man that hath this hope in him purifieth himself, even as he is pure" (1 John 3:3). Before enlarging upon this, let us point out where Christ is unique and beyond our imitation. He was *essentially* holy in His being, for He is "the Holy One of God" (Mark 1:24; Luke 4:34). He entered this world immaculate, pure from the least stain of pollution, "That holy thing which shall be born of thee" (1:35). Again, He was *effectually* holy, for He makes others holy. By His sufferings and blood there opened a fountain "for sin and for uncleanness" (Zechariah 13:1). He is also *infinitely* holy, as He is God, and no measure can be set upon His holiness as Mediator, for He received the Spirit without measure (John 3:34). In these particulars He is inimitable.

Notwithstanding these exceptions, the holiness of Christ is a pattern for us. He was truly and sincerely holy, without fiction or pretense. When the prince of this world scrutinized Him he could find no defect in Him (John 14:30). He was pure gold throughout. The Pharisee may pretend to be holy, but it is only in outward appearance. Now the Christian's holiness must be genuine, sincere, without simulation. Christ was uniformly holy, at one time and place as well as another. The same even tenor of holiness ran through the whole of His life from first to last. So should it be with His followers. "As he which hath called you is holy, so be ye holy in all manner of conversation" (1 Peter 1:15). What inconsistencies we have to bemoan; one part of our life heavenly, another earthly.

Christ was *exemplarily* holy, a pattern to all that came near Him, so that even those sent to arrest Him had to return to their masters and say, "Never man spake like this man" (John 7:46). We are to imitate Him in this respect. The Thessalonian saints were commended because they "were ensamples to all that believe in Macedonia and Achaia. For from you sounded out the word of the Lord not only in Macedonia and Achaia, but also in every place your faith to God-ward is spread abroad" (1 Thessalonians 1:7–8). Let none go out of our company without being either convicted or edified. Christ was strictly holy. "Which of you [convicteth] me of sin?" was His challenge (John 8:46). The most observing and unfriendly eye could pick no flaw in His actions. It is our duty to imitate Christ in this too: "That ye may be blameless and harmless, the sons of God, without rebuke, in the midst of a crooked and perverse nation, among whom ye shine as lights in the world" (Philippians 2:15).

Second, the *obedience* of Christ to His Father's will is a pattern for the Christian's emulation. "Let this mind be in you, which was also in Christ Jesus . . . [who] became obedient unto death" (Philippians 2:5, 8). Christ's obedience was free and voluntary, not forced and compulsory. "Then said I, Lo, I come: in the volume of the book it is written of me, I delight to do thy will, O my God" (Psalm 40:7–8). Nor did He waver, later, when suffering so grievously in the discharge of that will. "Therefore doth my Father love me, because I lay down my life" (John 10:17). So the Christian is to follow the steps of Christ, doing nothing grudgingly and counting not God's commands grievous. Our obedience must be rendered cheerfully if it is to be acceptable. See His perfect submission in Gethsemane. Here too He left us an example. We are to make no demur to the most unpleasant task God assigns us. Happy the Christian who can say with the apostle, "I am ready not to be bound only, but also to die at Jerusalem for the name of the Lord Jesus" (Acts 21:13).

The obedience of Christ was entirely disinterested. It was wrought for no self ends, but for the glory of God. "I have glorified thee on the earth: I have finished the work which thou gavest me to do" (John 17:4). Christ sought not honor of men, but the great desire of His soul was "Father, glorify thy name" (12:28). This quality must also characterize our obedience. "Look not every man on his own things, but every man also on the things of others" (Philippians 2:4). The streams of Christ's obedience flowed from the fountain of love to God. "But that the world may know that I love the Father; and as the Father gave me commandment, even so I do" (John 14:31). Let this also be true of us, for loveless obedience is of no value in the sight of God. The obedience of Christ was constant, continuing to His very last breath. Being not "weary in well doing" is required of us (Galatians 6:9; 2 Thessalonians 3:13). "Be thou faithful unto death" (Revelation 2:10).

Third, the *self-denial* of Christ is the pattern for the believer. "If any man will come after me, let him deny himself, and take up his cross, and follow me" (Matthew 16:24). Though there is to be a resemblance, there can be no exact equivalent. "For ye know the grace of our Lord Jesus Christ, that, though he was rich, yet for your sakes he became poor" (2 Corinthians 8:9). Who can gauge what Christ, for the glory of God and the love which He bare to the elect, gave up for us? How trivial in comparison is the greatest sacrifice we are called upon to make! Christ was under no obligation whatever to deny Himself for us, but He has placed us under the strongest obligation to deny ourselves for His sake. Though under no obligation, He denied Himself readily, making no objection to the severest part of it. Then let it not be said of us, "For all seek their own, not the things which are Jesus Christ's" (Philippians 2:21). Let not self be loved, petted, pitied, pampered, and indulged; rather renounce and mortify it, and make pleasing and glorifying Christ your great business.

Fourth, the *activity and diligence* of Christ in fulfilling the work of God committed unto Him was a pattern for all believers to imitate. It is said of Him that He "went about doing good" (Acts 10:38). What a glorious work He accomplished in so short a time!—a work which will be celebrated through all eternity by the praises of the redeemed, a work upon which His heart was intently set. "My meat is to do the will of him that sent me" (John 4:34). It was a work under which He never fainted, despite the greatest opposition. The shortness of the time provoked Him to the greatest diligence. "I must work the works of him that sent me, while it is day: the night cometh, when no man can work" (John 9:4). He improved all opportunities and occasions: granting Nicodemus an interview at night (3:1–21); preaching the Gospel to the woman at the well when He was exhausted from His journey (4:4–42). Nothing displeased Him more than to be dissuaded from His work. "Get thee behind me, Satan," He said to Peter when the apostle said, in effect, "Spare Thyself, Lord" (Matthew 16:23; Mark 8:33; Luke 4:8).

Shall His followers trifle their lives away in vanity? Shall we be slothful when He was so diligent? How great an honor God has placed on us by calling us to His service. Steadfastness in the work of obedience is our greatest security in the hour of temptation. "The LORD is with you, while ye be with him" (2 Chronicles 15:2). Diligence in prosecuting holiness is the way to get more (Luke 8:18). Graces grow by being used; spiritual acts lead to spiritual habits; talents faithfully employed are rewarded by an increase. Diligence in the work of God is the direct way to an assurance of the love of God (2 Peter 1:5–10). Diligence in obedience is the greatest security against backsliding. Coldness leads to carelessness; carelessness to negligence; negligence to apostasy. The more diligent we are in serving God, the more our likeness to Christ.

Fifth, the *inoffensiveness* of the life of Christ on earth is an excellent pattern to all His people. He injured none and never gave occasion for any to be justly injured by Him. He was not only holy, but also "harmless" (Hebrews 7:26). He waived His own personal rights to avoid giving an offense, as in the case of tribute money (Matthew 17:24–27). When he was reviled, He "reviled not again" (1 Peter 2:23). So circumspect was our Saviour that when His enemies sought occasion against Him they could not find any (John 19:4). Let us earnestly seek grace that we may imitate this blessed excellency of His life; that we may obey God's command and be "blameless and harmless, the sons of God, without rebuke" (Philippians 2:15). The honor of Christ, whose name we bear, is bound up in our deportment. The rule which He has laid upon us is "Be ye therefore wise as serpents, and harmless as doves" (Matthew 10:16).

Sixth, the *humility and meekness* of Christ is proposed by Himself as a pattern for His people's imitation. "Learn of me; for I am meek and lowly in heart" (Matthew 11:29). He abased Himself by taking upon Him the form of a servant. He stooped to the lowest office by washing the disciples' feet (John 13:1–16). When He presented Himself to Israel as their King, it was in humiliation, riding upon the back of a donkey. "Behold, thy King cometh unto thee, meek" (Matthew 21:5). He declared, "The Son of man came not to be ministered unto, but to minister" (20:28). He condescended to the lowest of men, eating with "publicans and sinners" (9:11). In all of this He left us an example to follow. Oh, to be "clothed with humility" (1 Peter 5:5) and thereby evidence our conformity to Christ.

Pride ill becomes one who professes to be a follower of the Lord Jesus. It not only betrays lack of communion with Christ, but also a woeful ignorance of self. Nothing is so provoking to God and more quickly estranges the soul from Him. "Though the LORD be high, yet hath he respect unto the lowly: but the proud he knoweth afar off" (Psalm 138:6). Pride is totally inconsistent with the complaints we make of our corruptions, and it presents a serious stumbling block to the children of God. Be not ambitious of the world's great ones, but content yourself as one of Christ's little ones. Learn humility at His feet. Evidence it in your apparel and deportment (1 Peter 3:3–4). Display it in cultivating fellowship with the poorest of the flock (Romans 12:16). Show it by speaking of and comporting yourself as "less than the least of all saints" (Ephesians 3:8).

Seventh, the *contentment* of Christ in a low and mean condition in this world is an excellent pattern for His people's imitation. His portion here was a condition of deepest poverty and contempt. The child of lowly parents; born in a manger. So deprived of the comforts of this world that, much of His time, He had not where to lay His head; so poor He had to borrow a penny to point out its superscription. Yet He never murmured or complained. Nay, so far from it, so perfectly content was He with God's appointments, that He declared, "The lines are fallen unto me in pleasant places" (Psalm 16:6). Under the most degrading sufferings, He never resisted: "He was oppressed, and he was afflicted, yet he opened not his mouth: he is brought as a lamb to the slaughter" (Isaiah 53:7).

> O that in this also the poorest Christians would imitate their Saviour, and learn to manage an afflicted condition with a contented spirit: let there be no complaints, or foolish charging of God heard from you, whatever straits or troubles He brings you into.
>
> The meanest and most afflicted Christian is owner of many rich, invaluable mercies (Ephesians 1:3; 1 Corinthians 3:23). Is sin pardoned and God reconciled? then never open your mouths any more. You have many precious promises that God will not forsake you in your straits (Hebrews 13:5). Your whole life has been an experience of the faithfulness of God to His promises. How useful and beneficial all your afflictions are to you! They purge your sins, wean you from the world, and turn to your salvation; then, how unreasonable must your discontentedness at them be! The time of your relief and full deliverance from all your troubles is at hand: the time is but short that you shall have any concernment about such things. Your lot falls by Divine direction upon you, and bad as it may be, it is much easier and sweeter than the condition of Christ in this world was. Yet He [was] contented, and why not you? (John Flavel)

"He that saith he abideth in him ought himself also so to walk, even as he walked" (1 John 2:6). The principal design of the apostle in this epistle is to exhibit certain signs and marks, both negative and positive, for the examination or trial of men's claims to being Christians (5:13). It is in that light our verse must be interpreted. The proof of a saving interest in Christ is our imitation of Him. Were this criterion faithfully insisted upon today from the pulpit much of the empty profession now abounding would be clearly exposed. A claim is made, "He that saith he abideth in him," which signifies an interest in and communion with Him. The only way that claim can be established is by walking as Christ walked, following the example He has left us.

> Every man is bound to the imitation of Christ under penalty of forfeiting his claim to Christ. The necessity of this imitation of Christ convincingly appears divers ways. First, from *the established order of salvation,* which is fixed and unalterable. God that hath appointed the end, hath also established the means and order by which men shall attain the ultimate end. Now conformity to Christ is the established method in which God will bring many

souls to glory. "For whom he did foreknow, he also did predestinate to be conformed to the image of his Son, that he might be the firstborn among many brethren" (Romans 8:29). The same God who has predestinated men to salvation, has, in order, predestinated them to conformity to Christ. This order of heaven is never to be reversed; we may as well hope to be saved without Christ, as to be saved without conformity to Christ.

Secondly, *the nature of Christ-mystical* requires this conformity, and renders it indispensably necessary. Otherwise, the body of Christ must be *heterogeneous*: of a nature different from the Head, and how monstrous and uncomely would this be! This would represent Christ to the world in an image, or idea, much like that, "The head of fine gold, the breasts and arms of silver, the thighs of brass, the legs of iron, the feet part of iron and part of clay" (Daniel 2:32–33). Christ, the Head, is pure and holy, and therefore very unsuitable to sensual and worldly members. And therefore the apostle in his description of Christ-mystical, describes the *members* of Christ (as they ought to be) of the same nature and quality with the Head: "As is the heavenly, such are they also that are heavenly. And as we have borne the image of the earthy, we shall also bear the image of the heavenly" (1 Corinthians 15:48–49). That image or resemblance of Christ, which shall be complete and perfect after the resurrection, must be begun in its first draught here by the work of regeneration.

Thirdly, this resemblance and conformity to Christ appears necessary from the communion which all believers have with Him in the same spirit of grace and holiness. Believers are called Christ's *"fellows"* or co-partners (Psalm 45:7) from their participation with Him of the same Spirit. God giveth the same Spirit unto us, which He more plentifully poured out upon Christ. Now where the same Spirit and principle is, there the same fruits and operations must be produced, according to the proportions and measures of the Spirit of grace communicated, and this reason is farther enforced by the very design and end of God in the infusion of the Spirit of grace: for it is plain from Ezekiel 36:27 that practical holiness and obedience is the scope and design of that infusion of the Spirit. The very innate property of the Spirit of God in men is to elevate their minds, set their affections upon heavenly things, purge their hearts from earthly dross, and fit them for a life of holiness and obedience. Its nature also is *assimilating* and changeth them in whom it is into the same image with Jesus Christ, their Heavenly Head (2 Corinthians 3:18).

Fourth, the necessity of this imitation of Christ may be argued from the design and end of Christ's exhibition to the world in a body of flesh. For though we detest that doctrine of the Socinians, which makes the exemplary life of Christ to be the whole end of His incarnation, yet we must not run so far from an error as to lose a precious truth. We say, the satisfaction of His blood was a main and principal end of His incarnation, according to Matthew 20:28. We affirm also, that it was a great design and end of the incarnation of Christ to set before us a pattern of holiness for our imitation, for so speaks the apostle: He "hath left us an example, that we should follow His steps" (1 Peter 2:21); and this example of Christ greatly obliges believers to His imitation: "Let this mind be in you, which was also in Christ Jesus" (Philippians 2:5).

Fifthly, our imitation of Christ is one of those great articles which every man is to subscribe, whom Christ will admit into the number of His disciples. "Whosoever doth not bear his cross, and come after me, cannot be my disciple" (Luke 14:27), and again "If any man serve me, let him follow me" (John 12:26). To this condition we have submitted, if we be sincere believers; and therefore are strictly bound to the imitation of Christ, not only by God's *command,* but by our own *consent.* But if we profess interest in Christ, when our hearts never consented to follow, and imitate His example, then are we self-deceiving hypocrites, wholly disagreeing from the Scripture character of believers. They that are Christ's are there described as walking not after the flesh, but after the Spirit.

Sixthly, *the honor of Christ* necessitates the conformity of Christians to His example, else what way is there left to stop detracting mouths, and to vindicate the name of Christ from the reproaches of the world? How can wisdom be justified of her children, except it be this way? By what means shall we cut off occasion from such as desire occasion, but by regulating our lives by Christ's example. The world hath eyes to see what we practice, as well as ears to hear what we *profess.* Therefore either show the consistency between your profession and practice, or you can never hope to vindicate the name and honor of the Lord Jesus. (John Flavel, Puritan)

From all that has now been before us we may draw the following inferences. First, if all who claim a saving interest in Christ are strictly bound to imitate Him, then it follows that Christianity is very unjustly charged by the world with the evils and scandals of empty professors of faith in Christ. Nothing can be more unreasonable, for Christianity severely censures loose and scandalous actions in all professors, and therefore is not to be blamed for them. "For the grace of God that bringeth salvation hath appeared to all men, teaching us that, denying ungodliness and worldly lusts, we should live soberly, righteously, and godly, in this present world" (Titus 2:11–12). Really, it is an argument greatly in favor of Christianity that even wicked men covet the name of it, though they only cloak their sins under it.

Second, if all professors forfeit their claim to a saving interest in Christ who endeavor not, sincerely and earnestly, to imitate Him in the holiness of His life, then how small a number of real Christians are there in the world! If flowery talking without strict walking, if common profession without holy practice, if church membership without denying self and treading the narrow way were sufficient to constitute a Christian, then a considerable percentage of earth's population would be entitled to that name. But if Christ owns none but those who follow the example that He left, then His flock is indeed a little one. The vast majority of those who claim to be Christians have a name to live, but are dead (Revelation 3:1). The demands of Christ are too rigid for them. They prefer the broad road where the majority are found.

Third, what blessed times we should witness if true Christianity once generally obtained and prevailed in the world! How it would humble the proud, mellow the self-willed, and spiritualize those who are carnal. A perverse world has often charged Christianity with being the cause of all the tumult in it; whereas nothing but pure Christianity, in the power of it, can cure those epidemics of evil. If the great majority of our fellows were regenerated by the Spirit and brought to walk after Christ in holiness, living in meekness and self-denial, then our prisons would be closed, armies and navies done away with, jealousies and animosities be removed, and the wilderness and solitary places be glad. The desert would rejoice and blossom as the rose. That is what constitutes the great difference between heaven and a world that lieth in the wicked one. Holiness is the very atmosphere of the former, whereas it is hated and banned here.

Fourth, it also follows that real Christians are the best companions. It is a blessed thing to fellowship with those who genuinely seek to follow the example of Christ. The holiness, heavenly mindedness, and spiritual graces which were in Him are, in their measure, to be found in all of His true disciples. They show the praises of Him who called them out of darkness into light. Something of the fruit of the Spirit is to be seen in all those whom He indwells. Yet it must be remembered there is a great deal of difference between one Christian and another; that the best is sanctified only in part. If there is something engaging and sweet, there is also that which is distasteful and bitter in the most mature saints. This is what gives us occasion to forbear one another in love. Nevertheless, notwithstanding all infirmities and corruptions, the Lord's people are the best companions on this earth. Happy are they who now enjoy fellowship with those in whom can be discerned the likeness of Christ.

Fifth, if no man's claim to being Christ's is warranted except so far as he is walking according to Him, then how groundless and worthless are the expectations of all unsanctified persons, who walk after their own lusts.

> None are more forward to claim the privileges of religion than those that reject the duties of it; multitudes hope to be saved by Christ, who yet refuse to be governed by Him. But such hopes have no Scripture warrant to support them; yea, they have many Scripture testimonies against them. "Know ye not that the unrighteous shall not inherit the kingdom of God? Be not deceived: neither fornicators, nor idolaters, nor adulterers, nor effeminate, nor abusers of themselves with mankind, nor thieves, nor covetous, nor drunkards, nor revilers, nor extortioners, shall inherit the kingdom of God" (1 Corinthians 6:9). O how many thousand vain hopes are laid in the dust, and how many thousand souls are sentenced to Hell by this one Scripture! (John Flavel, 1660)

Then how it behooves those of us who profess to be Christians to "be not conformed to this world," but to be "transformed by the renewing of [our minds]" (Romans 12:2). How we should strive to follow Christ's steps. That should be the great business of our lives, as it is the chief scope of the Gospel. If Christ has conformed Himself to us by taking upon Him our nature, how reasonable it is that we should conform ourselves to Him in a way of obedience. He came under the Law for our sakes (Galatians 4:4); the least we can do in return is to gladly take His yoke upon us. It was Christ's abasement to conform Himself to those who were infinitely beneath Him; it will be our advancement to conform ourselves to Him who is so high above us. Surely the love of Christ must constrain us to spare no efforts to "grow up into him in all things" (Ephesians 4:15).

If we will be conformed to Him in glory, how logical it is that we should now conform ourselves to Him in holiness. "We shall be like him; for we shall see him as he is" (1 John 3:2): like Him not only in our souls, but also our bodies too will be transformed like unto His (Philippians 3:21). What a motive this is to bring us into conformity with Christ here, especially since our conformity to Him in holiness is the evidence of our conformity to Him in glory (Romans 6:5). The conformity of our lives to Christ is our highest excellence in this world, for the measure of our grace is to be estimated by this rule. So far as we imitate Christ, and no farther, are we of any real help to those around us; contrariwise, the less we be conformed to Christ, the greater hindrances and stumbling blocks we are both to the saved and unsaved. What a solemn consideration this is! How it should drive us to our knees, seeking grace to be closer followers of Christ.

"That ye would walk worthy of God, who hath called you unto his kingdom and glory" (1 Thessalonians 2:12). By "worthy" the apostle had no reference to what is meritorious, but to that decorum which befits a Christian. As Davenant pointed out, "The word 'worthy' as used in Scripture does not always denote an exact proportion of equality between one thing and another, but a certain suitableness and fitness which excludes inconsistency." To walk worthy of God is to walk as Christ walked, and any deviation from that standard is a reflection on our profession and a reproach upon Him. It is for our own peace that we be conformed to Christ's pattern. The answer of a good conscience and the smile of God's approbation are rich compensation for denying the flesh. A comfortable death is the ordinary close of a holy life. "Mark the perfect man, and behold the upright: for the end of that man is peace" (Psalm 37:37).

In drawing to a conclusion let us consider a few lines of comfort to those who are cast down by the realization of how far short they come of measuring up to the standard Christ set before them. According to the yearnings of the new nature, you have sincerely endeavored to follow Christ's example. But being weak in grace and meeting with much opposition from the flesh and temptations from the devil, you have been frequently turned aside from the holy purposes of your honest hearts, to the great discouragement of your souls. You can say with David, "O that my ways were directed to keep thy statutes!" (Psalm 119:5); you have tried hard to follow after holiness, "if by any means" you might attain it (Philippians 3:11). But your efforts have been repeatedly thwarted, your aspirations dashed, and you have to cry, "O wretched man that I am! who shall deliver me?" (Romans 7:24).

First, let us assure the genuinely exercised soul that such defects in obedience do not invalidate your justification or affect your acceptance with and standing before God. Your justification is built not upon your obedience, but upon Christ's. However imperfect you are, you are "complete in him" (Colossians 2:10). Woe to Abraham, Moses, David, or Paul if their justification depended upon their own holiness and good works. Let not your sad failures dampen your joy in Christ, but rather be increasingly thankful for His robe of righteousness. Second, your heart anguish over your unlikeness to Christ, instead of being a proof that you are less sanctified than those who do not grieve over their lack of conformity to Him, evidences that you are more sanctified than they; for it shows you are better acquainted with your heart than they are, have a deep loathing of sin, and love God more. The most distinguished saints have made the bitterest lamentation on this account (Psalm 38:4).

Third, the Holy Spirit makes an excellent use of your infirmities and turns your failures into spiritual advantages. By those very defects He hides pride from your eyes, subdues your self-righteousness, causes you to appreciate more deeply the riches of free grace and place a higher value on the blood of the Lamb. By your many falls He makes you to long more ardently for heaven and gradually reconciles you to the prospect of death. The more a holy soul is buffeted by sin and Satan, the more sincerely he will cry, "Oh that I had wings like a dove! for then would I fly away, and be at rest" (Psalm 55:6). "O the blessed chemistry of Heaven, to extract such mercies out of such miseries" (John Flavel), to make sweet flowers spring up out of such bitter roots.

Fourth, your infirmities do not break the bond of the Everlasting Covenant; that holds firm, notwithstanding your many defects and corruptions. "Iniquities prevail against me" said David; yet in the same breath he added, "Thou shalt purge them away" (Psalm 65:3).

Fifth, though the defects of your obedience are grievous to God, yet your deep sorrows for them are well pleasing in His sight. "The sacrifices of God are a broken spirit: a broken and a contrite heart, O God, thou wilt not despise" (Psalm 51:17). Sixth, your grief is a conformity to Christ, for He was "the man of sorrows" (Isaiah 53:3). If He suffered because of our sins, shall we not be made to weep over them. Seventh, "Though God have left many defects to humble you, yet He hath given many things to comfort. This is a comfort, that the desire of thy soul is to God and the remembrance of His name. This is a comfort, that thy sins are not thy delight as once they were, but thy shame and sorrow. This is a comfort, that thy case is not singular, but more or less the *same* complaints and sorrows are found in *all* gracious souls through the world" (John Flavel, to whom we are indebted for much of the above).

INDEX
OF SUBJECTS

INDEX OF SCRIPTURE

Moody Press, a ministry of Moody Bible Institute,
is designed for education, evangelization, and edification.
If we may assist you in knowing more about Christ
and the Christian life, please write us without obligation:
Moody Press, c/o MLM, Chicago, Illinois 60610.